THE TIME OF LIFE

SUNY series in Contemporary Continental Philosophy
Dennis J. Schmidt, editor

The Time of Life

Heidegger and *Ēthos*

WILLIAM MCNEILL

State University of New York Press

Published by
State University of New York Press, Albany

For information, address State University of New York Press,
194 Washington Avenue, Suite 305, Albany, NY 12210-2384

Production by Ryan Hacker
Marketing by Susan M. Petrie

Library of Congress Cataloging-in-Publication Data

McNeill, William, 1961–
    The time of life : Heidegger and ēthos / William McNeill.
        p. cm. — (SUNY series in contemporary continental philosophy)
        Includes bibliographical references (p.   ) and index.
        ISBN 0-7914-6783-X (hardcover : alk. paper)
        1. Heidegger, Martin, 1889–1976. 2. Ethics. I. Title. II. Series.

B3279.H49M3763 2006
193—dc22   2005024121

13-digit ISBN: 978-0-7914-6783-1 (hardcopy : alk. paper)

10 9 8 7 6 5 4 3 2 1

Zu eng begränzt ist unsere Tageszeit
Wir sind und sehn und staunen, schon Abend ists,
Wir schlafen und vorüberziehn wie
Sterne die Jahre der Völker alle.

The time of our day is too narrowly spanned
We are and look and are astonished, already it is evening,
We sleep and like stars pass over
The years of all the peoples.

—Friedrich Hölderlin, "Rousseau"

Contents

Acknowledgments

Several chapters in the present volume have appeared in earlier form: Chapter 1 is a revised version of the essay "Life Beyond the Organism," which appeared in *Animal Others: On Ethics, Ontology, and Animal Life*, edited by H. Peter Steeves (Albany: State University of New York Press, 1999, 197–248). An early version of chapter 2 was published in the journal *Philosophy Today*, volume 42:1 (Spring 1998, 53–64). Copyright 1998 by DePaul University, all rights reserved. Chapter 4 was originally published as "The Time of *Contributions to Philosophy*" in: *Companion to Heidegger's Contributions to Philosophy*, edited by Charles E. Scott, Susan M. Schoenbohm, Daniela Vallega-Neu, and Alejandro Vallega (Bloomington and Indianapolis: Indiana University Press, 2001, 129–49). Portions of chapter 7 have appeared as "A Scarcely Pondered Word. The Place of Tragedy: Heidegger, Aristotle, Sophocles" in *Philosophy and Tragedy*, edited by Miguel de Beistegui and Simon Sparks (London: Routledge, 2000, 169–89).

The author is grateful to DePaul University for a period of research leave during the academic year 2002–03 that enabled this project to be completed. I thank DePaul University's College of Liberal Arts and Sciences for a summer research grant in 2002 that provided additional support, and for the opportunity to present publicly some of this work within the College. I am grateful to my research assistant, Kristina Lebedeva, for her careful reading of the manuscript, and to my reviewers for State University of New York Press, for their helpful comments and advice. Above all, I thank my wife Kim for her patience, understanding, and unflinching support. Finally, I wish to thank my graduate assistants Daw-Nay Evans and Maureen Melnyk for their generous help with indexing and proof-reading.

Introduction

The present study seeks to explore Heidegger's understanding of *ēthos*—of the originary dimension of the ethical and of human action—conceived in terms of the time of life and the temporality of human existence. *Ēthos* for Heidegger means our dwelling, understood temporally as a way of Being, yet such dwelling must be understood, on the one hand, in terms of our stance and conduct in the moment of action—the way in which we are held and hold ourselves, and thus "dwell," in the presence of the moment—and on the other hand, in terms of our more enduring way of Being that is brought about temporally in and throughout the unfolding of human experience. The essays that comprise this volume examine various dimensions of this tension between the moment of presence and the temporalizing of that moment as brought about and attuned by the antecedent claims of a greater whole.

The first chapter considers the phenomenon of life—of the Being of living beings—in relation to time and temporality by following Heidegger's phenomenological explorations of human and animal life in his Freiburg lecture course of 1929–30 entitled "The Fundamental Concepts of Metaphysics: World, Finitude, Solitude." The question of the relation between animal and human life is for Heidegger ultimately a question of *world*, of what "world" is and of what it means to "have" a world and to be "in" a world. However we understand the status of animals and of different modes of animal life, we always and inevitably do so in terms of an understanding of world. To be in the manner of human beings does not mean, on Heidegger's account, to be an entity of a certain species, with certain specifiable features and abilities (a conception that Heidegger views as a form of scientific reductionism that elides the very openness and indeterminability of our Being). It means, rather, nothing other than to be subject to, and addressed by, this antecedent claim of a historically determined world. The distinctive self-relation of human life, the ability to be (to dwell in) a relation to one's own Being, presupposes an "ekstatic" Being-outside-itself of our very Being, an ekstasis that is possible only as a relation to the phenomenon of world. Heidegger's investigation suggests, however, that *world*—understood as the open manifestness of beings as such and as a whole—is neither a purely ontological nor a transcendental phenomenon, but is temporalized historically in and as the unfolding of human existence. The poietic event of "world-formation" is, on this interpretation, not something that the human being accomplishes in and through his or her actions; rather, it first enables our very Being, our self-understanding and ability to relate to ourselves as beings that are already manifest. Indeed, the primary disclosure of world, Heidegger argues, is not at all an accomplishment of the already existent human being, nor, therefore, of human self-understanding or intellect. It is, rather, accomplished by the phenomenon of attunement, through which we are first disclosed to ourselves as being in this way or that, in the midst of beings as a whole. Attunement, as Heidegger had already argued in his 1927 work *Being and Time*, is primary in enabling our very dwelling, our *ēthos*. Even if such *ēthos* can subsequently be modified by understanding, by *logos* and by deliberation, such understanding nevertheless always remains responsive to an attunement and way of Being that is already given and situated, localized in a particular locale or site of dwelling. That *logos* (whether as language, thought, or understanding) neither originates nor coincides with the primary disclosure of our own Being is, however, on the positive side, our having always already departed from where we have been, our ekstatic Being-outside-ourselves as a being underway, a departure that is precisely able to leave be, to let be (*Seinlassen*)—in a letting that enables our very dwelling. A withdrawal from the site of presence, a dwelling in such withdrawal, enables our very return, our emergence into presence, even though such return is always bound to the moment. In the case of those beings we recognize and acknowledge as animals, their dwelling place, by contrast, coincides with a habitual haunt or environment, a habitat (and this is indeed an early root meaning from which *ēthos* derives).[1] The haunt of the human being, such dwelling in concealment, marks the human being as an exceptional site of disclosure and self-concealing, as having an *ēthos* that is truly haunting, altogether uncanny, *unheimlich*.

Chapter 2, "Care for the Self: Originary Ethics in Heidegger and Foucault," attempts, by way of a dialogue between Heidegger and Foucault, to open up the ontological dimension of the ethical in the work of both philosophers in terms of the ontological relation to self, shifting our understanding of "ethics" away from a set of theoretically constructed norms, principles, or rules governing practice, and toward an understanding of the ethical in terms of our concrete ways of Being in the world, our *ēthos*. The realm of *ēthos*, the chapter tries to show, is that of "originary" *praxis*, of a pre-theoretical and pre-philosophical dimension of worldly dwelling that exceeds, and indeed is prior to, the traditional theory/practice distinction in which theory is understood in advance as severed from practice, yet in such a way that it can and should be subsequently "applied" to ethical and political practice. In this traditional understanding, philosophy or theory is, implicitly or explicitly, understood as non-worldly, detached from the world—and thus from its own original grounds as itself a *praxis*, a concrete way of Being of the one philosophizing. By contrast, the philosophical cultivation of *ēthos* that this chapter discerns in both Foucault and Heidegger remains attentive to the singularity, the concrete uniqueness, of a particular existence, seeking to dwell in that very dimension otherwise eclipsed by our scientific understanding of the world, which from Aristotle on began to take hold of philosophy itself. In this second chapter, we attempt to approach this originary dimension of the ethical, or of *ēthos*, by bringing into view a constellation of issues that will be developed further in the remaining chapters. One's *ēthos* is not something permanent and unchanging: it is never entirely reducible to what Hans-Georg Gadamer has fittingly called "a living network of common convictions, habits, and values" transmitted by one's historical community and world.[2] Rather, it is constantly in transition, a manner of dwelling in being underway, and as such names a way of Being and dwelling in the world that can—and from a philosophical point of view must—be interrogated, understood, and transformed through various practices of the self. The Being of the self, as primarily an ontological relation to self for both Heidegger and Foucault, is not a theoretical abstraction from the ontic or concrete, but is, the present chapter tries to show, the concrete happening of an originary freedom that is never reducible to what one is or has been. The philosophical and "protoethical" task of care for the self (Foucault) or of authentic existence (Heidegger), a task that expressly takes up and engages this freedom in the knowing, questioning cultivation of one's *ēthos*, demands an understanding of selfhood in terms of the temporality of action, the phenomenon of world, and the historical determination of one's worldly Being.

It is these three moments that, taken together, articulate Heidegger's understanding of *ēthos*, an understanding that in many respects is indebted to Aristotle's account of *phronēsis* (practical wisdom, or excellence in deliberation pertaining to *praxis*). In Aristotelian ethics, we may recall, one's *ēthos* is determined by the ethical virtues that dispose us to act with courage, self-restraint, justice, etc.; by the deliberative virtue of *phronēsis* that enables us to deliberate well in the particular situation of action; and by our *theōria* or contemplation of the world afforded by *sophia*, or philosophical wisdom. Yet Heidegger, despite his admiration for Aristotle's account of *phronēsis* (as presented in Book Six of the *Nicomachean Ethics*), does not simply adopt Aristotle's understanding of human *ēthos*. As we have shown in a previous study, Heidegger indeed goes to great lengths to undermine the supremacy accorded to *theōria* both in Aristotle and in the philosophical tradi-tion.[3] What are the repercussions for Heidegger's understanding of *ēthos?* In chapter 3, we briefly examine how Heidegger's analyses of the temporality of human action, while drawing on Aristotle's insights into the temporality of *phronēsis* as critically oriented toward the *kairos* or opportune moment at which an action engages—what Heidegger will render as the *Augenblick*—nevertheless effect a certain displace-ment of Aristotle's conception of *ēthos*. Here we turn to an early lec-ture course, delivered in the summer semester of 1924, that Heidegger gave under the title "Fundamental Concepts of Aristotelian Philoso-phy." Whereas in chapter 2 the question of selfhood was examined primarily in terms of the ontological relation to self, and in terms of the question of freedom, our third chapter seeks to develop further the issue of the concrete practice of self-formation contributing to the cultivation of one's *ēthos*. Specifically, we shall try to follow this ear-lier, 1924 account of *ēthos* in Heidegger's work in raising the question of the relation between the moment of action and the role of ethical virtue in concretely bringing about one's ethical stance and conduct. In particular, how does Heidegger's understanding of the ekstatic temporality of human existence impact the traditional, Aristotelian understanding of virtuous *praxis* as entailing both ethical and intellec-tual virtues? Heidegger's early, phenomenological analysis, we try to show, initiates a certain displacement of an ontology of presence-at-hand operative in Aristotle's accounts of ethical *praxis*—an ontological perspective premised on the primacy of *theōria*, which tends to conceal the distinctive temporality in which the *kairos* of human action is enclosed—and does so in opening Aristotle's account of *ēthos* onto the fundamentally unsettled and unsettling dimension of the distinctive temporality and historicality of human existence.

Chapters 4 and 5 move into this dimension of historicality in seeking to make visible something of how Heidegger's understanding of the temporality of human *praxis* develops, in his work of the 1930s, into an understanding of the *Augenblick* or moment of action not only as the site of disclosure of a world, but as the site of the historical destining of world conceived as an event (or *Ereignis*) of Being. Chapter 4 begins with a recollection of Heidegger's characterization of the *Augenblick* in his 1924–25 reading of Aristotle's *Nicomachean Ethics*, as presented in his lecture course on Plato's *Sophist*, and traces its development in subsequent phenomenological works of the 1920s. It then shifts to a consideration of the reflections entitled *Contributions to Philosophy (Of Ereignis)*, dating from 1936–38, an extremely rich and productive period of Heidegger's work that is commonly regarded as marking a fundamental "turning" in his thought. The 1929–30 course "The Fundamental Concepts of Metaphysics: World, Finitude, Solitude" is, we suggest, a particularly important course in helping us to understand this turning or transition. What is at stake here is once again a certain displacement or shift in emphasis, in which the *Augenblick* is seen not only in regard to human action, but as belonging in advance, and always already, to a happening of world that exceeds human action and that indeed first calls it into Being. Not only is the time of the *Augenblick*—as already in the phenomenology of the 1920s—not that of a "now" or point in time that can be set before us or represented as one "moment" in a linear sequence of events; it is also now seen as historical in the sense of belonging to the *Ereignis* or event of the "history of Being," that is, to the way in which Being happens as world and is destined to human beings, in a destining that opens us to the necessity of our historicality. Chapter 5 seeks to examine more closely Heidegger's developing understanding, in the early to mid-1930s, of how worlds are historically determined, by focusing on the issue of historical beginnings. The task here is to shed further light on what Heidegger at one point describes as "the concealed moments [*Augenblicken*] of the history of Being" (GA 65, 92). The term *historical beginnings* is, we suggest, ambiguous: on the one hand, it implies that all beginnings, in the realm of human activity, are already and inevitably historically determined; on the other hand, it refers to the beginnings of historical worlds, epochs, or human actions, the moments of disruption and irruption in which those worlds, epochs, or actions emerge and are sent or destined into their own historicality. Our fifth chapter seeks to illuminate Heidegger's understanding of such ruptures, to which our *ēthos* is ineluctably exposed.

Chapters 4 and 5 also broach the topic of what Heidegger calls the "first beginning" of Western philosophy and the possibility of a transition to "another beginning." The first beginning, the Greek beginning, is marked above all by the discovery and ascendancy of *theōria*, conceived as a pure contemplation of the forms of all beings, a way of Being in which contemplation is increasingly severed from ethical and political *praxis*—separated out, abstracted and isolated to the point where it is no longer seen as being itself a worldly *praxis* at all—and the forms are likewise studied in abstraction from their sensuous, material embodiment. On both sides (sides that, in modernity, would eventually become "subject" and "object") what occurs is a removal and distancing of human dwelling from its exposure to the sensuous immediacy of things. We proceed as though we were not really, immediately or compellingly, claimed by and dependent on the sensuous. Yet this fantastical hypothesis—this story we tell ourselves of our not really belonging to the world, of our standing over and beyond it in all the glory of our dominance—has all too real repercussions. For Heidegger, the "first beginning" neither lies behind us in some remote, Greek past, nor is it the romanticized theme of some nostalgic longing. It is what continues to hold sway over us, that which dominates our future and unfolding actions, to the extent that our cultural *ēthos* is pervasively dominated by science and technology. Its repercussions affect not only those of us who engage directly in the production of science and technology, or those of us who, directly or indirectly, consciously or unthinkingly, have affirmed this way of life. They affect the entire world, all beings, which find themselves unable to resist the hegemonic force that imposes itself across the globe, eradicating other histories, other cultures, other languages, other ways of Being, other *ēthē*. Heidegger's work is not only a meditation on the power of this "first beginning" of Western culture, an attempt to understand it in all its dimensions; it is also thereby an attempt to prepare for the possibility of what he calls "another beginning."

In the final two chapters, 6 and 7, we seek to accompany Heidegger in his understanding of *ēthos* into the dimension of poetry and tragedy, a dimension of human dwelling that comes to be largely concealed and withheld in and through the ascendancy of the first beginning, yet which, if Heidegger is right, belongs no less assuredly to our destiny. It is striking that of the many studies concerned with Heidegger and ethics or Heidegger and "praxis," few venture to embrace the dimensions of poetic dwelling or tragedy.[4] Yet it is precisely these topics that become central to Heidegger's endeavors, from the 1930s onward, to think *ēthos* otherwise than from a theoretically skewed perspective. In both chapters, we attempt to consider—admittedly in an all too cursory and underdeveloped way—the conception of poetic dwelling that Heidegger embraces with respect to the poetry of the German poet Hölderlin (in whose work the theme of poetic dwelling is poetized) and in relation to Greek tragedy. Our interpretations focus in particular on the distinctive temporality that is brought to the fore both in Hölderlin's poetizing and in Greek tragedy.

Chapter 6 first attempts to situate the transition into the realm of poetic dwelling by recollecting a number of themes that emerged as central in previous chapters. In particular, we recall the primary disclosure of world through the phenomenon of attunement, as well as what the 1929–30 course already identified as the poietic moment of world-formation, understood as an antecedent event that first grounds our Being as dwelling. This formation and happening of a world, as the manifestation of beings as a whole in their Being, is, we suggest, the event of an originary *poiēsis* of which we are not the origin, yet which, happening in and through us, first enables our dwelling. A language and thought attuned to this arrival, to this coming to pass of a world, would presumably not yet be a discourse seeking to determine something "as" something—whether that of the apophantic discourse of science, the apophantic-hermeneutic discourse of Heidegger's early phenomenology, or indeed that of the hermeneutic deliberation of Aristotelian *phronēsis* itself, all of which are dianoetic, and concerned with determining that which already manifests itself in a certain way (with a view to constant laws determining the presence at hand of things; with a view to the existential-historical situatedness and engagement of the philosophizing self; or with a view to determining the best course of action under given circumstances in order to attain a certain end). It would, presumably, be a "simple naming" attuned to a letting-be disclosive of world in general, a letting-be that, as enabling presence itself, first enables vision, letting something be seen in its Being. It is in Hölderlin's poetizing above all, we try to indicate, that Heidegger finds precisely such a language and attunement. Yet Hölderlin's poetry is distinctive for Heidegger in that it seeks to poetize precisely the inaugural moment (or *Augenblick*) of this poietic disclosure and arrival of world. It poetizes, as Heidegger puts it, the "essence" or event of this poetizing itself, the time of poetizing. And in so doing, it poetizes the essence of human dwelling as an exposure to this dimension of that which, in its very withdrawal, exceeds such dwelling even as it calls it into Being—the dimension of what Hölderlin names the divine. The poietic accomplishment of human dwelling is thus, we try to show, called upon to unfold itself in a continual exposure to a not being at home, to what the Greeks called *to deinon*, which Heidegger—in keeping with his understanding of human Being as dwelling—translates as *das Unheimliche*: the "uncanny," or literally "that which is not of the home." Yet this very exposure, the tragic predicament of human action and *ēthos*, is what was once brought to the fore and celebrated in Greek tragedy.

In our final chapter, chapter 7, we pursue this line of thought in first examining what Heidegger might mean when, in his 1946 "Letter on 'Humanism,' " he claims that "[t]he tragedies of Sophocles . . . shelter the *ēthos* in their sayings more primordially than Aristotle's lectures on 'ethics' " (W, 184). Yet the same essay of Heidegger's also alludes to a statement made by Aristotle in the context of his discussion of tragedy in the *Poetics*. Heidegger writes: "But Aristotle's word in the *Poetics*, although it has scarcely been pondered, is still valid—that poetizing [*Dichten*] is truer than the exploration of beings" (W, 193). What kind of truth is it that is disclosed by poetizing? And why is the poetic disclosure of *ēthos* in Sophoclean tragedy "more primordial" than that disclosed by the philosophical-scientific discourse of Aristotle's *Ethics*? In seeking to address these questions, our final chapter presents a reading of the *Poetics* that argues that Aristotle's account there indeed preserves for us the thoughtful recollection of a more originary accomplishment of dwelling. In so doing, we give particular attention to the role of *theōria* in Greek tragedy—a *theōria* not yet philosophically distanced from sensuous immediacy—and to the affective dimension of attunement in which tragic presentation accomplishes its enigmatic *katharsis*. Central to understanding both, we argue, is the role of story or plot, of *muthos*, which Aristotle identifies as "the first principle and, as it were, the soul of tragedy" (1450 a38). The unfolding of human dwelling or *ēthos* in and before a world that always exceeds it is, we try to show, not simply depicted poetically in Greek tragedy, but is shown to be itself a poetic dwelling, accomplished in its Being by the *poiēsis* of a world that occurs in each case as *muthos*—as *muthos* that is at once singular and unique, and yet worldly, bringing about a belonging to a whole that will always exceed us, rendering our dwelling, as Heidegger understands it, forever *unheimlich, deinon,* "uncanny."

In its thematic orientation toward the moment or *Augenblick* and its tension with *theōria*, the present study may thus be viewed as a sequel to our earlier work *The Glance of the Eye*.

Abbreviations

WORKS BY ARISTOTLE

[DA] *De Anima*. Edited by W. D. Ross. Oxford: Oxford University Press, 1956. Translated as *On the Soul* by W. S. Hett. The Loeb Classical Library. Cambridge: Harvard University Press, 1957.

[M] *The Metaphysics*. 2 vols. With a translation by H. Tredennick. The Loeb Classical Library. Cambridge: Harvard University Press, 1933/35.

[NE] *Ethica Nicomachea*. Edited by L. Bywater. Oxford: Oxford University Press, 1894. Translated as *The Nicomachean Ethics* by H. Rackham. The Loeb Classical Library. Cambridge: Harvard University Press, 1934.

[P] *De arte poetica liber*. Edited by Rudolf Kassel. Oxford: Oxford University Press, 1965. Translated as *The Poetics* by W. Hamilton Fyfe. The Loeb Classical Library. Cambridge: Harvard University Press, 1932.

[PR] *Problems. Books I–XXI*. Translated by W. S. Hett. The Loeb Classical Library. Cambridge: Harvard University Press, 1953.

[R] *Ars rhetorica*. Edited by W. D. Ross. Oxford: Oxford University Press, 1959. Translated as *The "Art" of Rhetoric* by John Henry Freese. The Loeb Classical Library. Cambridge: Harvard University Press, 1926.

WORKS BY FOUCAULT

[FR] *The Foucault Reader*. Edited by P. Rabinow. London: Penguin, 1991.

WORKS BY HEIDEGGER

[BW] *Basic Writings*. Edited by David Farrell Krell. New York: HarperCollins, 1993.

[BZ] *Der Begriff der Zeit.* Tübingen: Niemeyer, 1989. Translated as *The Concept of Time* by William McNeill. Bilingual edition. Oxford: Blackwell, 1992.

[EM] *Einführung in die Metaphysik.* Tübingen: Niemeyer, 1953. Translated as *An Introduction to Metaphysics* by Ralph Manheim. New Haven: Yale University Press, 1959.

[GA 9] *Wegmarken.* Gesamtausgabe vol. 9. Frankfurt: Klostermann, 1976. Translated under the title *Pathmarks*, edited by William McNeill. New York: Cambridge University Press, 1998.

[GA 18] *Grundbegriffe der Aristotelischen Philosophie.* Frankfurt: Klostermann, 2002.

[GA 19] *Platon: Sophistes.* Gesamtausgabe vol. 19. Frankfurt: Klostermann, 1992. Translated as *Plato's Sophist* by Richard Rojcewicz and André Schuwer. Bloomington: Indiana University Press, 1997.

[GA 24] *Die Grundprobleme der Phänomenologie.* Gesamtausgabe vol. 24. Frankfurt: Klostermann, 1975. Translated as *The Basic Problems of Phenomenology* by Albert Hofstadter. Bloomington: Indiana University Press, 1982.

[GA 26] *Metaphysische Anfangsgründe der Logik im Ausgang von Leibniz.* Gesamtausgabe vol. 26. Frankfurt: Klostermann, 1978. Translated as *The Metaphysical Foundations of Logic* by Michael Heim. Bloomington: Indiana University Press, 1984.

[GA 29/30] *Die Grundbegriffe der Metaphysik: Welt—Endlichkeit—Einsamkeit.* Gesamtausgabe vol. 29/30. Frankfurt: Klostermann, 1983. Translated as *The Fundamental Concepts of Metaphysics: World, Finitude, Solitude* by William McNeill and Nicholas Walker. Bloomington: Indiana University Press, 1995.

[GA 34] *Vom Wesen der Wahrheit: Zu Platons Höhlengleichnis und Theäetet.* Gesamtausgabe vol. 34. Frankfurt: Klostermann, 1988. Translated as *The Essence of Truth: Plato's Cave Allegory and Theaetetus* by Ted Sadler. London: Continuum, 2002.

[GA 39] *Hölderlins Hymnen "Germanien" und "Der Rhein."* Gesamtaugabe vol. 39. Frankfurt: Klostermann, 1980.

[GA 45] *Grundfragen der Philosophie: Ausgewählte "Probleme" der "Logik."* Gesamtausgabe vol. 45. Frankfurt: Klostermann, 1984. Translated as *Basic Questions of Philosophy: Selected "Problems" of "Logic"* by Richard Rojcewicz and André Schuwer. Bloomington: Indiana University Press, 1994.

[GA 53] *Hölderlins Hymne "Der Ister."* Gesamtausgabe vol. 53. Frankfurt: Klostermann, 1984. Translated as *Hölderlin's Hymn "The Ister"* by William McNeill and Julia Davis. Bloomington: Indiana University Press, 1996.

[GA 65] *Beiträge zur Philosophie (Vom Ereignis).* Gesamtausgabe vol. 65. Frankfurt: Klostermann, 1989. Translated as *Contributions to Philosophy (From Enowning)* by Parvis Emad and Kenneth Maly. Bloomington: Indiana University Press, 1999.

[GA 66] *Besinnung.* Gesamtausgabe vol. 66. Frankfurt: Klostermann, 1997.

[GA 69] *Die Geschichte des Seyns.* Gesamtausgabe vol. 69. Frankfurt: Klostermann, 1998.

[H] *Holzwege.* Frankfurt: Klostermann, 1950.

[ID] *Identität und Differenz.* 8th ed. Pfullingen: Neske, 1986. Translated as *Identity and Difference* by Joan Stambaugh. Bilingual edition. New York: Harper and Row, 1969.

[NI, NII] *Nietzsche.* 2 vols. Pfullingen: Neske, 1961. Translated as *Nietzsche* (4 vols. in 2) by David Farrell Krell. San Francisco: HarperCollins, 1991.

[QT] *The Question Concerning Technology and Other Essays.* Translated by William Lovitt. New York: Harper and Row, 1977.

[SDU] *Die Selbstbehauptung der deutschen Universität.* Frankfurt: Klostermann, 1983.

[SZ] *Sein und Zeit.* Halle a. d. S.: Niemeyer, 1927. Translated as *Being and Time* by John Macquarrie and Edward Robinson. Oxford: Blackwell, 1987. Where reference is made to marginalia, I have used *Sein und Zeit*, 15th ed. Tübingen: Niemeyer, 1979.

[TK] *Die Technik und die Kehre.* 6th ed. Pfullingen: Neske, 1985.

[VA] *Vorträge und Aufsätze.* 5th ed. Pfullingen: Neske, 1985.

[W] *Wegmarken.* Frankfurt: Klostermann, 1967. Translated under the title *Pathmarks*, edited by William McNeill. New York: Cambridge University Press, 1998.

[WHD] *Was Heißt Denken?* Tübingen: Niemeyer, 1984. Translated as *What Is Called Thinking?* by J. Glenn Gray. New York: Harper and Row, 1968.

ONE

The Phenomenon of Life
Human, Animal, and World in Heidegger's 1929–30 Freiburg Lectures

[I]n what way, and whether, the Being of animals, for example, is constituted by a "time" at all, remains a problem in its own right.

—Heidegger, *Being and Time*

Do animals have Angst?

—Heidegger, *The Fundamental Concepts of Metaphysics*

Throughout his Marburg and Freiburg lecture courses of the 1920s, as in his magnum opus *Being and Time* (1927), Heidegger never ceased to emphasize the central importance of the phenomenon of world—a phenomenon that, he claimed, had never been adequately appreciated or understood in the history of philosophy, if indeed it had been seen at all.[1] As Hannah Arendt astutely noted, Heidegger's concept of world "in many respects stands at the center of his philosophy."[2] While *Being and Time* emphasized world as a referential totality of signification, enabling the disclosure of meanings that first "found the possible Being of word and language" (SZ, 87), and as a phenomenon to which Dasein was always already exposed in advance, that to which Dasein could only inevitably return in whatever degree of explicitness (76), it also highlighted the fundamental attunement of *Angst* as that which "first discloses *world as world*" (187). The "peculiar temporality" of *Angst* "holds" Dasein in the presence of its ownmost thrownness, yet in such a way as to hold the moment or *Augenblick* of possible decision "at the ready" (344). Such being held, the present study will argue, enables the distinctive phenomenon of human *ēthos*. For in disclosing Dasein in its "being toward" its ownmost possibility for Being, the temporality of *Angst* thereby first opens Dasein to the possibility of coming toward itself within and from out of its

1

thrownness, a "coming toward itself" that Heidegger elucidates as the originary phenomenon of the future (325), of Dasein's freedom, understood as a coming to be free for its ownmost potentiality for Being. We should note from the outset that, by contrast with Greek ontology, for which the world is disclosed by the *theōria* of philosophy and science, the primary disclosure of the presencing of a world is, on Heidegger's account, accomplished not by contemplative or philosophical knowledge, but by a fundamental *pathos* or attunement (*Befindlichkeit*); and such *pathos* is fundamental in attuning, in advance of any explicit deliberation or discursive understanding, the way in which we are held in the presencing of the moment—in short, in attuning our entire *ēthos*.

In this first chapter, concerned with the phenomenon of life and with the time of life, we seek to approach what is distinctive and unique about the temporality of human life—or in Heidegger's terms, about the relation between the finite Being (*Dasein*) of human life and the happening of a world—by accompanying Heidegger's phenomenological analyses of animal life as presented in his 1929–30 Freiburg lecture course, *The Fundamental Concepts of Metaphysics: World, Finitude, Solitude*. What emerges from these analyses is, we shall argue, that the very *sense* of life—the sense of presence and of the time of life—is quite different in the case of human being and animal respectively. In and of itself, of course, the claim that there is a decisive distinction between the Being of the human and that of other living beings is quite traditional and, where it issues in humanist or theological claims as to the superiority of the human species, not unproblematic, to say the least. Yet what is radical about Heidegger's phenomenological analyses here, we try to show, is that this distinction is never entirely reducible to an existing difference between different species of living being (and in this sense is not of the order of presence), but is itself temporalized in the "ekstatic" temporality of the world into which human Dasein is thrown. The happening of this temporal distinction not only enables the Being and worldly dwelling of human beings as intrinsically "protoethical," that is, as ethical in the originary sense of the word *ēthos*; it also implicates such dwelling in what Heidegger calls an event of world-formation (*Weltbildung*). With regard to human *ēthos*, the time of human life becomes visible as held in the tension between the presence of the moment and the poietic happening of a greater whole.[3]

The Soul, Unity of the Body

A living being is generally understood as an organism that has various organs. Yet what exactly is an "organism"? What is the relation between the unity of the organism, classically defined as the "soul," and the individual sense organs: eyes, ears, etc.?

The question of the relation between the unity of a living being and its various sense organs was raised in a decisive form by Socrates in Plato's dialogue *Theaetetus*, not with respect to living beings in general, but specifically with respect to the human being. The issue arises in the context of a dialogue concerning the essence of human knowledge. The initial answer proposed is that knowing is *aisthēsis*, sense perception, an apprehending via the senses. Yet what is it that does the perceiving in sense perception? Do we, Socrates asks, see with our eyes and hear with our ears? Or does the perception or apprehending of something necessarily involve something more than our specific sense organs? What does it mean to say that we see "with" our eyes? Is it the eyes as sense organs that do the seeing? Who or what is it that is seeing? Who or what is the "we" who see? Certainly, our specific sense organs are necessarily involved in all sense perception: we cannot see a sensible object without our eyes. Yet does this mean that it is the eyes as sense organs that actually do the seeing? Suppose that this were the case, says Socrates. Suppose that our eyes were what actually do the seeing, that it is our ear that hears sounds, our nose that does the smelling, our tongue that tastes. This state of affairs, as Socrates puts it, would be uncanny. For each particular sense organ perceives its own particular sense object: the ear hears sounds, the eye sees color; and even our sense of touch is different at different points of the body. The various capacities for sense perception are dispersed throughout different locations on the body. There would thus be vision at one point of the body, hearing at another, and so on. Such a state of affairs would be truly uncanny, since there would be no one there who could both see *and* hear *and* smell simultaneously. There would be no *one* there, no unity or unifying activity in which the various senses could belong together and be at one and the same time. Thus, Socrates argues, in order for there to be some*one* who sees, hears, smells, and so on, these senses must "reach toward something like one idea [*eis mian tina idean*], whether we call it soul [*psuchē*] or something else" (184 d).

Socrates' argument makes it clear that, in human apprehending at least, the sense organs (in Greek, *organon*) per se are not that which actively do the perceiving; rather, they are only that *through which* perception occurs. The sense organs are merely channels or "instruments" of perception, as the Greek *organon* (tool, implement) implies. The activity of perceiving as such is accomplished by the soul, by the apprehending or "seeing" (*noein*) of something more than the particulars disclosed by the various senses, namely, the unity of their belonging together in one *idea*, in one "vision." We cannot here examine the astonishing detail with which Heidegger in his 1931–32 course on Plato's *Republic* and *Theaetetus* (GA 34) analyzes the Socratic argument, but it is worth noting his emphasis that the Greek *idea* here (and the *noein* and *dianoein* it implies) does not yet refer to a nonsensible form opposed to the realm of *aisthēsis*. *Idea* means, rather, Heidegger argues, "something seen in its being seen" (*das Gesichtete in seinem Gesichtetsein*), the *being seen* of a unity that has been sighted (GA 34, 173). The apprehending (*noein*) of this unity throughout (*dia*) all differentiation of the senses and their objects is not simply an apprehending that occurs *by way of* the sense organs conceived as "instruments," but an apprehending that *stretches throughout* the various channels of sense perception, relates them to one another and holds them together in their unity. It is on the basis of such a unity that any dispersion of sense perception is possible, a perceiving of "this *and not* that." Our sensuous, bodily dispersion is a dispersion *in* gathering and a gathering or unifying *in* dispersion. As gathering and unifying in advance of any sensory apprehending of particulars, the soul (which is here not yet isolated as an entity, but conceived and seen as an "activity," a being-seen) is, as Heidegger puts it, nothing other than that stretching (*Erstreckung*) that stretches throughout the various sense organs, enabling a gathered relating to sense-objects. It is the presence of soul as this relational stretching (the striving of Plato's *erōs*) that first enables something corporeal to become organ-like, to be a body. "Only thus can something corporeal [*ein Körper*] become a body [*Leib*]," remarks Heidegger (GA 34, 177).

This Platonic view of the unitary Being of a living body in relation to its sense organs carries a certain truth and persuasiveness with respect to the human body and its manner of existing. But does it also have certain limitations? Furthermore, can this view legitimately be extended to apply to all living beings, human and nonhuman? May plants and animals also be said to "have" a soul in this manner? We know that Aristotle, in his *De Anima*, will subsequently understand the soul as the form (*eidos*) of a natural body that is able to live; as such, the soul is said to be the primary actuality or "entelechy" (*entelecheia*) of any body that has organs, whether plant, animal, or human (412 a20ff.). Although Aristotle provides an extremely careful phenomenological analysis of the differences between various genera and species of living being, and although he denies that animals or plants in general have *nous* (the capacity of *noein*), his analyses nevertheless open the way for understanding each and every living being as a kind of "organism."

THE ORGANISM AND ITS ORGANS

In his Freiburg lecture course from winter semester 1929–30, *The Fundamental Concepts of Metaphysics: World, Finitude, Solitude*, Heidegger attempts to indicate what is problematic about the Platonic-Aristotelian approach to understanding living beings, and especially animals, in terms of a fundamental form and principle called the soul. More precisely, he problematizes not so much the Platonic or Aristotelian conceptions per se, but their modern interpretation that makes itself known in contemporary scientific and technical conceptions of living beings as "organisms." According to such conceptions, an animal is basically an organism that has various organs. Each of the organs perform various functions that serve the underlying end of maintaining the organism itself as a whole. What the organism itself is and is capable of appears to be determined by the organs that it has. For example, it is evident that only those living organisms that have eyes can see. Having eyes is clearly a precondition of seeing, it makes vision possible.

But what does it mean to "have" eyes? And is seeing simply a result of having eyes? In the 1929–30 course, Heidegger begins his elucidation of the essence of the organism by trying to extricate our understanding of the organism and its organs from any instrumental conception. Yet the very word *organ*, stemming from the Greek *organon* ("working instrument," or *Werkzeug*, as Heidegger translates it), and related to *ergon* ("work," in German: *Werk*), itself suggests that an instrumental conception of living beings has been in play since the Greeks (GA 29/30, 312). An "instrumental" interpretation may be defined as one that views the function of the organs in terms of an extrinsic end, purpose, or *telos,* and by extension regards the relation between the accomplishments of the organism (for example, seeing) and its organs (having eyes) as being "organized" in terms of cause and effect or means–end relations (we see because we have eyes; the eyes are a means to seeing).

Yet to what extent is an organ not an instrument? Both the organ and the instrument accomplish something; both are characterized by an end or purpose, by being "for something" or "in order to do something." A pen is for writing; the eye is for seeing. Yet may we conclude from this that both are pieces of equipment or instruments? *Is seeing produced by the eye?*, Heidegger asks. Does the eye have a *telos,* an end or purpose, *in the same way* that an implement does? Not at all. Seeing is not produced by the eye as the end of the activity of seeing in the manner that the use of a pen produces a piece of writing. For in the case of writing, the use of an instrument produces an end product that is other than the productive activity itself. The terms of Heidegger's analysis here are clearly Aristotelian, appealing to Aristotle's distinction between *praxis* and *poiēsis.* Writing is a form of *poiēsis,* a *technē* where the end product lies beyond (*para*) the activity of producing. In seeing, by contrast, there is, according to Aristotle, no remainder outside of or beyond the activity itself at the moment it is accomplished. Thus, vision, both perceptual and speculative (*horasis, theōria*), is a paradigm for *praxis* in the highest, ontological sense. For here the end or *telos* of the process is included in the activity itself: at the same time we both see and have seen. And life (*zēn*), the living of living beings, is also a *praxis* in precisely this sense of being an end in itself: at the same time (in the same moment), notes Aristotle in the *Metaphysics,* we are at once living and have lived (1048 b18ff.).[4]

This distinction between the organ and the instrument in terms of the ontological status of their activity in each case is therefore indicative of a fundamental distinction that must be made with regard to the manner of Being belonging to these beings themselves. For whereas an instrument or piece of equipment is an independent entity, something independently present at hand or ready to hand and available for different people to use, the organ such as the eye is in each case incorporated into a unique and singular living being. As Heidegger elucidates:

> The pen is an *independent* entity, something ready to hand for *several different* people. By contrast, the eye, the organ, is, for those who need and use it, *never* present in *this* way. Rather every living being can in each case see only with *its* eyes. These eyes, and all the organs, are not independently present at hand like an item of use, a piece of equipment, but are incorporated into that entity which makes use of them. (320–21)

Thus, Heidegger proceeds to distinguish the organ, as having a capacity (*Fähigkeit*) for something, from the instrument or piece of equipment as having a readiness (*Fertigkeit*) for something. Readiness, he emphasizes, is here meant in a double sense: The piece of equipment is ready both as completed or finished, and in the sense of being ready or usable *for* something. Heidegger is here pointing to an ambiguity in the meaning of "end." For "end" can mean either completion or purpose. (This corresponds to the ambiguity of the Greek meaning of *telos*.) Both the organ and the piece of equipment can serve some further end, and their essence is determined by this end in each instance. As we have just indicated, the nature of the end or "purpose" is fundamentally different in each case. Nonetheless, both the organ and the instrument might be said to serve some end, to be "ready for" something in the most general sense. But the instrument lies ready for doing something in lying independently before us; moreover, it is itself, qua instrument, a *product* of a prior *technē*, whereas the living organ of the body is neither a product of human *technē*, nor is it an independent, self-subsistent thing.[5] It is therefore highly questionable whether we may consider the organ as something independent, since the eye taken by itself does not have the capacity to see, just as a piece of equipment taken by itself is not capable of anything at all, but requires the human hand to actualize its potentiality. The question to be raised is:

> Can the animal see because it has eyes, or does it have eyes because it can see? Why does the animal have eyes? Why can it have such things? Only because it can see. Possessing eyes and being able to see are not the same thing. (319)

It is *being able to see*, the potentiality for seeing, Heidegger points out, that first makes the possession of eyes possible and necessary. "An eye taken by itself is no eye at all" (323). The eye is not an

instrument that exists on its own, only to be subsequently incorporated into an organism. Rather, organs, and their essence as organs, that is, as having capacities, always belong to the organism
and develop out of the organism. We must therefore say, not that
organs have capacities, but that capacity belongs to and proceeds
from the respective organism as a whole. The presence of a particular capacity as such thus precedes the organ corresponding to
it: the organ develops out of the capacity. Heidegger illustrates this
by reference to protoplasmic amobae and infusoria, whose organs
continually form themselves as and when required, and then dis-
appear. Yet may one not conclude, from the fact that specific organs develop out of the organism, that the organism itself *produces*
its own organs, indeed produces, reproduces, and renews itself
within certain limits? Such a conclusion seems difficult to deny;
moreover, it allows us to perceive a major difference between an
organism and a machine. A machine has to be constructed by human
beings, and also regulated by them, whereas an organism is able to
regulate itself.

Nevertheless, there is something about this conclusion that
Heidegger wishes to resist. His resistance concerns the further conclusion that is normally drawn from these observations, namely
the conclusion that, on account of its capacity for self-production,
self-renewal, and self-regulation, the organism must have within it
a specific active force or vital agent, an "entelechy." This conclusion, Heidegger insists, closes off the problem of the essence of life.
For it implies some kind of efficient cause that originates and con-
trols the movement and development of the organism, producing
its organs (Heidegger speaks of an "effective agency" or "causal
factor," a *Wirken* or *Wirkungsmoment* [325–26]). It is questionable,
indeed, whether we may speak of a *producing* of organs on the part
of the organism at all. For the organs are not produced in the way
that an item of equipment is made ready. Heidegger underlines
the independent character of the produced thing as opposed to a
living, emergent, or disappearing organ by pointing out their different relatedness to *time*. In the case of, say, a hammer, it is in a
certain way a matter of indifference how long the hammer is actually present or whenever it is destroyed. In the case of an organism
such as a protoplasmic organism, the time at which the organs
appear is, by contrast, critical. In the protoplasmic creature, each
organ appears as and when it is needed. The organs are bound to

the *duration and time of life*, the time of the living organism itself, and not in the first instance to an objectively ascertainable time (the time of something present at hand). The organs are bound to the lifetime and life process of the organism, to its capacity for living.

Heidegger examines various cases of protoplasmic organisms because they are best suited philosophically to the task of understanding the essence of the organ and its relation to the organism. Such life-forms appear to have no organs, or no enduring organs; at most their organs are "momentary organs." Although Heidegger does not develop the question of the *time* of the living being here, this critical temporal nature of the organs which emerges clearly in the case of protoplasmic cells helps to ward off an illusion that "repeatedly misleads" existing approaches to understanding the essential nature of organs. For in the case of those so-called "higher" animals which have an "enduring animal form," the illusion arises that the organs are something present at hand, something that remains constant, and that can be regarded independently and understood by analogy with instruments. Yet the temporal distinctions that become apparent when considering protoplasmic animals make it evident that the specific manner of Being pertaining to living entities is fundamentally different from the Being of the present at hand or ready to hand piece of equipment. "Organs, even though they appear to endure and to be present at hand, are nevertheless given only in *that manner of Being* which we call *living*" (329).

On the basis of these considerations, Heidegger argues that the "purposive" or teleological character of equipment and organ is fundamentally different in each case. The eye does not serve vision in the way that the pen serves to write. Whereas that which has been made ready serves or is "serviceable" (*dienlich*) for some (extrinsic) end, the organ as capacity must be understood as "subservient" (*diensthaft*) to the *potentiality* of the specific organism to which it is bound.

This distinction between the Being of equipment, or instrumentality, and the Being of the organ now enables Heidegger to characterize more precisely the nature of capacity pertaining to the potentiality of the organ as opposed to the readiness of equipment. To say that something is ready-made (*fertig*) means not only that (1) it is completed; and (2) it is ready to serve for something; but means also (3) that "in its Being it is at an end," it cannot proceed

any further. The piece of equipment *in itself* is unable to do anything; the pen, for example, in itself cannot write, just as the hammer in itself cannot hammer. Writing or hammering require that
an additional action be brought to the pen or the hammer from the
outside, from beyond them: the possibility of them serving some
end must, as Heidegger expresses it, first be "torn from the piece
of equipment." In sum, "being a hammer is *not a pushing toward*
hammering, the ready-made hammer lies outside a possible hammering" (330–31). This lying outside or beyond is to be contrasted
with the way in which an organ such as the eye *belongs to* the
capacity to see, because the capacity has the intrinsic character of
subservience. Capacity, as Heidegger now formulates it, *"transposes itself into its own wherefore, and does so in advance with respect
to itself"* (331). This pushing toward and transposing itself into its
own end in advance indeed characterizes what is "properly peculiar" to capacity; the hammer in its Being, by contrast, "knows
nothing of the sort."

The self-transpositional character of the capacity of a living
organ marks its very Being as living, as a kind of bodying-forth.
Whereas using a piece of equipment for a particular end subordi-
nates the equipment to a prescription that has in advance pre-
scribed its possible usage (this being taken from the idea [*idea,
eidos*] or "plan" in view of which the equipment was first produced), the living capacity itself requires no such external prescription. It is intrinsically self-regulating, and this self-regulation of its
pushing toward its own end or "wherefore" characterizes capacity
as *driven*. Capacity accomplishes itself as drive, as a driving itself
forward or being driven forward that regulates in advance the
possible range of accomplishment of the specific organ. Moreover,
in its self-driving or driven character, each capacity traverses a
particular dimension: its dynamic occurs as *traversal*. Yet the self-
regulating traversal of a dimension is not to be taken in the spatial
sense; the drives that are triggered in and as the actualization of
various capacities are not merely extrinsic "occasionings" of the
spatial movements of the living body. Rather, the dimensionality
in question is that traversed by the capacities of the organs as
living; the dimensional traversal is the very Being of the living
body, the pulse of living tissue. This traversal, as the movement of
driven capacities, drives and extends in advance right through the
unfolding of a capacity. The movement of living drives, Heidegger

adds, can therefore never be understood along the lines of a mechanical or mathematical model, except by neglecting what is specific to the organs and organism *as living*.

These reflections allow us to address once more the question raised earlier: Can the animal see because it has eyes, or does it have eyes because it can see? What the animal's eye can accomplish in each case, and the structure of the eye as organ, must be understood in terms of the capacity for seeing. The capacity for seeing, on the other hand, cannot adequately be determined in terms of the eye and its anatomical structure. This does not mean, of course, that empirical observation of the organ is irrelevant or could simply be disregarded. The anatomical structure of the bee's eye, for example, can help us to understand how the bee "sees" only if we consider it on the basis of the *specific* manner of Being of the bee and its capacities. Heidegger cites a striking experiment in which the retinal image appearing in the eye of a glow worm was photographed. The photograph allows us to identify relatively clearly various features of a window within the glow worm's field of vision. The insect's eye, Heidegger comments, is capable of forming an image or "view" of the window. But does this tell us what the glow worm *sees*? "Not at all. *From what the organ accomplishes we cannot at all determine the capacity for seeing, nor the way in which whatever is accomplished by the organ is taken into the service of the potentiality for seeing*" (336). Indeed, we cannot even begin to problematize the relationship between this insect's eye as organ and its capacity for seeing until we have considered the glow worm's *environment*, and the way in which the animal in general can have an environment. For the insect's eye is as it were "inserted," as something nonindependent, between its environment and the seeing animal, where "inserted" means existing in the manner of the drive-like traversal pertaining to capacity.

Yet not only the environment must be taken into account, but also the animal or *organism as a whole* that "has" capacities. What constitutes, or what is the essence of, an organism as such? The question of the essence of the organism, which Heidegger approaches most cautiously, may be considered from two perspectives: first, in terms of the nature of capacity; and second, in terms of the relation between organs and the environment. Heidegger does not himself tease out these two threads so cleanly in his analysis; we do so here in order to show the intrinsic complexity of the analysis and the multiplicity of perspectives in play.

Regarding the first of these threads, the subservience that characterizes the nature of capacity as such has made it clear that each *specific* organ must be understood in terms of the way it is incorporated into and belongs to the specific organism under consideration. In analyzing the nature of an organ, which as it were constitutes the "between" or the "interface" between the organism as a living being and its environment, the analysis has thus had tacit recourse to a certain understanding of what it means to be an organism in general. The analysis of the nature of capacity pointed back to an understanding of the capacity for something in terms of a drive-like traversal in which the capacity transposes itself into its own end or "wherefore," that is, *into its own Being.* For in being actualized, the capacity (for example, the capacity to see) does not lose itself or exhaust itself as capacity, but precisely retains itself as such a capacity, and does so in and throughout its driving traversal (seeing). This self-like character, however, does not belong to the specific organ as such, but to the capacity that the organ itself subserves and into which it is drawn. The specific capacities belong to and are regulated by the organism itself as a whole: it is the organism as a whole that appears to be constituted by this *self-like* nature. The organism is as it were the site or locus of the various capacities which, in turn, unfold from out of and subserve the organism as a whole. We have already encountered this self-like character of the organism, Heidegger reminds us, in noting that what is peculiar to the organism as opposed to a machine is that the organism (within certain limits) is *self*-producing, *self*-regulating, *self*-renewing. It is, as we say, *self-preserving.*

With regard to the second thread, this self-like, self-preserving character of the organism may also be considered in relation to the environment. Earlier, while discussing the features of certain protoplasmic creatures, Heidegger had noted that not only do the "momentary organs" that appear remain bound to the living process of the animal (unlike produced equipment), but that these organs never pass over into another body or substance. In the case of pseudopodia, for example, these protoplasmic creatures produce apparent limbs by which to propel themselves. "Yet when one of these apparent limbs of the animal comes into contact with that of another consisting of the same substance, it never flows over into the other or combines with the cellular content of the other. This means that *the organ is retained within the capacity* of touch and movement and indeed can only be superceded or replaced through this capacity" (329). The organs of a particular organism, even where they are highly fluid and changing (without the apparent permanence of the human or so-called higher organisms), never pass over into or lose themselves in the substance of another organism. In other words, the organs belong to an organism that, even at the fluid level of a protoplasm, has the character of self-retention and self-differentiation from other substances, including substances that are generically the same.

The question remains of how this self-like character of the organism is to be conceived. For the self-regulating and self-retaining nature of the organism has led, Heidegger argues, to a precipitous explanation of the selfhood of the animal "by way of analogy with our own selves," so that we speak of an animal "soul," a vital force, an entelechy, or even ascribe consciousness to animal life (332). We should not deny a certain self-like character pertaining to the organism, for this lies in the very essence of capacity as such: in its driving traversal, a capacity does not depart from itself, but retains itself in and as the very movement into its wherefore. And yet it does so "*without* any so-called *self-consciousness* or even *reflection*, without any relating back to itself" (340). Every living organism exists in the manner of being "proper to itself," of being "properly peculiar" (*sich-zu-eigen, eigentümlich*), in other words, of belonging to itself. Yet not every living being belongs to itself in the manner of a human being or "person," that is, in the manner of *selfhood*. Heidegger thus now proposes to reserve the terms *self* and *selfhood*, taken in the strict sense, to characterize the way in which human beings belong to themselves, in contrast to the "proper Being" (*Eigentum*) peculiar to the animal. With regard to the translation of these difficult terms, it should be noted that *Eigentum* normally means one's "property," what one owns, and *eigentümlich* would ordinarily be rendered as "peculiar." In the present context, both words thus carry the sense of something withheld from others, withdrawn or even refused, even something secretive. As we shall see, a certain refusal will shortly be identified by Heidegger as belonging to the Being of the animal.

The organism as a unity of the living body that is constantly articulating itself into various capacities and yet retaining itself as a unity amid this multiplication and apparent dispersion of capacities unfolds and sustains its very Being (living) as this unity. An organism does not simply "have" capacities as extrinsic properties, but thrives amid this articulating of itself into capacities. It lives as *capability* and *potentiality*. Its living is the very ability to articulate such potentiality into a self-traversing movement into living capacities, a movement of traversal that is also a self-retention, a being "organized." Capability characterizes the essence of life. "Only that which is capable and remains capable, lives" (343). An organism, therefore, Heidegger insists, is not to be thought of as a present at hand entity that "has" various properties, capacities, and organs: "The term 'organism' is therefore no longer a name for this or that entity at all, but rather designates *a particular and fundamental way of Being*" (342).

Thus far, Heidegger's analyses have served to put in question the instrumental view of the relation between organs and their activities. By emphasizing the unique way in which the organ is embedded in the living activity of the organism as a whole, Heidegger shows that the relation between an organ and its accomplishment is not an extrinsic means–ends relation, as reductively conceived by mechanistic models of life. The organs are not simply instruments of the living body. Yet although this technical or instrumental teleology of the Being of living organs, as the Being of the organism itself, is readily refuted, there remains the possibility of a teleology of living Being that is not so much technical (modeled around so-called efficient causality) as practical (oriented toward final causality). According to this teleology, the Being of the living entity or organism constitutes an end in itself. The relation between the organism, its organs, and their accomplishment is indeed not one of an *extrinsic* instrumentality conceived along productionist lines, but rather constitutes an *internal* teleology whereby the organs and their activities subserve the higher, organizing end of the Being (living) of the organism itself.[6] This end is both *origin* and *telos* of every moment of living activity; it is origin and *telos* of itself, of its own Being and subsisting qua living.

This schema of a "practical," internal teleology is indeed that proposed by Aristotle in his classical treatise on the essence of life, the *De Anima*. Although he initially appeals to "technical" analogies to approach the issue of life, Aristotle is careful to emphasize that these are merely analogies, which are not appropriate to characterizing the nature of the living. It is the concept of *entelecheia*, rather, appropriate to the realm of *praxis*, that Aristotle chooses in order to characterize the living being as an end in itself (the *psuchē*). According to Aristotle, the soul or *psuchē* is the primary entelechy of the living body, and such will be any body that has organs. As having (being) its own end in advance (namely, in advance of any particular moment of actualization), which is the sense of *entelecheia*, the living being is also precisely "in itself" (*en heauto*) *archē* of its own movement and rest (412 b17f.). Thus, Aristotle conceives of life in the most general sense, encompassing both animal and human, as *praxis*, as being an end in itself. For Aristotle, the decisive distinction between animal and human is of course that humans can relate to that being-an-end as such, via *logos*, and thus be ethical and political beings. Yet leaving aside for the moment the question of whether this characterization of *praxis* is appropriate even to understanding the essence of human existence, the first question that needs to be raised in the present context is whether the conception of internal teleology is indeed appropriate or adequate to living beings in general. Or is perhaps something about the otherness of other living beings obscured in adopting a schema (itself highly questionable) from the realm of human affairs in order to characterize all living beings?

In Heidegger's text, the possibility of this internal teleology has thus far been maintained precisely in the insistence that the organs and their capacities in each case *subserve* the Being of the organism as a whole. But to what extent can an "organism" be characterized as being a self-contained, self-regulating whole? Is an organism origin and end of its own proper Being, of its being gathered into "itself" in such a way as to have and dispose over the possibility of self-movement and rest? The viability and phenomenological appropriateness of this schema depend on the organism "itself" being accessible in its self-like character, or in its own "proper" Being. And if the "organism," as a *living* being, is not adequately conceivable as something purely "present at hand" (a schema that, Heidegger suggests, is borrowed from the realm of *technē*, equating being complete (being-at-an-end) with the completedness of the produced "work" or product), if its own proper Being is *not fully manifest* as such, how can we gain access to the living of this other being as such? Does the Aristotelian notion of the soul as *eidos* still import a technical or productionist

approach into our understanding of other living beings, an approach
that tends to obscure the character of their own proper Being?

The Animal as Other

In showing the shortcomings of a technical-instrumental interpretation of the organs of an organism, the ontological inappropriacy
of this schema came to light fairly readily. It soon became apparent
that the application of an instrumental teleology was unsuitable,
because it is taken from a realm of beings that are obviously not
living (or at least not normally regarded as such). The Being of
equipment or tools (presence-at-hand and readiness-to-hand) is
evidently not the same as the Being of living beings. Of course, the
predominance of a productionist-instrumental understanding of
Being in Western scientific and philosophical thinking has not
prevented this schema from being applied to living beings also. By
contrast with this first schema, the second, that of an internal-
practical teleology, appears initially much less problematic with
regard to its ontological appropriacy. For we recognize immediately that this schema is indeed more properly attuned to understanding the Being of an entity as living. An indication of this is
also the fact that, whereas in our initial discussion of the organism
and its organs, concerned with refuting equipmental teleology, the
interpretations of the organism and its organs could in principle
apply to *any* living being, raising the question of the appropriacy
of an internal teleology of life immediately involves us in appealing to a possible distinction between *different kinds* of living being.
Our concern now is not whether this schema is suitable for characterizing living beings in general, but whether it is phenomenologically and ontologically appropriate to those living beings that
we regard as other than human (and, in this context, particularly
those that seem most human-like, namely, animals). For we recognize that human existence can to some extent, and within certain
limits, anticipate its own Being and thus be an origin and end of
its own actions, of itself as *praxis*.

In analyzing the relation between organs, their accomplishment, and the organism, Heidegger did not simply overlook or
ignore the possibility and even necessity of distinguishing between
the living Being of the human and that of other beings. Rather, this

issue was constantly kept in the background as it were, occasionally surfacing by way of a critical caution or reminder of the preliminary and tentative status of these analyses. As a question, the human/animal distinction thus serves as a critical limit to the preliminary analyses of the organism and its organs. For example, after recounting the glow worm experiment and recalling the need to consider the glow worm's relation to its environment before drawing any conclusions as to what it sees, Heidegger cautions:

> The difficulty is not merely that of determining *what* it is that the insect sees, but also that of determining *how* it sees. For we should not compare our own seeing with that of the animal without further ado, since the *seeing and the potentiality to see of the animal* is a *capacity*, whereas *our potentiality to see* ultimately has a *character of possibility quite other* and possesses a *way of Being that is quite other*. (337)

Of course, claiming that our way of Being is "quite other" than that of the animal seems to raise the objection: but how then can we know anything about the Being of the animal, without falling into a naive anthropomorphism? Will not our interpretation of the animal necessarily be anthropocentric? How do we know what it is like to be an animal? If the animal is truly other, will not any attempt on our part to define its Being necessarily reduce and erase its otherness? The question of access to the animal and to living beings that are nonhuman thus proves uncircumventable; moreover, the prospect of our knowing what it is like to be an animal seems doomed from the outset. Yet perhaps such objections, which raise themselves repeatedly in contemporary debate, are themselves historically conditioned by the epoch of subjectivity. What is striking about such objections is that they presuppose that our perspective is at once subjective and purely human. They presuppose as unquestioned that human beings, through the subjectivity of their thinking, are undeniably at the *center* of the world, and that the "world," here conceived as the sum-total of beings (objects) in their Being, is merely a result and "function" of human representation. The said objections presuppose both that we know what the human being is, and that this conception of the world as our "representation" is unquestionable. Not only are these presuppositions historically determined, they are also phenomenologically and ontologically reductive with respect to the essence of life in general, whether human, animal, or other. In the remainder of this chapter, we shall try to indicate how Heidegger's account of animal life in the 1929–30 course undermines such subjectivity by shifting our perspective away from any supposed "interiority" of life and toward a transformed conception of *world*.

If the Being of animals and that of humans were absolutely other, such otherness would of course not even be conceivable. The otherness of the animal remains, as Hegel would say, an otherness "for us." (How this "we" is to be determined can remain an open question for now; Heidegger's understanding of the Being of the human being is not that proposed by Hegel.) It is an otherness that is manifest within the element of the Same, the element of *Being*, an element which in the 1929–30 course is thought under the title *world*.[7] Thus, in claiming that, for animals and humans respectively, "Seeing and seeing are not the same thing" (320), Heidegger is not claiming that there are *no* grounds whatsoever for comparison. It is a question, rather, of drawing critical distinctions that are first enabled by a certain underlying sameness, a sameness that is not to be conceived ontically (in terms of the underlying similarity of two entities) but ontologically, in terms of ways of Being, and in relation to world. In the case of seeing, for example, the seeing of animals and that of humans manifests a sameness in that both are evidently *ways of apprehending something* (using the word *apprehending* very loosely here), and as such, ways of Being and of being in relation to other entities in the world. This does not preclude the possibility and even necessity of making distinctions with respect to the *way* in which something is apprehended in each case. (Heidegger will even claim that the animal does not "apprehend" anything, in a more strictly defined sense.)

In order to help clarify the grounds on which a comparison between the different ways of Being of animal and human is possible, let us turn to the framework of the proposed "comparative examination." Heidegger's initial discussion of this issue, which occurs before the preliminary analysis of the organism and its organs, already brings to bear certain insights that will be decisive for addressing the question of access to beings other than ourselves.

The stone is "worldless" (*weltlos*); the animal is "poor in world" (*weltarm*); humans are "world-forming" (*weltbildend*): three "theses" which Heidegger proposes in order to frame his inquiry into

world (263). The three theses recall the possibility and perhaps
even the necessity of distinguishing between humans, animals, and
inanimate objects as fundamentally different kinds of entity. However obscure their grounds, these distinctions initially appear self-
evident for us. Yet in terms of what criteria do we make such
distinctions? Heidegger first considers the relation between the
second and third theses: the animal is poor in world; man is world-
forming. If by *world* we mean something like the accessibility of
other beings, then what the theses are proposing seems straightforward: Humans have greater access to other entities, their world is
richer, it encompasses a greater range of accessibility; the animal
has less access, it is "poor" in world compared to the richness of
the human world. Yet may we simply understand poverty here as
being intrinsically of lesser significance with respect to richness? Is
the human a higher being than the animal? The reverse might well
be true, notes Heidegger. Especially if we stop to compare the
discriminatory capacity of a falcon's eye with that of a human
being, or ponder the fact that "the human being can sink lower
than any animal. . . . No animal can become so depraved as a human being" (286). Yet the fact that human existence bears ethical
responsibility, and could in this sense be said to be "higher," need
not be taken to imply that the human world is intrinsically more
perfect or complete, or of intrinsically greater significance, but indicates only its radical otherness. All of which initially indicates
only that "the criterion according to which we talk of height and
depth in this connection is obscure" (286).

The thesis of poverty in world as characterizing the animal
indeed suggests, according to Heidegger, that animals are in some
way deprived of world, yet such deprivation must not be taken as
equivalent to having no world whatsoever. This becomes clear via
a comparison with the first thesis, which depicts the stone as
worldless. At the same time, the comparison helps us to understand
positively the phenomenon of world as the accessibility of beings as
such. We may say that the stone is worldless, that it has no world:
This means that in principle it has no access to those beings in whose
midst it is located. The stone may be in contact with the ground, but
does not touch it in the way that the lizard sitting on the stone
touches the stone. Above all, Heidegger emphasizes, neither of these
ways of "touching" is the same as "*that* touching which we experience when we rest our hand upon the head of another human

being" (290). For the earth upon which the stone rests is not given
for the stone; the stone has no access to anything *other* that surrounds it. The stone has no access to other beings. It gives no sign
that other beings are present for it in any way.

In the case of the animal, the situation is more complicated.
Whereas the surface upon which the stone rests is not accessible to
the stone at all, the rock on which the lizard sits is indeed given in
a certain way for the lizard—but, Heidegger hypothesizes, it is not
given to the lizard "*as* a rock." This does not mean that it is given
as something other than itself, but means: "not accessible *as a being*
[*als Seiendes*]" (291–92). The thesis that the animal is poor in world,
then, cannot mean that it is altogether without access to other beings.
"Its *way of Being,* which we call '*living,*' is not *without access* to what
is around it . . ." (292). The animal is not utterly deprived of world,
if "world" means the *accessibility of beings.* To this extent we must
say that the animal in some sense "has" world. On the other hand,
if poverty in world indicates a deprivation, and deprivation means
"not having," then it seems that the animal does not have world.
Yet is the conception of world being used in the same sense when
we say that the animal has, and yet does not have, "world"? It
seems not. When we say that the animal "has world" then we
mean world as the accessibility of beings, as some kind of openness for encountering other beings in general. This sense of world
would therefore encompass both humans and animals as living
beings. When we say that the animal does not "have world," we
mean that it does not have access to other beings *in the way that
humans do* or in the way that "we" do. Yet this makes it highly
problematic as to whether the thesis that the animal is poor in
world can be a coherent thesis at all.

These reflections on accessibility serve initially to indicate the
fundamentally different ways of Being that pertain to the human being, the animal, and the stone. They have, Heidegger tells us, the
sole purpose of eliminating the naive approach that might think
we were concerned with three beings "all present at hand in exactly the same way" (296). Human beings, animals, and stones are
indeed all beings that appear and are present at hand *within* the
world. Yet their respective *ways of Being,* which in each case include a certain presence-at-hand (or possible presence-at-hand, at
least for us), are not at all identical (*gleich*). These comparative
(*vergleichende*) considerations help to highlight both proximity and

difference with respect to the different ways of Being in each case. On the one hand, the Being of the animal, insofar as it is characterized by having access to other beings, is not entirely other than that of humans. Access to other beings, as Aristotle already saw, is a fundamental characteristic of both humans and animals. On the other hand, in this respect neither the human nor the animal have the same kind of Being as the stone, which has no access to other beings. Likewise, the sense in which the animal does *not* have world cannot be understood in the same way as the sheer deprivation or not-having pertaining to the stone. From what perspective do we make such comparisons?

The question of our perspective upon each of the beings referred to in the three theses is primarily concerned not with the danger of anthropocentrism (which, Heidegger suggests, could perhaps be compensated retrospectively), but with a question of principle regarding transposability—that is, regarding our ability as questioners to transpose ourselves *into* each of the beings to be investigated. Heidegger approaches the issue by way of three correlative questions: Can we transpose ourselves into an animal, into a stone, or into another human being? Insofar as we ourselves are human beings, and exist in our own particular manner of Being, the question is whether we are able to transpose ourselves in each case into an entity that is other. Yet the very talk of "transposition," Heidegger stresses, is misleading. For transposing oneself cannot here mean factically entering the supposed "interior" of the other entity (thus taking on its very Being), nor substituting oneself for the other entity. Rather, the point is, Heidegger notes, that transposing oneself, as a way of understanding the Other, must precisely *let* the Other *be other*. With respect to the fundamental problematic it seeks to address, transposition is better understood as a "going along with" (*Mitgehen mit*) the Other in its way of Being. The "decisive *positive* moment" of self-transposition does not consist in our relinquishing or abandoning ourselves, but "in we ourselves being precisely ourselves, and only in this way first bringing about the possibility of ourselves being able to go along with the other being while remaining *other* with respect to it" (297). The very term *transposition* is misleading because it suggests that the beings in question are in the first instance isolated spheres, each with their own interiority, between which a relation of access and mutual interaction would subsequently have to be established.

Among other things, such a model—essentially a variant of the subject–object schema so central to modern representation—leaves unthought the possibility that a relation to the Other (however the latter is determined) may *precede* and even be *co-constitutive* of the so-called self and the possibility of its relation to itself. Allowing this possibility does not deny that each of the entities in question is, in its own specific Being, indeed determined by selfhood (here understood in a purely formal sense).

Yet how are we to understand transposition as a going-along-with the Other? Heidegger begins by discussing the first question: Can we transpose ourselves into an animal? What is really being asked here is: Can we go along with the way in which the animal sees and hears things? It is self-evident for us in asking this question that the animal indeed relates to other things such as its food, its prey, its young, and so on. When we ask this, Heidegger remarks, we are assuming without question that "in relation to the animal something like a going-along-with, a *going along with it in its access and in its dealings within its world* is possible *in general*, and does not represent an intrinsically nonsensical undertaking" (299). The only question is whether we can factically succeed in this going-along-with the animal. We make this assumption, it seems, because we can see that both animals and we ourselves indeed have access to other beings, because we have access to animals and they have access to us, and it ought therefore to be possible in principle (or so it seems) for each to *share* such access, precisely in going along with, in sharing and participating in, the Being of the Other.

What of the second question: Can we transpose ourselves into a stone? The answer quite clearly seems to be "no," in this instance not because of any inability on our part, but because the stone itself has no sphere of transposability—no possibility of another being accessing its specific manner of Being, which seems to be that of sheer presence-at-hand. Note that Heidegger adds a qualifier: there are nonetheless ways in which we are able to regard purely material or "inanimate" things not as such, but rather to "animate" them, namely via *myth* and *art*. What is at stake in deciding whether a kind of transposability is possible here, says Heidegger, is "the distinction between fundamentally different *kinds of truth*." The current investigation, we are reminded, is to remain within the bounds of the possible truth belonging to "scientific and metaphysical knowledge" (300).

In the case of the third question—Can we transpose ourselves into another human being?—the very question, Heidegger indicates, is meaningless. Not because a going-along-with the other human being is impossible, but because we as human beings are *already* transposed into other human beings in the very manner of our existing. Insofar as the Being of human beings is *Dasein* (as analysed in Heidegger's 1927 treatise *Being and Time*), and *Dasein* intrinsically entails *Being-with-others*, it is fundamentally unquestionable for us that we can, for example, "share with one another" the same comportment toward the same things, and indeed do so without this comportment being fragmented in the process. As a specific way of Being that we ourselves in each case are, Dasein, as Heidegger explained in *Being and Time,* is neither an isolated sphere nor an interiority, but is, as its manner of Being, an always-already-being-in-the-world with other beings of its own kind (and in the presence of other non-Dasein-like entities). Of course, this possibility of community, of Being-with (*Mitsein*), does not preclude our having factical difficulties in going along with the other human being. It does not exclude difference, but must precisely allow for difference within (and indeed as first enabling) community. Being with (others), as Heidegger puts it, "belongs to the essence of human existence, that is, to the existence of every unique individual in each case" (301). There is no human individual who would not always already have been exposed to being in a world, to a Being-in-the-world that is also a Being with other human beings. Heidegger does not spell it out here, but the "unquestionability" of the sharing (*teilen*) at issue is due to the fact that "our" world of Being-with-one-another is a world that is first disclosed in and through discourse, which itself enables communicative disclosure to others, a "communicating" (*Mitteilung*: literally, a separating and sharing-with) of our own Being. The significance of this will become apparent later.

Where do such reflections leave us? An initial comparative consideration of the second guiding thesis, "the animal is poor in world," suggested that the animal has and yet does not have world. If we now consider what this means in terms of transposability or going-along-with, it now seems that we as human beings are in some way and to some extent already transposed into the sphere of animal life, into the realm of access to other worldly entities that characterizes living beings in general. Yet does this necessarily mean that the animal *has a world*? A series of difficult, yet crucial questions arises here:

> However, if an original transposedness on the part of human beings is possible in relation to the animal, this surely implies that the animal also has its world. Or is this going too far? Is it precisely this "going too far" that we constantly misunderstand? And why do we do so? Transposedness into the animal can belong to the essence of human beings without this necessarily meaning that we transpose ourselves into an animal's world or that the animal in general has a world. And now our question becomes more incisive: In this transposedness into the animal, where is it that we are transposed to? What is it we are going along with, and what does this "with" mean? What sort of going is involved here? Or, from the perspective of the animal, what is it about the animal that allows and invites human transposedness into it, even while refusing human beings the possibility of going along with the animal? From the side of the animal, what is it that *grants the possibility of transposition and necessarily refuses any going-along-with*? What is this *having* and yet *not having*? (308)

The animal at once admits the *possibility* of a certain transposedness of human beings into it, and yet necessarily *refuses* our going along with it. We cannot go along with the way in which the animal sees something in the way that we can go along with the manner in which another human being sees something. The animal has, or better *is*, a certain sphere of transposability, and yet does not appear to have what we call world (which for us is always that of a historical community). Yet the animal's not having world, its refusal of our going along with it, is possible, notes Heidegger, only where there is a potentiality for granting transposability and having world. Such refusal is not a sheer not-having (not having even the possibility, as with the stone). The term *poverty* (*Armut*) designates precisely this "not having *in* [or *while*] being able to have [das Nichthaben *im* Habenkönnen]." Nevertheless, the refusal in question, Heidegger emphasizes, is not due to any inability intrinsic to the finitude of human knowing, but "is grounded in the essence of the animal" (309).

THE BEING OF THE ANIMAL: ORGANISM AND ENVIRONMENT

The above considerations have helped to set into relief the way in which the Being of animals manifests its own specific otherness to us, the way in which the animal's own proper Being announces itself within our world. Heidegger's formulation of this otherness as a "not having in being able to have" indicates that this otherness of animal Being is neither absolute otherness, nor a dialectical determination that would represent the Being of animals and that of humans as different stages of one underlying order of Being, of the Same conceived in the manner of the Hegelian Absolute. Indeed, Heidegger's formulation here seeks precisely to resist such a homogeneous ordering of living beings. For this reason, the "poverty in world" that names the aporia of animal Being also resists any hierarchical ordering of the Being of the animal compared to that of the human with regard to such criteria as completeness or perfection. Before considering this issue further, however, let us turn to Heidegger's concluding discussions of the Being of the animal and of the organism.

Following his preliminary analysis of the organism and its organs, Heidegger develops a complex and nuanced interpretation of the "self-like" character of the animal organism, of the "peculiarity" of its proper Being. We cannot here recount the detailed analyses of animal Being as "driven" and drive-like, analyses which the 1929–30 course unfolds in relation to certain results of experimental biology, but shall merely summarize the main conclusions. The organism's self-retaining is its remaining "with" itself (*bei sich selbst*), and this without any self-reflexivity. But in the case of animals, their remaining with themselves and keeping to themselves is also an "eliminative" moving away from, or assimilation of those entities that manifest themselves to the animal. Heidegger characterizes this strange absorption (*Eingenommenheit*) of the animal in and into itself as *Benommenheit*, captivated behavior or "captivation." Captivation designates the Being of the animal, "the inner possibility of animality itself," and yet it is quite different for each animal species (349). Such captivation is still an openness, since the animal is after all open to encountering other things; it has access to other entities in general. But is this openness the same as our openness for other entities, is this access the same as our access? Heidegger cites some results from experimental biology in arguing for a decisive difference between the openness of the animal's Being and that of the Being of humans. The animal is certainly open for and can be affected by other things around it; it is open for an environment in general, but, Heidegger argues, it can never ascertain, grasp, or apprehend these other things *as such*, as being what they are and as being present in the way that they are. Its captivation is such that it cannot apprehend other entities *as beings*, in their being present at hand. The animal has taken or removed from it (*genommen, benommen*) the possibility of apprehending something *as* something. Yet its captivation is not "some kind of rigid fixation on the part of the animal, as if it were somehow spellbound" (361). Rather, captivation enables the kind of "leeway" specific to the animal's openness for its environment, its openness for encountering things within the limits of its driven behavior.

To say that the animal is unable to apprehend beings as such, as beings (*Seiendes*), is to say that it is unable to apprehend them in their Being (*Sein*), that is, in respect of the fact that they "are": that they are this or that, that they are present here now and not absent, and so on. Yet this in itself implies something further:

> This driven behavior does *not* relate itself—and as captivated behavior cannot relate itself—to *what is present at hand as such.* What is present at hand as such means what is present at hand in its *being* present at hand, as a *being*. Beings are *not manifest* for the behavior of the animal in its captivation, they are not disclosed to it, and for that very reason are *not closed off from it* either. Captivation stands outside this possibility. As far as the animal is concerned, we cannot say that beings are closed off from it. Beings could only be closed off if there were some possibility of disclosure at all, however slight that might be. But the captivation of the animal places the animal essentially outside of the possibility that beings could be either disclosed to it or closed off from it. . . . (361)

Taken in itself, in what is most proper to it, the animal in its living moves outside of the play of disclosedness and concealment, beyond the possible alternative of Being or not Being. This means, more precisely formulated, that in the animal's behavior there is "*no letting be* of beings as such—none at all and in no way whatsoever, not even any not-letting-be" (368). Its openness is certainly an access to things outside of it, yet it is also characterized as an inability to attend to (*sich einlassen auf*) things as such. Rather, in its specific openness, the animal is driven around within its manifold drives in such a way that it "finds itself suspended, as it were between itself and its environment, even though neither one nor the other is experienced *as* being [*als Seiendes*]" (361). The animal is enclosed within an encircling ring (*Umring*), within which it is open for whatever can disinhibit its drives, for whatever can "affect" it or "trigger" its capacities. The animal "always intrinsically bears this disinhibiting ring along with it and does so as long as it is alive. More precisely, the animal's living is precisely the struggle [*Ringen*] to maintain this ring or sphere . . ." (371). This self-encircling is a way of living that is a strange absorption in itself; but this does not mean that the animal is absorbed in some so-called "interiority" (371). On the contrary, the animal lives and moves, it "behaves" (*benimmt sich*), precisely in a continual openness for whatever manifests itself to the animal in its environment. The Being of the animal, as driven behavior that is responsive to the entities that show themselves to it, is not at all enclosure in a capsule or closed sphere (377). And yet this manner of living appears to close itself off, or be closed off from, our way of Being.

We shall consider the validity and wider context of these claims in the final section of this chapter. But first let us pause to consider, within a somewhat broader perspective, the implications of this characterization of the Being of the animal with respect to our earlier question of the unity and self-like character of the organism—what Heidegger referred to as the peculiarity of its own proper Being. Heidegger's analyses appear to be conducted at a certain limit of scientific and metaphysical inquiry; more precisely, they appear to take such inquiry regarding this theme to a certain limit. In so doing, they not only problematize the mechanistic and physicalist conceptions of life, which reduce life to mechanistic or purely material processes, but also complicate a certain naivity in prevailing Darwinist and neovitalist approaches.

Our earlier consideration of the living being as an organism, while rejecting mechanistic conceptions of the organism and its organs as reductive and inappropriate, was nevertheless led to assert the necessity of a certain "self"-like unity of the organism. This appeared necessary simply on account of the organism's self-retention, its retaining itself as such despite all interaction with its environment. Of course, this character of being self-maintaining is in a purely formal sense found in every entity that is *this one* entity and not another. Yet the self-like character of an organism is unlike that of a stone, insofar as the organism, in its way of Being, is open for being affected by other entities around it, and indeed in such a way as to move itself in response to them, to "behave" accordingly. The pressing question is what kind (if any) of relation to "itself" the animal has in such behavior; what kind of "movement" this is (especially since it is not simply movement in space, but also a movement of living, of the living "process" as such—something Heidegger notes is crucial to understanding animal life, but which he does not pursue at length in this course);[8] and what it means to say that the animal moves "itself."

In general it can be said of scientific studies of animal or organismic life that they begin by regarding the animal as an *entity* and proceed from there to examine (via experiment, observation, and so on) its specific *way of Being*. Depending on the presuppositions at work, this way of Being may be regarded in advance in a mechanistic manner, that is, as "functioning" in terms of laws of extrinsic cause and effect; or it may be regarded in terms of an internal purposiveness and teleology, whereby the animal's way of Being is intrinsically self-regulating (self-causing, self-producing), unfolding in accordance with an "entelechy" (vitalism). Both of these approaches are inherently metaphysical, insofar as they proceed from an entity to discover its Being, its concealed truth and ground. *What* the animal, as an entity, truly *is*, in the *manner of its Being*, is to be uncovered by observing and inferring the hidden laws that govern and regulate its Being. These laws in their unity and coherence are to be made visible in language, in the *logos* of scientific discourse, which thereby formulates the formerly concealed *eidos* of the entity in its own proper Being, in the Being of itself, its "being-a-self." In Aristotelian metaphysics, such an approach ultimately arrives at the permanent truth of the Being of the entity; in modern metaphysics (science), such observation, in keeping with a transformed sense of *theōria*, is in advance subservient to the essence of technology: it discovers "truths" that serve only an ongoing production of "truth," of language, of Being, and of beings (not least of "living," "genetic" "material"). What is problematic about both approaches is that they presuppose in advance and from the outset that entities *in themselves* have the character of *eidos* ("form") and of *logos*, that the *Being* of entities (here, of living beings) has in the first instance and in general the character of a *"self"* (of self-subsistence and identity) that is reducible to and accessible as *logos*. With respect to determining the Being of living beings as "organisms," both mechanism and vitalism from the outset presuppose as known what is in fact most enigmatic, the enigma of living beings as such.

How does Heidegger's approach in the 1929–30 course problematize such approaches to understanding the Being of living beings? From the beginning, Heidegger's analysis takes the "organism" not as an already existing, fully determinate entity whose definitive Being is presupposed to be accessible in the presence-at-hand of its *eidos* (whether conceived as outward, empirical form, or as concealed "entelechy"), but as the *way of Being* of an entity that, existing in and as this way of Being, is fundamentally *open* to an environment, yet in the case of the animal in such a way as not to be open to itself, that is, to its own way of Being as such, in such openness. This fundamental openness of the organism as a way of Being means not only that the animal should not be conceived as an isolatable entity that then "has" a way of Being; but that the holistic and self-like character of an organism cannot be properly conceived as already circumscribed in advance in the manner of entelechy, of being in advance its own end. The self-like character of the animal as organism, rather, must be conceived as a finitude of Being, but a finitude that—as we shall attempt to clarify in the next section—is not accessible to the animal as being such.

The extent to which Heidegger's analyses in the 1929–30 course, in engaging with contemporary theories of biology, at once extend and radicalize prevailing late-nineteenth and early-twentieth-century conceptions of the organism is clarified in particular in section 61 of the course in the context of his remarks on the research of two leading biologists, Hans Driesch and Jakob Johann von Uexküll. In the research of Driesch, the mechanistic and instrumentalist conception of the relation between the organism and its organs is surpassed in favor of a holistic view of the organism. According to this view, "Wholeness means that the organism is not an aggregate, composed of elements or parts, but that the growth and the construction of the organism is governed by this whole-ness in each and every step" (380). Although this approach avoids the naive mechanistic conception that tries to recompose the living organism out of elementary cells, themselves conceived in physico-chemical fashion, it leads Driesch to regard the organism in terms of purposiveness, as governed by a certain force or entelechy. But a decisive shortcoming in this vitalist or neovitalist approach (which, Heidegger remarks, is "just as dangerous as mechanism" with regard to biological problems) is that the organism is isolated in advance from its environment: "[T]he organism is certainly grasped as a whole here, yet grasped in such a way that the animal's rela-tion to the environment has not been included in the fundamental structure of the organism. The totality of the organism coincides as it were with the external surface of the animal's body" (382). By contrast with the research of Driesch, the investigations of Uexküll adopt a more "ecological" approach that emphasizes the animal's relation to its environment. Despite the wealth and importance of Uexküll's empirical observations, however, the philosophical and theoretical interpretation of the organism's intimate relation to and interdependence upon its environment, is, Heidegger suggests, barely adequate. Not only is it problematic to speak, as Uexküll does, of an "environing world" (*Umwelt*) and an "inner world" (*Innenwelt*) of animals (since to do so meaningfully presupposes that the meaning of "world" has been adequately clarified); but the approach to understanding the organism's relation to its environ-ment is continually led astray by the prevailing Darwinistic inter-pretation of adaptation. "In Darwinism such investigations were based upon the fundamentally misconceived idea that the animal is present at hand, and then subsequently adapts itself to a world that is present at hand, that it then comports itself accordingly and that the fittest individual gets selected" (382). Nevertheless, claims Heidegger, Uexküll's investigations indeed prepare the possibility of "a more radical interpretation of the organism, according to which the totality of the organism would not merely consist in the corpo-real totality of the animal, but rather this corporeal totality could itself only be understood on the basis of that original totality which is circumscribed by what we called the *disinhibiting ring*" (383).

These remarks help to clarify the sense in which Heidegger's analyses problematize neovitalist conceptions of the organism, which ultimately appeal to an entelechy, but also problematize more fundamentally the ascription of an intrinsically self-like character and of a world to the animal precisely by the way in which the animal's open relation to its environment is taken up into the fundamental characterization of the animal's Being. As a way of Being, the animal is neither an entity that is simply present at hand "within" an environment or surrounding world that is also present at hand, and to which it *then* relates (375), nor is its Being an already present end in itself. Rather, as organism the animal is a fundamentally open way of Being (living) in relation to its environment, a manner of being open to the approach of other entities—a peculiar way of Being that does not hold itself back as such in the face of such approach (cf. the bee experiment described at 350–62), but is absorbed and captivated in the manner of assimilative and eliminative behavior.

We can see already from these reflections that Heidegger's analyses problematize from the outset any attempt to understand the Being of the organism or of the animal on the basis of a presupposed *eidos*. Not only is it reductive to regard the organism from the outset as an entity circumscribed by its already existing, present at hand form or figure, the "morphological unity" of its corporeal body; it is no less reductive to presuppose that an organism, in its way of Being, simply "has" or is an already existing "organization," fundamentally present at hand and that would be accessible in principle to an eidetic *logos*, that is, to a theoretical discourse that would simply describe what is already given and present at hand. Whether and to what extent Heidegger's own discourse, in claiming to describe the Being of the animal, is also problematized through these very analyses is something we shall have to consider in our concluding remarks.

On the basis of this characterization of animal Being as open for those things that disinhibit its drives, yet unable to attend to them as such, Heidegger identifies what now appears to have been misleading in the initial thesis that the animal is poor in world. When it was said that the animal both has and does not have world, the concept of *world* was being used in an equivocal and "underdetermined" sense. In saying that the animal has world, we meant that it has access to other things around it, unlike the stone. In saying that the animal does not have world, we meant that the animal refuses our going along with it in the way that *we* can go along with other human beings, in the sense of sharing a common comportment toward the same things, toward things to which we have a common access. Heidegger's claim concerning captivation, however, now suggests that the animal does have access to things that actually are, but that only *we* are able to experience these things and attend to them *as beings*:

> On the basis of our interpretation of animal *captivation*, however, we can now see *where the misinterpretation lies*. The animal certainly has access to . . . , and indeed to something that actually is. But this is something that *only we* are capable of experiencing and having manifest *as beings*. When we claimed by way of introduction that amongst other things world means the accessibility of beings, this characterization of the concept of world is easily misunderstood because the character of world remains underdetermined here. We must say that world does not mean the accessibility of beings, but rather implies *amongst other things* the accessibility of beings *as such*. (390–91)

If this insight is correct, then it seems we must conclude that the animal in fact *has no world*. This cannot of course mean that its Being coincides with the worldlessness of the stone. The animal indeed has something that the stone does not have; its being open in captivation is "something the animal *essentially has*" (391). We can therefore now provide a more appropriate formulation of the enigmatic "having and not having" of the animal: the animal displays a not-having of world in having an openness for whatever disinhibits its drives (392).

Does the clarification that *world* means not simply the accessibility of beings, but (inter alia) the accessibility of beings *as such* enable us to clarify the proper Being and proper peculiarity of the animal? We can now see—or so it seems—that the thesis that the animal is poor in world goes too far. For it is only from *our* perspective that the animal can be said to be poor in world. If by *world* we mean the human world, then we cannot say that the Being of the animal *in itself* is constituted by poverty in world. The thesis does not represent an interpretation of the specific essence proper to animality, but "only" a "comparative" illustration (393). It seems, therefore, says Heidegger, as though we must discard our thesis altogether, since it gives rise to the mistaken opinion that "the Being of the animal in and of itself" is deprivation and poverty (394).

Nevertheless, Heidegger does not hasten to this conclusion, but insists on the need for a critical caution. For is not this suspicion of a misinterpretation again based upon a metaphysics of subjectivity, itself derived from the medieval interpretation of the Being of beings as substance, an interpretation prepared in part by Greek philosophy? Does it not presuppose that the animal could in principle be accessible as it is *in itself*, isolatable from its intrinsic relations to other entities and thus determinable in its Being—precisely a presupposition that Heidegger's analyses have been at pains to refute? And have we not once again presupposed a naive anthropocentrism when we say "it is only from *our* perspective . . . ," only from the perspective of "our," "human" world? In what sense do we "have" this perspective, in what sense do we *have a world*, given that "we" are not simply entities that crop up among others, but are more fundamentally characterized by an access to other beings as such? What does it mean that we "stand" in an openness to other beings as such, that we apprehend other entities in their Being? Who are the "we" who, according to the third thesis, are said not merely to have a world or (as in *Being and Time*) to be "in" a world in the manner of "dwelling" in the presence of other beings, but to be "world-forming"? Is "world" adequately determined as an openness to or accessibility of beings as such?

Given that we still know very little of the essence of world, remarks Heidegger, we have no right at this stage to alter the thesis that the animal is poor in world, or simply to reduce it to the statement that the animal has no world, which might lead us to regard this not-having as "a mere not-having, rather than a deprivation" (395). Rather, we must leave open the possibility that the animal's not having world must indeed be understood as a deprivation. The present stage of the analysis invites a renewed meditation on what is meant by world.

The Phenomenon of World

Thus far, Heidegger's analyses have sought to understand the organism in terms of its living, and not as a mere entity: "the organism" is not meant to refer simply to a present at hand entity; and the specific Being of the animal organism (the animal as a way of Being, as "captivation") is not to be understood as presence-at-hand. Indeed, nature in general is inadequately conceived as "the wall which it becomes when turned into an object of scientific-theoretical observation" (403). It is characteristic of theoretical and scientific inquiry that it levels out distinctions in ways of Being pertaining to different kinds of entities, investigating all entities only insofar as they can be thematized and objectified in their presence at hand. That different kinds of entities do have fundamentally different ways of Being is, by contrast, precisely what we presuppose in our worldly actions and comportment toward other beings: we do not (for the most part) relate to another human being in the way that we might relate to an animal or to a stone. Moreover, in beginning with entities that are *isolated* and objectifiable in their presence at hand, the modern scientific worldview constructs retrospectively a "world" that (schematizing somewhat rapidly and without taking full account of the transformation of science into technology) consists of the subsequent linking and coordinating of these isolated elements in mathematically conceived space and time. In such a "world," there is no space or time for the irreducibly finite action of the individual, whose originary world is historically and ethically determined; the finitude of space and time is excluded in this theoretico-technical construct. In short, what is always and necessarily excluded in the scientific worldview are the worlds from which science itself originates (worlds that are intrinsically differential and which do not first need to be constructed): the finite action and activity of the scientist never enters the scientific "picture" as such; as a finitely acting being, the living individual is a matter of indifference to the force of scientific truth. Every scientist can in principle be substituted by another who can verify exactly the same results.

We have seen that in characterizing the Being of the animal as captivated behavior or *Benommenheit*, Heidegger not only denies that animal Being should be reduced to that of a present at hand entity; he also insists that the animal's multiple relations to its own environment are co-constitutive of, and must be incorporated into any theory of, the Being of the animal. Given that the "organism" is a fundamentally *open* way of Being, it is evidently problematic even to claim that one could conclusively define, that is, delimit in a definitional *logos* that would circumscribe its Being, *what* "the animal" in its essence "*is.*" Even Heidegger's characterization of the *way of Being* of the animal as *Benommenheit* neither claims to be a conclusive theory of animality that would be valid for all time, nor does it present a blanket theory of animal Being that could simply be "applied" indifferently to all animals. Nor, finally, does it present a definition that would simply allow us to oppose animals on the one side to human beings on the other.

The first point, which follows simply because the Being of language is itself intrinsically historical, that is, finitely temporal, is made by Heidegger himself with respect to a very specific history. Just following his summary of what is meant by *Benommenheit*, Heidegger remarks:

> Certainly we do not mean to imply that this represents the definitive clarification of the *essence of animality* beyond which there is no need to ask any further for all time. Yet it does represent a *concrete characterization of that fundamental conception in relation to the essence of life* within which every consideration of the essence of life moves. It was one which was long neglected precisely in the nineteenth century . . . because it was suppressed by the prevailing mechanistic and physicalist approach to nature. (378)

This remark relates to an earlier comment which we recalled above, namely, that the present inquiry is "for the moment" to remain within the bounds of scientific and metaphysical truth—kinds of truth that, he adds, "have together long since determined the way in which we conceive of truth in our everyday reflection and judgment" (300). In the 1929–30 course, Heidegger not only engages with contemporary scientific theory of animal life, but seeks to ground such theory philosophically: on the one hand, showing some of the fundamental presuppositions of such theory (ontological presuppositions concerning the very concept of biological life, and which are not accessible to the science of biology as such, but only to philosophizing); and on the other hand, grounding such presuppositions in a more fundamental experience of "world." In so doing, however, the 1929–30 course not only retrieves in a critical and transformative manner a fundamentally Aristotelian, ontotheological framework; it also problematizes the foundational primacy attributed to theoretical contemplation as our originary mode of access to the world.

Regarding the second point, the characterization of animal Being as captivated behavior would represent a metaphysical theory of "the animal" in general only if all animals, in this manner of

Being, were present at hand in the same way. But the thesis concerning animal Being as "poverty in world" and as captivated behavior is meant precisely to deny this reductionism (although this does not mean, of course, that a certain kind of presence at hand does not also pertain to the animal in each case): In characterizing the Being of the animal as *Benommenheit*, Heidegger is insistent that "animals for their part are *not something present at hand for us* in their Being . . ." (402). That is, they are not present at hand for us *in the way that scientific theory conceives them to be from the outset*. And this also means that Heidegger's thesis on animal Being is itself not reducible to a "theory" of animality. Rather, it provides us with a way of seeing and approaching animal Being that draws attention to what is suppressed and excluded by any scientific theory (not just those theories of the late nineteenth century).

The way in which Heidegger's thesis transgresses the "dimension of truth pertaining to scientific and metaphysical knowledge" becomes fully visible only toward the end of his reflections on animal Being, as the phenomenon of world is brought increasingly into view. Resisting any notion that the thesis of animal Being as captivation could simply be applied indifferently as a blanket theory, Heidegger stresses the need for attentiveness to the quite specific differences between various animal species. The encircling ring that constitutes the animal's captivation varies from animal to animal. Every animal and animal species is encircled by its own encircling ring, which in each case determines the openness of the animal for whatever things within its environment can disinhibit its specific drives. Yet not only is the encircling ring of the woodpecker different from that of the squirrel, which differs in turn from that of the woodworm; these encircling rings are themselves not present at hand spheres "laid down alongside or in between one another." Rather, they *intermesh* with one another:

> The woodworm, for example, which bores into the bark of the oak tree is encircled by *its own* specific ring. But the woodworm itself, and that means together with this encircling ring of its own, finds itself in turn within the ring encircling the woodpecker as it looks for the worm. And this woodpecker finds itself in all this within the ring encircling the squirrel which startles it as it works. Now this whole context of openness within the rings of captivation encircling the animal realm is

not merely characterized by an enormous wealth of contents and relations which we can hardly imagine, but in all of this it is still fundamentally different from the manifestness of beings as encountered in the world-forming *Dasein* of man. (401)

The encircling rings of living animals intermesh with one another and are "transposed" into one another in a way that differs fundamentally from all mere presence-at-hand. The Being of living beings, moreover, is such that in it there becomes manifest "*an intrinsically dominant character of living beings amongst beings in general*, an intrinsic elevation [*Erhabenheit*] of nature over itself, a sublimity that is lived in life itself" (403). Yet none of this intersecting of the encircling rings that constitutes the Being of living beings is simply present at hand for us human beings. Rather, human existence or *Dasein*, Heidegger emphasizes, is *itself* transposed in a peculiar way into the encircling nexus of living beings. Yet does this mean that we humans perhaps find ourselves circumscribed by our own specific encircling ring that grants us our peculiarly human perspective upon things, just as other living beings have theirs—"as if we were now on the same level as the animals, both them and us standing over against a wall of beings with the same shared content, as though the animals amongst themselves and we amongst them simply saw the same wall of beings in different ways, as though we were simply dealing with manifold aspects of the same" (403)? It is precisely this kind of theoretico-analogical relativism (which is also the essence of scientific objectivity, that is, of the metaphysics of representational subjectivity) that Heidegger's analysis seeks to resist:

> No, the encircling rings amongst themselves are not remotely comparable, and the totality of the manifest enmeshing of encircling rings in each case is not simply part of those beings that are otherwise manifest for us, but rather holds us captive [*hält uns . . . gefangen*] in a quite specific way. That is why we say that humans exist in a peculiar way *in the midst* [*inmitten*] of beings. In the midst of beings means: Living nature holds us ourselves captive as human beings in a quite specific way, not on the basis of any particular influence or impression that nature exerts or makes upon us, but rather from out of our essence, whether we experience that essence in an originary relationship or not. (403–404)

The claim that the ways in which entities are originarily given and show themselves are fundamentally different among living beings, whether animal or human, cautions us against the prejudice that there is simply one world, composed of a sum-total of present at hand entities, to which different beings would have different access depending on their individual perspective. The honey that appears to a bee as its food may not appear to a cat at all—not even as something toward which it could be indifferent (for this would presuppose the cat being able to adopt a stance toward the honey, as well as the honey being given for the cat *as being honey*). But this does not at all mean that the way in which something appears is primarily dependent upon a "subject" or upon the particular living being in question—not even in the case of the human being. Furthermore, as Heidegger here indicates, human beings are not above or beyond nature in the sense of being different, as beings, from living nature (the fundamental or originary difference between human and animal is not an ontic difference); rather, the point is that living nature (as *phusis*) in us, which indeed "holds us captive in a quite specific way," exists in a way of Being that is other than that of other kinds of living being. It is ontologically other, other by virtue of its being "ontological," or better, historical. In Heidegger's understanding of "essence" (*Wesen*), the claim that the animal is other in essence than the human does not refer to essential essence in the sense of "whatness" or substance (*essentia, ousia*) characteristic of metaphysics, but to the respective ways of Being of human and animal, the kind of presence each displays.

In order to substantiate and clarify these claims, we must examine more closely the concept of world and its relation to selfhood, keeping in view Heidegger's earlier claims about animal Being as captivation. Here we shall also go beyond what is explicitly said in the text of the 1929–30 course.

In examining the claim that "the animal is poor in world," Heidegger indicated provisionally that this thesis is sustainable only if by "world" we mean not simply the accessibility of beings, but ("amongst other things") the accessibility of beings *as such*, as beings. Yet this determination too is not sufficient to fully comprehend the phenomenon of world. What is meant by "world"? For us, entities are not only given and accessible to us as manifest beings, as being in each case this or that; they are also simultaneously given *as a whole*, in a certain togetherness and unity. They belong together in such a way that no entity is ever given in iso-lation, and yet each and every entity is manifest in its particularity, as being the entity that it is. But this "whole," which we under-stand as our *world*, is not at all reducible to the sum-total of mani-fest beings, nor to a totality of beings that exist in themselves. Rather, this "whole" must already be given *in advance* in order for it to be possible for us to have access to any entity *as being this particular entity*. The possibility of beings first being given and appearing as such, in their specific Being, is first enabled by this prior forming of a whole. For to have access to any particular entity as being this entity is *already* to see it *in an originary relation to* other beings, as being *this* entity *and not another*. "Originary" here means, among other things: prior to ascertainment by a theo-retical *logos*. A differential unity, a belonging together in mutual difference, always already precedes any appearing of identity. In the 1929–30 course, Heidegger relates the prevailing of this differ-ential unity to Aristotle in identifying it with the simultaneous *sunthesis* and *diairesis* that first enables (i.e., temporalizes) the spe-cific openness in which apophantic discourse (the *logos apophantikos*) is grounded. Apophantic discourse is discourse that makes the spe-cific claim solely to point out and manifest that which already is in its presence at hand (and such is precisely the theoretical discourse of science). The happening, or temporalizing, of this differential belonging-together, that is, of the openness of beings as a whole at each moment, is equally an event of freedom: it first enables our being free for other beings as other. As the prior formation of world, this event first enables not only the *logos apophantikos* as such, but every *logos*. For every discourse speaks, knowingly or not, from out of and into this prior forming of a whole.

We do not have the occasion here to pursue at greater length this rootedness of *logos* in the happening of world.[9] But granted that *world*, at least for us human beings, entails not only the accessibility of beings as such, but the accessibility or manifestness of beings as such and *as a whole* in the specific sense indicated (412); granted also that there is a prior forming of world—prior, that is, to the manifestness of particular beings as such—the pressing question remains of *how* this "forming" of world occurs. Is it the human being that in each case forms the world, as Heidegger's third thesis, "man is world-forming," might seem to claim? If so, are we not after all trapped in a kind of anthropocentric perspectivism in which human beings, whether as individual or collective subjects, somehow form and thus "have" their human world, from which they could know nothing of the "world" or "worlds" of animals? Is not the world, in which we already find ourselves, "our world" after all, as we put it above?

That the world is not at all simply "our" world, that it is neither the property of, nor something first formed by the activity of, human beings, is indicated by the fact that the only human beings that exist are individual beings that have already become manifest as such, within and in the midst of a world of others, a world that for its part already exists in preceding them. Only within an already prevailing world can individual beings first become manifest as such, not only to others, but to themselves as individual beings. The Being of an individual human being is first enabled by this precedence of a world (which is to say, by the precedence of history). Thus, Heidegger writes, "For it is not the case that the human being first exists and then also one day decides amongst other things to form a world. Rather world-formation is something that occurs, and only on this ground can a human being exist in the first place" (414). As Heidegger also indicates here, "world" is not simply a phenomenon that already exists, but an *event* that occurs and continues to occur: it forms itself, it is intrinsically poietic, transformative. But this event does not happen without or somewhere beyond human beings either: it occurs in and through human beings, who partake in the happening of this event, although they do not originate it as "subjects." Thus, Heidegger explains, it is not the individual, existent human being who is world-forming; rather, the human being in his essential humanity, in his (futural and historical) Being (*Sein*)—in his openness to and for a possible world, in the happening of disclosedness in and through him—is first enabled by something else: "the *Da-sein in* the human being is world-forming" (414).

In what way do we in each case first come to ourselves and first become manifest to ourselves as such, as an individualized, existing self, through this event of world-formation that occurs through the *Da-sein* in us, that is, through the historical disclosure of worldly freedom? Not through any self-reflection or theoretical speculation, but more originarily through the phenomenon of attunement (*Stimmung*). For the happening of attunement holds and maintains us in the thrownness of our concrete, bodily existing: In its originary unity with world-formation, it manifests us in our already having been, in our having been thrown in each case into the finite happening of a particular, situated historical world. Such happening of attunement is the way in which we originarily approach and find ourselves as precisely *ourselves* in each instance, and not others. It is the event of our emergence into the manifestness of a finite world, a happening of the manifestness of a whole into which we are held in advance, and thereby held open to others and to ourselves. As such, attunement is the specific way in which living nature "holds us captive" in the midst of beings as a whole:

> Dasein places us ourselves before beings as a whole. In attunement, one *is* in this way or that—and this therefore entails that attunement precisely makes manifest *beings as a whole* and makes us manifest to ourselves as we find ourselves situated in the midst of beings as a whole. Attunement and being attuned is by no means a taking cognizance of psychological states, but is rather a way of *being borne out* into a manifestness of beings as a whole that is in each case specific, and that means: into the manifestness of Dasein as such, as it finds itself situated in the midst of this whole in each instance. (410)

The primacy of attunement in the disclosure of our Being entails that living nature, in holding us captive, is never entirely reducible to an object of theoretical contemplation. Rather, it is that to which we are always already bound in advance, that which binds us prior to all our activities and actions. Yet it binds us in the peculiar and enigmatic manner that this binding character of those beings that surround us and press upon us *first approaches us* from out of the openness of a finite, historical world. By contrast, the German for "poverty" in the animal's alleged "poverty in world," namely, *Armut*, implies the lack of a certain kind of *pathos* or attunement, of a certain mood, even of a certain courage or gathering of oneself, of a certain "cheer" or "spirit"—all of which are suggested by the German *Mut*.[10] The manifestness of beings as a whole in each case approaches us as a manifestness that *precedes us in already having been*, such that the disclosure and openness of living nature for us is always already historical. If the happening of world is itself an emergence, a coming into Being, and indeed one that first enables our own historical emergence as a self in each case, this futural character of world-formation is nevertheless always bound in advance to manifestation in and through particular living beings whose existence is at once finite and historical.[11] The happening of world is thus "bound" in the twofold sense of being tied to and borne by a particular, factical situatedness in the midst of beings, and in that the possibilities it enables are in each case *restricted* in advance to possibilities that are projected and come toward us *from out of* a disclosedness of beings that have already been, that is, that are manifest in a worldly and historical manner (cf. 527–28). The event of world-formation frees beings as a whole to manifest themselves temporally and historically, and only thereby frees us to respond to and take up a stance toward beings as a whole amid this situated happening of worldly freedom. Freedom, as Heidegger would later emphasize, is not the property of human beings.

These considerations, which go somewhat beyond the explicit text of the 1929–30 course, make it apparent that a peculiar *poiēsis* happens in and through human beings, a *poiēsis* of which they are not the origin (Heidegger relates it to Aristotle's so-called *nous poiētikos*). Nevertheless, this originary *poiēsis* itself *enables* that peculiar manner of being an origin that is proper to human beings: the possibility of *action*, of coming into Being in freely responding to that which has already been. Our everyday actions, as in each case a factical response to that which already is, presuppose a more originary responsiveness and responsibility in and through which beings first manifest themselves and come to be, come to stand in the light of a particular historical world; in short, they presuppose what Heidegger would later call the event (*Ereignis*) in which language comes to pass. The Being of world itself indeed presupposes, or rather *is*, this always already having been drawn into language as an event that precedes us, as the precedence that history itself is. The coming to be of a world is in each case first enabled by our being held open in our bodily attunement (prior to any self-disclosure or presence as such) for the happening of language. For language is that which has always already been in being always yet to come.

The Time of Life: Self and World

We cannot pursue these themes at length here, themes that, emerging from the 1929–30 course, clearly foreshadow the discussion of the strife between world and Earth in "The Origin of the Work of Art" (1936) and the more explicit writings on the *Ereignis* of world as the *Ereignis* of language in Heidegger's later work. We shall broach some of these issues in our later chapters. In the present chapter we shall try, rather, in our concluding remarks to reconsider some of Heidegger's claims concerning animal Being in the light of the preceding discussion of world, specifically in relation to the question of selfhood.

According to the characterization of animal Being as captivated behavior, such captivation entails among other things an absorption (*Eingenommenheit*) of the animal into itself (367). But this does not mean that the animal in its way of Being (living) is preoccupied with itself or even has access to itself, that is, to its own way of Being, as such. Quite to the contrary. The animal neither has nor exists as a self in the way in which we do. The animal's captivated behavior is absorption in the sense of a being absorbed into "the totality of interacting instinctual drives," a totality in which the unity of the animal's body as a living body is grounded (376). As we have seen, this absorption does not, however, mean enclosedness or encapsulation in an interiority. It is precisely an *openness*—a way of living that is a remaining open for whatever is accessible. As a consequence of this very openness of the activity of living, the animal is always more than it already is: it exceeds every "already" in an incalculable manner that can never be theoretically discerned. Which is also to say that the animal in its living is in each case a specific kind of emergence and approach: as Heidegger puts it, the animal "approaches" or "comes toward" the Other in "opening itself" to the Other (369). And yet, according to Heidegger, this Other is never manifest as a being (*Seiendes*), that is, in its Being (*Sein*). Whatever disinhibits and triggers the animal's driven behavior in affecting its specific sensibility "withdraws itself as it were constantly and necessarily" from the specific openness of the animal's captivated behavior (370). This self-withdrawal of that which appears and presents itself to the animal implies that the animal is in effect captivated by the ongoing flow of presentation of whatever presents itself, of that which it "deals with" in the manner of "elimination" (*Beseitigung*)—the German term here implying moving things aside, letting them pass to the side. This "elimination" precisely lets the animal maintain its ongoing activity as living, lets its own specific emergence move on, so to speak.

But this moving on—as the ongoing opening up and self-maintaining of driven capacity in its self-traversing movement—is a continual exposure to and dependence on whatever presents itself even
as it withdraws, presents itself in its very withdrawal. This entails
that the animal, "taken" as it is by the ongoing flow of presentation, borne along and carried along by it, is unable to take up a free
stance outside the presence of whatever is present as its environment. Neither the specific Being (presence) of the animal itself, nor
that of whatever appears and presents itself to the animal, are able
to attain any permanence in the midst of this temporal flow of
presentation. Thus Heidegger writes that, for the animal,

> that which disinhibits . . . must constantly in accordance with
> its essence withdraw itself. It is *nothing enduring* that could
> *stand over against the animal as a possible object* [kein Bleibendes,
> das dem Tier als ein möglicher Gegenstand gegenübersteht]. . . .
> The self-withdrawal of that which disinhibits corresponds
> to the essential *inability to attend* to it which is involved in
> behavior. . . . (372)

Correlatively, the Being of the animal itself lacks the specific enduring or remaining that enables an attentiveness to whatever is
present as such, as being present:

> Since that which disinhibits behavior essentially withdraws
> and eludes it [aus dem Wege geht], so too the relation of behav-
> ior to that which occasions it is a *not attending to it*. No perma-
> nence as such is ever attained [Es kommt nie zu einem Bleiben als
> solchem], nor indeed any change as such. (370)

In order for a living being to be able to achieve an endurance
beyond or in excess of the temporal flow of presentation, it (its
living presence) would have to take up an independent stance in
relation to something outside of and beyond not only that which
is presenting itself, but beyond the present of whatever is presenting itself at each moment. Such a stance, constitutive of our *ēthos*,
is, for us, a dwelling in the element of language. It is what we call
Being. In being brought to language, things too first attain a certain
endurance and permanence of presence, they come to stand over
against us (our own presencing) in various kinds of presence at
hand. For only where there is language can that which presences

come to stand in the relative and unitary constancy of its manifold presentations. Such permanence is not atemporal or eternal, but an enduring in the manner of the specific temporality of *historical* time: it is a coming to stand, for a while, for a time, in a coming that is at once a return, and, in the temporality of its very return, something new.

What does this imply with respect to the activity of the animal in each case? The beginning of the animal's activities, such as moving, feeding, and so on, is never a free origination in the manner in which humans can freely initiate and thus be an origin of their actions. This is because the animal does not exist in a free (world-forming) anticipation of Being in general, whether its own Being or that of others; it does not come to stand within the freedom of and openness to a world, that is, to that whole that first enables something to be apprehended as *being* what it is, as being in such and such a way, or as being in relation to something else. The animal's activities and movements are always responsive to and triggered by whatever presents itself in the animal's immediate environment. Yet none of this entails that the animal is a purely passive being, merely at the mercy of whatever presents itself to the animal as it withdraws. The animal is still able to move and "act" in a manner that is not *wholly* or exclusively determined by its immediate environment. Although Heidegger, so far as we are aware, nowhere clarifies this sufficiently, the animal (or at least some animals) in fact has and must have a certain ability (again different for each specific animal according to the manner of its behavior and captivation) to relate to something *as* something, although not, indeed, *as being* something. It is indeed a precondition of the animal's being able to move that it has an ability to relate to something beyond the field of its own specific presence at any particular moment. Aristotle already understood this necessity for a living being to exist in a differential relationship to the momentary field of presence of its immediate environment if it is to be able to move. A cat responds to the presence of a mouse *as* its potential dinner, or *as* something to play with; it responds to the presence of a dog *as* a potential threat—*and not* as its food (but this "and not," which in the case of the animal occurs not through the free element of *logos*, but is bound to the momentary presence of the particular, is presumably not open to the animal *as such*). This entails that what is not immediately present (in the latter case, its food) is and can indeed also be present *in a certain way* for the animal—which is also a precondition of the fact that certain animals can be trained and acquire "learned behavior."[12] (Aristotle called this faculty *phantasia*.) But in what way? For the animal, the presence of that which is not immediately given in its environment is a presence by association: it is triggered precisely by that which is present at a given moment. The animal is exposed to the presence of what presents itself in the immediate moment in the sense of being captivated by it and having to behave accordingly in response. This response would of course be very specific, dependent on the way in which the animal's previous exposure to various entities has been "incorporated" into its driven behavior, and on what transpires in the free play of presence and absence to which the animal is exposed on each occasion; animal response does not follow the rule of cause and effect. But this precisely means, as we can now see more clearly, that it would indeed be going too far to say that the animal either has or does not have world: its living entails the forming of a certain whole, of a wholeness of its relations that is the openness of an encircling ring—and yet this living does not irrupt or break out into the taking up of a *free stance* in the midst of this whole, a stance that would free it for its own presence.

The implications of these reflections become clearer if we consider the question of whether the animal has a relation to *itself* or not. The above considerations imply that the animal indeed has something like a *sense* of self. The animal senses itself, that is, its embodiment, in emerging out of itself and in moving, but only in response to whatever is immediately given to it within what Heidegger calls the encircling ring of its specific openness for being affected. But such a sense of self is quite other than the human sense of selfhood. In its absorption into its own living, into its own openness for . . . other entities, the animal is never "with itself [*bei sich selbst*] in the proper sense" (374), the German preposition *bei* here implying "in the presence of. . . ." Rather, Heidegger writes,

> The specific selfhood [*Selbstsein*] of the animal (taking "self" here in a purely formal sense) is its being proper to itself, being its own [*Sich-zu-eigen-Sein, Eigentum*] in the manner of its driven activity. The animal is always driven in a certain way in this activity. This is why its being taken [in the sense of given over to, or "preoccupied" with whatever it is ab-

sorbed in: *Hingenommensein*] is never a letting itself attend to beings, *not even to itself as such*. But this driven activity does not occur within a self-enclosed capsule; on the contrary, on the grounds of the way in which the instinctual drives themselves are preoccupied [*aufgrund der Hingenommenheit der Triebe*] it is always related to something else. (376–77, emphasis added)

The claimed inability of the animal to attend to itself as such (that is, as being itself) is not disproven by the fact that birds preen themselves or that cats clean their fur. The claim is that the animal is unable to let itself (its own Being) be, because it is unable to let be in general. Letting be (*Seinlassen*) in the sense of attending to . . . is not at all to be understood as a passive disregard, but as a taking into care in the manner of entering into the historical happening of a world. The animal's absorption into itself means that the animal cannot exist in the manner of being-a-self (or of self-consciousness), even though it "has," or rather, "is" its own proper way of Being (living), which is intrinsically retained in this absorption. This means that the animal, as a way of Being, is indeed "outside of itself," but not in such a way as to have a *free* relation to its own Being, that is, to *stand* outside itself in its own Being. For this reason, its Being is not "ekstatic" in the strict sense of the word (as used in *Being and Time* to characterize the temporality of *Dasein*), which entails *stasis*, that is, having assumed a *stance* (*Haltung*) outside of its own Being, a stance or "holding" of oneself (*Sichhalten*) that nevertheless enables a free presence-to-self in the manner of human existing or *ēthos*. Thus, Heidegger remarks, human activity is "comportment" or conduct (*Verhalten*) rather than behavior (345–46). "But all comportment is possible only in being held in a certain restraint [*Verhaltenheit*], maintaining a stance [*Verhaltung*], and a stance [*Haltung*] is given only where a being has the character of a self or, as we also say, of a person" (397–98). Such presence is (among other things) a remaining "with" (*bei*), that is, in the presence of oneself in each case, which is to say, in the presence of one's own having-been, of oneself as other—not as any arbitrary other, but as the other in and of oneself, the still indeterminate Other that in each case "holds us captive" in our historical thrownness in the midst of beings as a whole. It is a futural openness for one's own having been, an openness that is "held" (*gehalten*), as presence, in the manner of the *Augenblick*, the momentary "glance of the eye" that catches sight of beings as a whole in their worldly presence and that stands at the heart of both *Being and Time* and the 1929–30 course (and indeed of all of Heidegger's work). "Oneself" here means, therefore: thought as and in terms of *Dasein*, as Being-in-the-world, that is, as the having-been of a *world* that includes the Being one has and will have been in one's worldly appearing to others. Assuming a free relation and stance toward one's own Being presupposes a free yet binding relation toward the Being of beings as a whole, toward the phenomenon of world that first lets beings appear and be as such, in their singularity.

By contrast, the animal in its absorption displays a peculiar non-remaining with either its own (thrown) Being or that of others, that is, with Being as that which has been (historical). The animal's "thrownness," its being captivated as a particular emergence in living nature, is ahistorical. The animal shows an openness to what is to come in a turning away from, a non-attending to, presence— in a non-tarrying in the presence of others. The Being or *Dasein* of human beings, by contrast, is precisely this tarrying and dwelling in the presence of others (including oneself as "other"), *a presence that exists only as having-been*. This tarrying in being held in a presence and toward other beings as a whole can be understood as the happening of an always indeterminate future, as an originarily responsive letting-be (*Seinlassen*). In enabling beings to arrive and while in presence, it entails a holding oneself in this presencing, an originary letting-happen (or letting-arrive) of *world*, as completion (*Ergänzung*). This forming of a whole enables the togetherness of other beings in keeping to themselves while presencing: a belonging together as a coming to be (to presence) together in having-been.

With regard to the time of life, one can thus say that whereas the animal, in its radical openness, is refused the possibility of any return to its own having-been as a having been in the presence of others—which, as we can now better appreciate, is precisely the *refusal* in which the animal shows itself to us in its specific otherness—and is thus excluded from an active participation in the temporality of the world as such, human beings are necessarily held in and drawn into this possibility. Their presence can only ever be a presence that has already been; their future presence will always be a presence that will have been: with respect to the presence of what is present, they exist in an essential absence. And this is the possibility and necessity of their actions, of their existing futurally and, from out of what has been, bringing forth in their actions what has never yet been—of their being an origin that remains indebted to a historical world as a world of others. In the concluding remarks of the course, Heidegger characterizes the occurrence of this held presence, of the moment of human existing and acting, as the happening of an essential absence that is at once worldly, historical, and finite:

> In the occurrence of projection world is formed, that is, in projection something erupts and irrupts toward possibilities, thereby irrupting into what is actual as such, so as to experience itself as having irrupted as an actual being in the midst of what can now be manifest as beings. It is a being of a properly primordial kind, which has irrupted to that way of Being [*Sein*] which we call *Da-sein* and to that being [*Seienden*] which we say *exists*, that is, *ex-sists*, is an exiting from itself in the essence of its Being, yet without abandoning itself.
>
> Man is that inability to remain and yet is unable to leave his place. In projecting, the *Da-sein* in him constantly *throws* him into possibilities and thereby keeps him *subjected* to what is actual. Thus thrown in this throw, man is a *transition*, transition as the fundamental essence of occurrence. Man is history, or better, history is man. Man is *enraptured* in this transition and therefore prevails as "*absent*." Absent in a fundamental sense—never simply at hand, but absent in the essence of his prevailing, in his *essentially being away*, removed into *essential having been and future*—prevailing in absence and never at hand, yet *existent* in his essential absence. . . . (531)

What does this absence intrinsic to the momentary presencing of human existence imply with respect to the divergence between human and animal ways of Being? In recalling his earlier analyses of the fundamental attunement of boredom from the same course, an attunement that brings us before beings as a whole and thrusts us into the momentary necessity of having to act, Heidegger recalls how the *Augenblick*, or authentic moment of presence, shows itself as the opening up of "the entire abyss [*Abgrund*] of *Dasein* in the midst of *Dasein*" (411). It is the abyss of our historical Being, of the task of having to be historical even in the thrownness and finitude of our living singularity (for us, the inevitable "solitude" [*Einsamkeit*] and individuation [*Vereinzelung*] in our having to be with others), the abyss of our manner of being held captive in the midst of living

nature. This being held captive (*gefangen*) is, Heidegger insists, quite
different from the animal's captivation (*Benommenheit*). For between
these two manners of Being "there lies an abyss that can be bridged
by no mediation whatsoever" (409). The anti-Hegelian tenor of this
claim should not, however, mislead us into thinking that there is
no belonging together of these diverse and different ways of Being.
More precisely, as becomes apparent by the end of the course, we
should say that the abyss in question *is the "between"*: it is the
happening of that between which enables a finite, differential belonging together in distinction, the happening of a historical world.[13]
In the concluding paragraphs, Heidegger identifies the happening
of this "originarily *irruptive* 'between' " as the irrupting into the
midst of beings of the ontological difference itself (the difference
"between" Being and beings), or better, of the *event* of originary
difference that occurs as the formation of world and that first lets
beings become manifest as such, in their Being (530–31). It is the
event of that distinction which "ultimately . . . *makes possible all distinguishing and all distinctiveness . . . ,*" all *krinein* (517–18). Nevertheless, if our insight into this "abyss," the happening of worldly
freedom itself, calls for "the complete divergence of the two theses
[concerning the animal and the human being]" (409), this does not
mean that the theses are unsustainable as such. The thesis of the
animal's world-poverty as "not having in/while being able to have"
world, in its divergence from the thesis that the human being is
world-forming, precisely lets "the essence of world light up" (409).
The entire analysis of animal Being, we must recall (and Heidegger
is emphatic about this), is subservient to this leading task.[14] Only
if one isolates the analyses of animal Being from their proper context, as tends to happen in contemporary debate, does the thesis
that the animal is "poor in world" appear to merely reinscribe a
fundamentally traditional, metaphysical "theory" distinguishing the
animal from the human. (This does not of course mean—as the
present chapter has tried to indicate—that the thesis does not retrieve traditional philosophical resources; the point is that in so
doing, it also critically transforms and rethinks such resources.) By
contrast, attentiveness to the way in which the thesis is situated in
relation to the phenomenon of world shows why the Being of the
animal and that of human *Dasein* cannot simply be opposed to one
another as present at hand realms being described by a purely
theoretical discourse. The "abyssal" opening up of the happening

of world, as the happening of historical freedom, is not that of a present at hand abyss or difference that exists between two already existing entities. It is the opening of the ongoing and never completable task of our ethical responsibility toward not only other humans, but all others, living and otherwise. The momentary event of presencing that lets beings be is in this sense protoethical, the criterion of all criteria.

Heidegger's attentiveness to the poietic, world-forming occurrence of this "momentary" event indicates that the *Augenblick* not only names the way in which we are held in having-been and future, and thus exist and come to presence only in and as the "essential absence" of a displacement or removal that is also an ekstatic rapture or transport; it also marks the site of the opening up of a world that has always already called us into Being, called upon us to irrupt into the freedom of a world and to assume a free stance toward the beings manifest within this happening of world. Having entered a world, we are always already absent in the sense of having-been, of dwelling in advance in the happening of a world whose presence calls us from beyond our time. Existing in the world, our "own" time is always already that of others, both of the others of other historical worlds and of other beings whose way of Being is not historical, that is, does not carry the weight or burden of our responsibility. In acting, in coming to be ourselves, we have always already exited from any time that could be exclusively our own in entering the time of others as the time of a world. The time of life, "our" time, will always have been that of others in whose presence we dwell. Such dwelling, and the stance that it assumes at a given moment, is precisely our *ēthos*.

TWO

Care for the Self
Originary Ethics in Heidegger and Foucault

Our first chapter has made visible the Being or *Dasein* of human beings as a dwelling in the presence of other beings, a dwelling first enabled by Dasein's being held, through the attunement of *Angst*, in a futural openness for its own having-been, an openness in which the moment of action, the *Augenblick* of a possible decision, is held at the ready. This openness, as *Being and Time* already indicated, is itself temporalized as Dasein's *being free for* its ownmost potentiality for Being—that is, as its being free for the freedom that it itself potentially is—and only thereby as a being free for the possibility of this or that determinate decision. Attuning Dasein in its factical, thrown situatedness in the midst of beings as a whole, *Angst* first discloses and brings Dasein "before" the world as world, as that which always already exceeds it, opening Dasein to and for its thrown Being-in-the-world as such. The phenomenon of world shows itself to be this prior or precedent forming of a whole, of a freedom for presence, from out of which beings can first be uncovered as such, as being this or that, in the determinacy of their possible presence. In the same way, the phenomenon of world temporalizes itself as the horizon from out of which the possibility of a particular decision can first be discerned in its determinacy. Thus, as Heidegger indicates in *Being and Time,* that in the face of which, or "before" which, Dasein is attuned by *Angst*—the phenomenon of world as such—is itself altogether *indeterminate*, an openness that opens the possibility of this or that moment of presence. With respect to particular beings themselves, it is *nothing*, and yet this "nothing" of beings is the most primordial "something," the phenomenon (or phenomenality) of all phenomena (SZ, 186–87). Dasein's dwelling, its being held in the possibility of presence, is thus intrinsically a being held out into the "nothing," as Heidegger would put it in the 1929 lecture "What is Metaphysics?" (W, 12). Yet this also means that Dasein's dwelling, its being "at home" in the world, is always exposed in advance to a "not being at home," to an *Unheimlichkeit*, an uncanniness that, Heidegger emphasizes, is "the more primordial phenomenon" with respect to all dwelling (SZ, 189). Thus, as Heidegger would subsequently express it, *Unheimlichkeit* does not first arise as a consequence of humankind; "rather, humankind emerges from uncanninness and remains within it . . ." (GA 53, 89); the essence of *Unheimlichkeit* is "presencing in the manner of an absencing, and in such a way that whatever presences and absences here is itself simultaneously the open realm of all presencing and absencing" (GA 53, 92). Exposed in advance to, and grounded in, a not being at home, Dasein's dwelling thus shows itself to be, fundamentally, not at all a secure and fixed abode amid the familiar, but a task that must be accomplished ever anew: the task of coming to be at home in, all the while, not being at home.

We shall later return to this theme of *Unheimlichkeit* in considering the theme of poetic dwelling in Heidegger's dialogue with Hölderlin and with Sophocles. For now, let us dwell for a moment on what Heidegger in *Being and Time* identifies as the *peculiarity*, or *Eigentümlichkeit*, of *Angst*: the "peculiar indeterminacy" of that in the presence of which Dasein finds itself attuned in *Angst* (188); the "peculiar temporality" of *Angst*, such that "it is originarily grounded in having-been, and future and presence are first temporalized from out of this" (344). This peculiarity corresponds, indeed, to what we have seen Heidegger note toward the end of the 1929–30 course: With respect to his Being, the human being is "that inability to remain," to dwell, "and yet is unable to leave his place." For the attunement of *Angst* at once discloses Dasein in the radical individuation of its thrownness, of its being bound, as this singular Dasein, to this having been here and now in this factical situatedness, from out of which it—and it alone—has to act. Yet the thrownness of this having been, Dasein's inability to leave its place, is at the same time delivered over to having *yet to be*—thus, to the most radical indeterminacy, to the openness of the future that happens or temporalizes from out of this having been, thus in turn giving rise to the present. *Angst*, says Heidegger, "discloses Dasein *as being possible*," discloses its very Being as possibility (and not as this or that possibility), manifests it in its "*being free for* the freedom [or possibility] of choosing itself," but this freedom for . . . a determinate possibility, although thrown and factical, is not itself determinate. What is this strange, uncanny freedom to which Dasein is exposed amidst its very thrownness? And is it really Dasein's "ownmost" potentiality for Being? Does it belong to Dasein as its already existent, albeit ontological and abyssal, ground? Or is it not rather the case that, in its very happening, such freedom resists all appropriation by Dasein, exceeding it in the direction of that future that will never be its own? Is this freedom for myself, for my possibilities, in the end a freedom *of* myself? And how does such freedom relate to questions of selfhood and *ēthos?*

The present chapter attempts to approach such questions by way of an apparent parallel between Heidegger and the work of French philosopher Michel Foucault concerning the question of ethics, the important differences between these two thinkers notwithstanding. One cannot but be struck by the proximity of certain of Foucault's formulations in one of his last works, namely, the 1984 interview published under the title "The Ethic of Care for the Self as a Practice of Freedom," and Heidegger's early thought from the period surrounding *Being and Time.* Our purpose in the following remarks is not to argue that Foucault and Heidegger are saying the same thing, but to try to show that their thinking shares a common issue, to which and from which each of them speak, and in terms of which they may be brought into dialogue. This dialogue, we shall try to show, sheds light on the ways in which, for both thinkers, the practice of freedom, enacted as a free, knowing, and self-critical cultivation of one's *ēthos*, demands an understanding of selfhood in terms of the temporality of action, the phenomenon of world, and the historical determination of one's worldly Being.[1]

The title of Foucault's interview immediately suggests a common ground between these two thinkers: the theme of "care for the self," prominent in Foucault's last phase, at once recalls the central term by which, in *Being and Time*, Heidegger designates the Being of *Dasein*, of the entity that each of us ourselves is in each case. And yet no sooner do we make this connection than we sense within us an immediate resistance. For one thing, Heidegger emphasizes that "care" (*Sorge*) designates the very Being of Dasein, and is not to be taken as a particular ontic comportment. In being ahead of itself in its already being in the world, Dasein's Being has always already been taken into care, whether or not Dasein, at the ontic-existentiell level, chooses to "care" about its Being or not. Furthermore, where, in his early work, does Heidegger have anything to say about the practice of freedom? And is it not evident enough from Foucault's later studies that care for the self is to be taken as a very concrete practice? Is not his work on the last two volumes of the *History of Sexuality* in effect an extensive study of various concrete, historically conditioned practices of such "care"? Whereas in Heidegger one would appear to find, as do most commentators, merely an ontological "theory" of selfhood or of Dasein's Being that not only has nothing to say about concrete practice, but expressly distances itself from any ethics.

Yet matters are far from being so simple. Not only should one stop to ask what kind of "ethics" is being resisted in Heidegger's analytic of Dasein as care, one should also pause to take the measure of the radicality of Foucault's conception of ethics in his later work, which is far from what modernity understands under that name. We need to address attentively, in other words, what is meant by "the subject" or "the self" in each of these two thinkers, and within the periods of their work being considered here.

HEIDEGGER: SELFHOOD AND THE FINITUDE OF TIME

For those who would remain content with opposing the concreteness of Foucault's problematic to the ontological or supposedly theoretical status of Heidegger's analytic, Foucault's interview itself presents a complication, for the distinction between the ontological and the ontic or concrete articulates the entire issue and central argument of the interview.[2] A few examples:

> "Liberty is the ontological condition of ethics. But ethics is the deliberate form assumed by liberty." (712/4)

> "One must not have the care for others precede the care for self. The care for self takes ethical precedence in the measure that the relationship to self takes ontological precedence." (715/7)

> "[I]f you care for yourself correctly, i.e., if you know ontologically what you are, if you also know of what you are capable, . . . if you know, finally, that you should not fear death, well, then, you cannot abuse your power over others." (716/8)

> "[T]he care for self appears like a pedagogical, ethical, and also ontological condition for the constitution of a good leader." (721–22/13)

The central tenor of all of these statements appears to show a remarkable consonance with the path taken by Heidegger's analytic
of Dasein. The argument that the relationship to self takes ontological precedence over care for others is made by Heidegger himself in the thesis that Dasein's Being is constituted by mineness
(*Jemeinigkeit*). This thesis was, and continues to be, so misunderstood that Heidegger immediately felt the need to undertake a
number of clarifications.[3] The most important of these appear in
The Metaphysical Foundations of Logic (1928), in the essay "On the
Essence of Ground" from the same year, and in *The Fundamental
Concepts of Metaphysics: World, Finitude, Solitude*, from 1929–30.[4]
    What is at issue in the misunderstandings to which this thesis
of Dasein's mineness was exposed is a persistent confusion of the
ontological with the ontic. The statement that "Dasein is in each
case mine" is an existential-ontological determination of Dasein's
Being, its selfhood or Being-a-self, and not an ontic assertion that
opposes the self to the Other. To say that Dasein exists "for the
sake of itself" (*umwillen seiner selbst*) is not to assert an "existentiell
or ethical egoism" (GA 26, 240), but is an ontological statement of
essence that pertains to any Dasein as such, to Dasein "*in each
[or any] case.*" Thus, as Heidegger explains in the essay "On the
Essence of Ground":

> The statement: *Dasein exists for the sake of itself,* does not con-
> tain the positing of an egoistic or ontic end for some blind
> narcissism on the part of the factical human being in each case.
> It cannot, therefore, be "refuted" for instance by pointing out
> that many human beings sacrifice themselves *for others* and
> that in general human beings do not merely exist alone on
> their own, but in community. The statement in question con-
> tains neither a solipsistic isolation of Dasein, nor an egoistic
> intensification thereof. By contrast, it presumably gives the
> condition of possibility of the human being's being able to
> comport "himself" *either* "egoistically" *or* "altruistically." Only
> because Dasein as such is determined by selfhood can an I-self
> comport itself toward a you-self. Selfhood is the presupposi-
> tion for the possibility of being an 'I,' the latter only ever being
> disclosed in [relation to] the 'you.' Never, however, is selfhood
> relative to a 'you,' but rather—because it first makes all this
> possible—is neutral with respect to being an 'I' or being a
> 'you,' and above all with respect to such things as "sexuality."

> All statements of essence in an ontological analytic of the Dasein
> in the human being take this entity from the outset in such
> neutrality. (W, 53–54)[5]

Heidegger's point here is that the *Being* of Dasein's self, of its being
a self, is not to be confused with the 'I.' Selfhood or mineness is not
on the same level as the 'I' versus 'you' distinction, but is the
ontological structure of Being that determines every 'I' or 'you' in
its Being in each case prior to, or in excess of, any ontic determi-
nations. And yet, this ontological neutrality that characterizes the
Being of the self is not merely that of a formal, abstract essence. If
that were the case, the statement that Dasein, in its Being, exists for
the sake of itself would be no different from the Kantian determination of man as an end in himself—a universal and purely formal
definition that reduces all human beings to the purely rational and
self-grounding self-determination of subjectivity. Although
Heidegger's statement of essence is meant to be a universal one, it
is not formal in the sense of an abstraction, just as the "essence" of
Dasein departs from the classical notion of essence in understanding Dasein's "essence" in terms of its way of Being, its existence,
in its ontological relationship to itself. Heidegger elsewhere explains that all statements of essence are "formal" only in the sense
of being formally *indicative*: "[T]hey point in each case into a concretion of the individual Dasein in the human being, but never
bring the content of this concretion along with them . . ." (GA 29/
30, 429). In short, the "mine" or "self" in the mineness or selfhood
of Dasein is indeed indicative of this concretion of a particular
Dasein in each case, and yet the Being of this self is never simply
individuated, is never reducible to such individuation.

Selfhood or mineness is thus to be understood as an *ontological
relationship to self*, that is, as a relation of Being. The Being of the self
is neither the constant presence at hand of a body we see before us;
nor is it the permanent substratum of a transcendental self that lies
behind every act of positing, thinking, or acting, and that can never
become an object; nor, finally, is it the self-positing, self-regulating
relation to self that is an activity of the self upon the self, as formulated in exemplary manner by the Kantian law of autonomy and
subsequently conceived as absolute subjectivity by Fichte. The Being
of the self as relation to self in the analytic of Dasein is indeed the
ontological condition of any particular ontic act: "[B]eing a relation

to self, as being a self, is the presupposition for various possibilities of ontic comportment toward oneself," as Heidegger notes (GA 26, 244), but what is remarkable in this determination of Dasein is that such relation to self is not the relation *of a self* to the self. The relation to self is indeed a relation to the thrown, embodied self that appears and is present in the world, but it does not proceed from an already existing self. It proceeds, rather, from Dasein's openness to the *world*, an openness that is simultaneously an openness of world in Dasein, an openness of the temporal horizon that world itself is. In the statement that Dasein exists for the sake of itself, "itself" is to be understood as Being-in-the-world: the "for the sake of" articulates, as Heidegger clarifies in "On the Essence of Ground," the fact that it is a transcendence to world that first temporalizes selfhood; it is world that "shows itself to be that for the sake of which Dasein exists. World has the fundamental character of the 'for the sake of' . . . and does so in the originary sense that it first provides the intrinsic possibility for every factically self-determining 'for your sake,' 'for his sake,' 'for the sake of that,' etc." (W, 53).

To say that Dasein in its Being is a relation to self is thus to say that Dasein exists primarily as *possibility*, that is, as freedom.[6] Yet such freedom is at once indeterminate, irreducible to a determinate way of existing at any moment, and also in each case mine, not in the sense of it being an existent property of the self, but in the sense of being bound to the singularity of existence, to the insubstitutable existence of a particular embodiment at a particular time and place. This ultimate freedom of Dasein only truly *is*, in other words, when taken up and engaged by a particular concrete, embodied existence in a particular instance. And this is what Heidegger calls the existentiell engagement or commitment [*Einsatz*] of the self.[7] Engagement or commitment here refers to the singularity of a concretion that exceeds, and is quite other than, the particularity that is merely the correlate of a formal universal. Such engagement implies, moreover, that the relation to self is not just another possible example of an ontic relation: it is not of the same order as the relation to another.[8] Rather, it is an utterly singular, and utterly binding, ontico-ontological relation that announces itself here. In other words, it is the originary site of the ethical, or what might be better referred to as the protoethical.

To say that selfhood, or being a self, is an ontological relation to self, to an ontically existing concretion that is in each case *mine*, is thus to indicate in a formal manner the singularity of concrete existence in each case. The ontological relation to self is *primary*, it has priority over any relation to the Other, because every ontic relation to self or other is always the taking up of a *determinate* relation that presupposes as its element the singularity of ontological indeterminacy, or in other words, of ontological freedom.[9] Thus, Heidegger writes, in *The Metaphysical Foundations of Logic*:

> In its expressly choosing itself there lies essentially the full self-engagement [of Dasein], not in the direction of where it has not yet been, but in the direction of where and how it always already is as Dasein insofar as it exists. To what extent this factically succeeds in each case is not a question for metaphysics, but a question and issue for the individual. Only because Dasein, on the basis of its selfhood, can expressly choose itself is it able to engage itself for an Other, and only because Dasein, in being in relation to itself, can in general understand anything like a "self" can it in turn listen at all to a "you-self." Only because Dasein, constituted by a "for the sake of . . . ," exists in selfhood—for this reason alone is anything like human community possible. These are primary, existential-ontological statements of essence, not ethical theses about the relative priority of egoism and altruism. (GA 26, 245)

Expressly choosing oneself here refers to authentic existence, as Heidegger goes on to indicate, which demands "full self-engagement," that is, expressly enacting one's own finitude, the finitude of the concretely existing, embodied self. This explicit enactment of full self-engagement entails coming to see, and to assume as the grounds of one's actions, the finitude that Dasein "always already is, so far as it exists." Here we see how the analytic of Dasein unfolds as a hermeneutic of existence. It demands of each individual that he or she disclose, via the interpretation of Dasein as self-interpretation, what he or she always already was, yet which was concealed in the dominant interpretations underlying the everyday way in which "people" (*das Man*) talk—such interpretations (e.g., the self as "subject") being those passed down by the dominant philosophical tradition. When Heidegger speaks of the ontological relation to self as the "presupposition" for different possibilities of ontic comportment, such presupposition is not to be understood as a theoretico-transcendental "condition of possibility," but existentially (that is, as we shall indicate in a moment, in terms of the primacy of the originary, ekstatic future). Because such existing always unfolds factically as a singular relation of embodiment, it is irreducible to a formal or abstract determination of human existence that could simply be *applied* to particular cases. This not only means that, as a hermeneutic, the analytic of Dasein is intrinsically protoethical; it also means that it calls for, and calls upon each individual to engage in self-transformation, to attend to, as Nietzsche puts it, "How one becomes—what one is."[10]

Indeed, this ontological engagement in self-transformation is what is demanded if the ontological analytic of Dasein is not to become a merely theoretical discourse. To read it as such, as a theoretical description of human existence, is to fail to hear from the outset the claim addressed to us in the statement that Dasein is the entity that we ourselves *in each case* (*je*) are. It is to misunderstand the entire import of the analytic. It is the hermeneutic nature of the discourse of the analytic of Dasein in *Being and Time*, of its *logos*, that resists reduction to a merely theoretical *logos*. This discourse, as a discourse of "existential-ontological statements of essence," does not present "ethical theses" about the priority of egoism or altruism because its statements are not reducible to the positings of a theoretical or representational *logos*. In other words, the kind of ethics that is being resisted is precisely that conception of ethics which would regard proper ethical conduct as dependent simply (or even primarily) on the application of a formal theory, whether of particular rules or general regulatory principles. And this is what is at stake in the insistence that the ontology of Dasein not take as its object a "worldless" 'I' or "subject." Thus, Heidegger emphasizes in *Being and Time*: "The object we have taken as our theme is *artificially and dogmatically foreclosed* if one restricts oneself 'in the first instance' to a 'theoretical subject,' in order then to supplement it 'on the practical side' by tacking on an 'ethics' " (SZ, 316). Similarly, in the 1946 "Letter on 'Humanism,' " when taking up the question addressed to him shortly after the publication of *Being and Time*, the question "When are you going to write an ethics?," Heidegger shows the naivity of the question by indicating that, despite certain shortcomings,[11] the analytic of Dasein is already protoethical, just as his later thinking of Being is "neither theoretical nor practical" (W, 183–88).

It is in the 1929–30 course *The Fundamental Concepts of Meta-physics: World, Finitude, Solitude*, however, that Heidegger points most clearly to the transformative element of protoethical engage-ment. And what is at issue here is precisely the response of the individual to the discourse of the analytic—a question, in short, of whether a singular possibility of freedom is taken up, creatively transformed, or overlooked. Just as no one can see for another, just as no human being can live the existence of another, so too no discourse can *of itself* accomplish an existing relation to possibility, or to human life as *bios*, as ethico-political life. Thus, in the said course, Heidegger reiterates that the concepts at play in the ana-lytic of Dasein do not refer to the qualities of something present at hand or already existing independently,

> but are to be taken as *indications* that show how our under-standing must first twist free from our ordinary conceptions of beings and expressly transform itself into the Da-sein in us. The claim [*Anspruch*] upon us to undertake this transformation lies within each one of these concepts—death, resolute open-ness, history, existence—yet not as some additional, so-called ethical application of what is conceptualized, but rather as a prior opening up of the dimension of what is to be compre-hended. These concepts are indicative because, insofar as they have been genuinely acquired, they can only ever address this claim upon us to undertake such transformation, but can never bring about this transformation themselves. They point toward Dasein itself. But Da-sein—as I understand it—is always *mine*. (GA 29/30, 428–29)

How one responds to the claim of the discourse, of its conceptuality, of the knowledge at work in it, is ultimately a matter of the indi-vidual (but not necessarily *for* the individual—and here is the role of pedagogy or *paideia*), a matter in which the individual him- or herself is at stake and in play. At stake is the relation to self as a relation of *possibility*, that is, of power in each case: What interpre-tations have power over me, govern me in my very existence at any particular moment? What possibilities in relation to self or in relation to others are opened up or closed off? Above all: What is this primary power over myself that is the ontological relation to self, this strange freedom *for* myself that is not a freedom *of* myself? The ontological relation to self is not only the presupposition of listening to a "you-self"; it is also the possibility of listening to language—of hearing the possibilities that address and claim us in any particular discourse. One might in this sense recall the claim from the Introduction to *Being and Time*: "Higher than actuality stands *possibility*. Understanding phenomenology lies solely in taking it up [or seizing it: *Ergreifen*] as possibility" (SZ, 38). Notably, Heidegger does not say here that phenomenology should be taken up as *a* possibility; phenomenology itself is conceived here as the disclosure (in Da-sein as understanding) of possibility itself; as such it is not just one possibility, but, as the letting-be-seen via *logos* of that which shows itself in concealing itself (Being itself), it is the explicitly engaged unfolding of Being (not just of one's "own" Being) as possibility. As the "destruction" (*Destruktion*) of the history of ontology dominated by the philosophical *theōria*, it can be seen as a protoethical response to the claim of a tradition, of a history, a response that already belongs to the history of Being.

On the basis of our brief remarks, we can now begin to see also why Heidegger insists, in *The Metaphysical Foundations of Logic*, that the neutrality of Dasein, which is also a neutrality in respect of sexuality, is "the originary positivity and power of its essence," "not the negativity of an abstraction, but precisely the power of the *origin* that sustains the inner possibility of any concrete, factical human existence" (GA 26, 174). "Origin" here refers not to an ontic source, but to possibility as exceeding in advance any determinate actuality, and being thought otherwise than as the ground of such actuality. It is neither a Kantian transcendental-practical self, nor, however, the absolute self-actuality of spirit. Genuine metaphysical universality, Heidegger remarks, does not exclude concretion, "but is in one respect what is most concrete, as Hegel already saw, although he exaggerated it" (GA 26, 176). It is a matter of avoiding this Hegelian exaggeration that reduces or recuperates the finitude of time to the self-presencing of existing actuality. On the other hand, one must take care not to fall prey to an opposite exaggeration or misunderstanding, namely, that of regarding this particular existentiell engagement (the extreme engagement of the philosopher, attuned to Being) as such as the only essential issue or possibility, since, Heidegger remarks, it is in the projection of Dasein's fundamental ontological constitution that this engagement itself becomes manifest as irreducible to and nonbinding for the singular individual, for the factical existing of a finite self (GA 26, 176–77).

Nevertheless, it is precisely *this* projection of the ontological-metaphysical constitution of existence, and one's existentiell commitment to *this* possibility, that "first reveals the essential finitude of Dasein, which in existentiell terms can be understood only as the inessential character of the self . . ." (GA 26, 176). In short, the *relation to self* that becomes manifest in and through the analytic of Dasein is neither simply ontic, nor purely ontological, and to reduce it to either one is to overlook its temporal finitude. For the moment of engagement is always in each case an *Augenblick* of temporal singularity that cannot be appropriated by a theoretical *logos*. It is the engagement, rather, of a temporal hermeneutic of existence that maintains an openness to possibility.

That it is indeed the temporality of existence that is at issue here is indicated by Heidegger when he states that the metaphysical neutrality of Dasein is "not an empty *abstractum* from the ontic, a neither-nor, but what is properly concrete in the origin, the 'not yet' of factical dispersion" (GA 26, 173). In this originary concretion of its ownmost or proper possibility, Dasein in its embodiment is neither of the two sexes, but maintains a certain neutrality or freedom in respect of sexuality; yet such concretion is authentically engaged only when Dasein is able to attain an authentic relation to self—and this is something that demands a certain practice of the self: here, the practice of a critical philosophical existence. Likewise, this is also to say that one's sexuality is always open in principle to possibilities of transformation through various practices of the self. One must not, therefore, regard such neutrality as a given fact or property of a supposed human nature or essence. Thus, Heidegger remarks, "This neutral Dasein is never an [already] existing one; Dasein exists in each case only in its factical concretion" (GA 26, 172). And yet, as we have just seen him remark on the following page, the metaphysical neutrality of Dasein is precisely what is "properly concrete." It is a matter, therefore, of avoiding an overly reductive interpretation of Dasein's concretion that would simply reduce it to the merely or purely ontic.[12] By contrast with the *already* existing or existent, factical concretion of a particular Dasein, its factical appearance and presence at hand within the world, Dasein's *originary* concretion is precisely maintained in the opening of its futuricity, which is also, therefore, its most originary, ontologically indeterminate facticity. Its actuality in any given case presupposes the openness of a protoethical, ontological relation to self that is the relation of one's own thrownness to the originary future, that is, to the possibility of action qua originary *praxis*, the possibility of being an origin. Such thrownness encompasses not only one's embodiment, but one's having been born and thrown into a tradition of discourse, interpretation, and history, as well as the particular situation of *praxis* or ethical engagement in any given instance. The ontological neutrality of Dasein is precisely the "not yet" of factical dispersion, in other words, the ontological relation to the originary future which remains indeterminate as long as I exist in this thrownness that "is" never simply mine, but which, in the moment or *Augenblick* of ethical engagement, I can choose—if only for a moment. This reflects the priority of the ekstasis of the future that belongs to the ontological meaning of "care." As "care," Dasein is always already ahead of itself; but the "self" here is always only the thrown self, the self whose existence has already been decided in some way, the "oneself" (*Man-selbst*) that already knows itself (SZ, 193). In its "averageness," it tends to exist inauthentically, that is, for the sake of a self that it (and others) has already been. The authentic relation to self, by contrast, is an existing for the sake of a future that is that of the world, that has yet to be, and that is, as such, always unknown. Such existence takes upon itself the ethical injunction "know thyself" as the task that does not seek a conclusive answer, but that acknowledges and engages its own finitude as its only relation to the future. Just as the ontological relation *to* self is not a relation *of* the self, but a relation of the transformative power of the finitude of time, so Heidegger intimates already in *Being and Time* that the ontological structure of care as ekstatic temporality is intrinsically poietic. As the "originary 'outside-itself,' " ekstatic temporality does not temporalize as a relation *of* self to self (such as in the manner of transcendental or dialectical-historical selfhood): there is no substratum here, only the finitude of ekstatic temporality that will later be thought in terms of the Earth, concealment, in its strife with world. Temporality "is not in the first place an entity that then steps outside of *itself*, rather its essence is *Zeitigung* in the unity of the *ekstases*" (SZ, 329). The German word *Zeitigung* means temporalizing, but also suggests maturation, flourishing, the Greek *genesis*, coming into being (*phusis*). Whereas ekstatic time is at once originary and finite, the ordinary understanding of time regards time only as "a pure sequence of nows *without beginning or end*."[13]

Thus, in "On the Essence of Ground," Heidegger emphasizes that it is "in coming toward itself from out of the world that Dasein first temporalizes and gives rise to itself [*zeitigt sich*] as a *self*, i.e., as a being entrusted with the task *of Being.* . . . [I]t is a surpassing in the direction of world that first temporalizes and gives rise to [*sich . . . zeitigt*] selfhood" (W, 53). Dasein is thus essentially "world-forming" (55): a theme that, as we have seen in chapter 1, would subsequently be further developed in the 1929–30 course.

The question of authentic existence, in conclusion, can never be a matter of telling others what the right measure is, or of positing some theoretical or regulatory ideal of ethical existence. It is a matter, rather, of the possibility of a singular response to one's own thrownness, of an explicit affirmation of how one becomes—what one has been. "Only seldom do we take hold of time, which possesses us ourselves in a metaphysical sense, only seldom do we become master of this power that we ourselves are, only seldom do we exist freely" (GA 26, 257–58). Or, as Heidegger would later express it, "we are free only in coming to be free" (NI, 400).

FOUCAULT: *ĒTHOS* AND THE PRACTICE OF FREEDOM

The above remarks, despite their brevity, perhaps help to shed light on the complexity of Foucault's prioritizing of what he himself calls the ontological relation to self. Yet Foucault's analysis also supplements Heidegger's ontological analytic of existence by extending it in the direction of what he calls ascetic or ethical practices of concrete self-formation. This is something that appears to be largely neglected or left unsaid by Heidegger, although it is not altogether missing from his work. It is implicit, for example, in the factical ideal of authentic existence as a task that has to be accomplished ever anew.[14] An authentic relation to self entails an anticipatory (or future-oriented) understanding of one's ownmost potentiality for Being, that is, of one's ownmost freedom, from out of an openness to world and to the beings disclosed therein. Such understanding, as we shall see in the next chapter, is intimately involved in the ongoing and concrete cultivation of one's *ēthos*.

Let us briefly consider the theme of the self in Foucault's late period. One of the reasons we experience such resistance, at least initially, to the language of "the self" is that for us moderns the self is still predominantly understood as something transcendental or ontological. But for both the early Heidegger and the later Foucault, the self is not at all ontological; rather, it is the *relation to self* that is ontological, and "ontological" here means, not transcendental in a metaphysical sense, but if anything "practical," that is, conceived as a *way of Being*. And it is the way in which one takes up or neglects this relation to self that is to be understood as originary ethics. As Foucault emphasizes in a 1983 interview "Politics and Ethics," "[E]thics is a practice; *ēthos* is a manner of being" (FR, 377). Thinking ethics as *ēthos* recalls the predominant Greek sense of ethical existence. In "The Ethic of Care for the Self . . . ," Foucault states:

> [*Ē*]*thos* was a manner of being, a way of conducting oneself [*la manière d'être et la manière de se conduire*]. It was the subject's mode of being and a certain manner of acting visible to others. One's *ēthos* was seen by his dress, by his bearing, by his gait, by the composure with which he reacts to events, etc. For them, that is the concrete expression of freedom. (714/6)

Yet the relation one assumes toward one's self in any given instance, and the alternative possibilities that one rejects, neglects, or remains ignorant of, are determined in part by knowledge. And because one's very Being at any moment is determined in part by knowledge, this means, for Foucault, that having freedom as a formal property of the will (autonomy), and being free, are not at all the same. Consider the following exchange from the same interview:

> Q: You say that freedom must be practiced ethically?
>
> MF: Yes, for what is ethics if not the practice of freedom, the deliberate practice of freedom [*la pratique réfléchie de la liberté*]?
>
> Q: That means that you consider freedom as a reality already ethical in itself?
>
> MF: Freedom is the ontological condition of ethics. But ethics is the deliberate form assumed by freedom. (711–12/4)

Freedom, Foucault here indicates, is not at all to be conceived as "a reality already ethical in itself," but as the "ontological condition" of the possibility of the ethical. For ethical practice to be possible, one must first be free for the possibility of assuming a specific relation to self or to others: "[T]here cannot be relations of power unless the subjects are free" (720/12). In this sense, factical liberation is a prerequisite for the practice of ethical freedom. Ethics is thus "the deliberate form assumed by freedom." "Ethics" here does not refer to a theoretical system, nor to reflection on moral principles. Rather, "ethics" means the situated and finite engagement of one's freedom, of one's existence as possibility, in each case. Such engagement is ethical when it occurs as a result of a certain form of deliberation, when one's potentiality for Being unfolds in a certain relation to knowledge, to a *logos*, by way of discursive practice.

What kind of knowledge of self is called for in a care for the self that is truly ethical, and to what extent, in what measure, does it determine the ethical relation to self? Such knowledge is situated, historical, and finite in its claim. Like Heidegger, Foucault emphasizes that what he rejects is first setting up a theory of the subject, and then posing the question of how such a subject comes to know the world. Rather:

> What I wanted to try to show was how the subject was itself constituted, in such and such a determined form, as a mad subject or as a normal subject, through a certain number of practices which were games of truth, applications of power, etc. I had to reject a certain *a priori* theory of the subject in order to make this analysis of the relationships which can exist between the constitution of the subject or different forms of the subject and games of truth, practices of power, and so forth. (718/10)

The human subject or self is never simply the given fact of a permanent self-identity; it is not at all an identity, but, at any given moment, a particular way of Being, a relationship to self that is constituted as a response not only to a given practical situation, but to an entire background of historically conditioned interpretations (interpretations of the human being and of the world), as well as other historically conditioned ethical, political, and institutional practices of power.

> Q: That means that the subject is not a substance?

> MF: It is not a substance; it is a form and this form is not above all or always identical to itself. You do not have towards yourself the same kind of relationships when you constitute your-

self as a political subject who goes and votes or speaks up in a meeting, and when you try to fulfill your desires in a sexual relationship. There are no doubt some relationships and some interferences between these different kinds of subject but we are not in the presence of the same kind of subject. In each case, we play, we establish with one's self some different form of relationship. And it is precisely the historical constitution of these different forms of subject relating to games of truth that interests me. (719/10)

The specificity of the kinds of knowledge at work in the constitution of these different relationships to self, these different ways of Being, also means that for Foucault an extreme caution has to be exercised when speaking of "care for the self," for this theme has a very complex history of meanings that are still at work in us today when we use this expression. For both Foucault and Heidegger, the analysis of this concrete issue demands a genealogical, hermeneutic approach that cultivates an intense awareness of its own history, that is, of the history of Being. Just as there is no way of Being that does not have its history, that is not always already a response to history, so too the history of Being exceeds infinitely one's own way of Being at any particular moment. In both Heidegger and Foucault, the Being of the "self" refers to a story that will have been very largely both written and read by others to whose time one belongs in precisely this manner. Foucault warns us against the temptation to take the theme of care for the self as a theoretical answer to the task of ethical existence:

> Q: Should we actualize this care for self, in the classical sense, against this modern thought [namely, against the scientific ideal of modern rationality]?

> MF: Absolutely, but I am not doing that in order to say: "Unfortunately we have forgotten the care for the self. Here is the care for the self. It is the key to everything." Nothing is more foreign to me than the idea that philosophy strayed at a certain moment of time, and that it has forgotten something, and that somewhere in her history there exists a principle, a basis that must be rediscovered. (723/14)

Foucault's response here is simply a way of saying that there can be no definitive response to history, since history is not a series of facts concealing a firm ground, but that which has always yet to come, that which claims us in advance, configuring in a temporal-historical, and thus finite, manner the understanding in terms of which we first approach and relate to ourselves. Above all, the "classical sense" of care for the self (as the interviewer refers to it) is not so easy to discern. Thus, in response to the question "Is ethics then what is realized or achieved in the search or care for self?," Foucault counters by discussing a specific historical configuration of care for self, namely, that extending from "the first Platonic dialogue up to the major texts of the later Stoics," noting how "beginning at a certain moment in time . . . the care for the self becomes something somewhat suspect. Caring for the self was, at a certain moment, gladly denounced as being a kind of self-love, a kind of egoism or individual interest in contradiction to the care one must show others or to the necessary sacrifice of the self." This transformation occurred during the Christian era, but, Foucault remarks, is not due exclusively to Christianity. In the Greek and Roman period, by contrast, "[w]e have . . . an entire ethics which turned about the care for the self and which gave ancient ethics its very particular form." And only now comes Foucault's tentative answer: "I am not saying that ethics is the care for the self, but that in antiquity, ethics, as a deliberate practice of freedom, has turned about this basic imperative: Care for yourself" (712–13/4–5).

Is ethics then what is realized in care for the self, assuming one has adequately specified the latter? Foucault's response, the cautious formulation that ethics, as a deliberate (that is, concrete and knowing) practice of freedom "turned" or "pivoted" about care for the self indicates the unstable and tentative role of knowledge in such care; this very instability, however, reflects a growing tension between contemplative and practical knowledge during the period in question, a tension in the role of philosophy itself. On the one hand, care for the self in the Greco-Roman world, as a transformative practice of ontological knowledge of self, is itself intrinsically ethical. "Care for self ethical in itself . . ." (7). But one cannot, therefore, simply say that ethics *is* the care for the self, for ontological knowledge of self is not something attainable once and for all, nor is it a knowledge that, once attained, could then simply be "applied" to *praxis*. Rather, it must be attuned to and engaged in the moment of *praxis* itself. In other words, it is not reducible to a theoretical knowledge of self that could constitute a permanent bedrock for ethical practice. Care for the self is not simply a matter of knowledge. Which is another way of saying that no one simply *is* ethical; rather, ethical existence is precisely what remains a *task*, one that has never been accomplished by anyone.[15] Thus, the ethical imperative that Foucault formulates here is not a categorical imperative grounded in a theoretical *logos* that pretends to have discerned once and for all what the Being of the self is, for example, as the actuality of presence to self (Kantian autonomy), but a *historical* imperative that formulates ethical existence as a task, as a relation to the future: "Care for yourself"—for whom? for what? who or what might that be? That is precisely the question.

Indeed, even Foucault's brief qualifications here concerning the historical specificity of the theme of care for the self are very broad and potentially misleading. In another interview from the same period (April 1983), entitled "On the Genealogy of Ethics: An Overview of Work in Progress," Foucault provides a further caution on interpreting "care for the self" too narrowly, a caution that invokes greater historical specificity, and that implies that one should not regard Foucault's later work as simply embracing or affirming a Platonic or Stoic conception of care for self. Care for the self, and the *technē* it demands, should be seen, rather, with respect to their political import:

> What I want to show is that the general Greek problem was not the *technē* of the self, it was the *technē* of life, the *technē tou biou*, how to live. . . . And I think that one of the main evolutions in ancient culture has been that this *technē tou biou* became more and more a *technē* of the self. A Greek citizen of the fifth or fourth century would have felt that his *technē* for life was to take care of the city, of his companions. But for Seneca, for instance, the problem is to take care of himself. (FR, 348)

In other words, the transformation of discourse and of *theōria* that issued in the practice of philosophizing is problematically involved in the transformations of the relation to self that lead to Stoicism, to early Christianity, and eventually to the establishment of the Cartesian *cogito* and the modern positing of an Archimedean point from which the world becomes representable as a picture. Although philosophy in Plato and Aristotle emerges in the context of a political concern for the sustainability of the *polis*, the characterization of thinking as a *theōria* turned toward the nonsensible, and of *technē* as grounded in the *theōrein* of nonsensible ideas, already announce the beginnings of a turn away from the exteriority of a concern with freedom in its worldly, political reality and toward the interiorizing of freedom as a withdrawal from the world.[16] The relation to self becomes grounded in a relation to the "soul," "the prison of the body," as Foucault described it almost a decade earlier.[17] By contrast, both Foucault and Heidegger emphasize the primacy and importance of a worldly engagement of one's freedom.

We have seen, then, a number of striking similarities in the understanding of the self in the early Heidegger and the later Foucault: (1) The self is conceived ontologically, as a relation to self that is grounded in the possibility of freedom. "Care for the self" in Foucault, or authentic existence in Heidegger, designate a care for Being, for the Being of one's self in its finite openness to a historical world. (2) An understanding (which need not be explicit or self-critical, i.e., philosophical understanding) of the practico-ontological relation to self is a precondition for assuming an ethical relation to others. (3) The critical practice of ontological knowing is an explicit mode of care for the self that continually recoils upon itself, putting its own Being constantly in question through a hermeneutic attentiveness to its own genealogy. (4) Such practice is intrinsically protoethical, unfolding as a singular engagement with and of one's own existence in each case. (5) As such, protoethical engagement is a transformative participation in one's own thrown Being, a participation in the formation of the self as a worldly response to history. (6) Finally, for both Foucault and Heidegger, knowledge of the practico-ontological relation to self is attainable in a critical manner only through the practice of philosophizing.

CARE FOR THE SELF AND THE TASK OF PHILOSOPHIZING

A few words by way of conclusion. As a kind of antidote to philosophy's withdrawal from its originary task, that is, as a warning concerning the theoretical appropriation of *technē*, a brief historical recollection of that task may be helpful. Philosophizing as a *praxis* had originally no other task than to further the human capacity for free and open deliberation, the one capacity that perhaps distinguishes us from other beings. For deliberation is authentic thoughtfulness. It means the ability to think something through by way of *logos*, and to arrive at the right *logos*, the right command

and law of one's forthcoming action and decision. Yet arriving at the right *logos*, the appropriate measure of one's action, so as to be able to act *well* demands of us several different abilities. First, one must have a general knowledge of the Good as it relates to one's own place in the world, in the midst of beings as a whole. One must have contemplated (*theōrein*) the unity and harmony of the *kosmos*, awakening a sense for how all beings belong together in it. This is what Aristotle called "theology." Its beginning and end is wonder, *thaumazein*, for through such wonder one first comes to experience one's own limits, one's own place and finitude in the midst of other beings. But this alone is not enough. Second, one must, again by way of contemplation, have acquired a general knowledge of each particular kind of being, in its own particular kind of existence. One cannot act well without knowing beforehand something about the beings one is relating to. Together, these first two kinds of knowledge comprise what Aristotle calls *sophia*, wisdom, for which the philosopher strives. Yet these two kinds of contemplative knowledge, whose results can be communicated and thus taught as universal laws or *logoi*, as "scientific" or epistemic truths, have a beginning and an end, which is also where they encounter their limit. Their beginning and end is human existence itself, in its singularity in each case as a *praxis*—and here science can tell us nothing. For each human existence is something that is chosen and enacted anew and differently at every moment: it is free precisely insofar as it is not bound in advance to follow any already chosen path, any given *logos*. This means, on the one hand (as Aristotle well understood), that there can be no adequate or binding theoretical knowledge of what the Good for human beings is—for this will be different in each case, at each moment—and, further, that there can be no adequate theoretical or scientific knowledge of what *praxis* itself is; for *praxis* "*is*" only in its enactment. Moreover: insofar as contemplation, whether scientific or philosophical, is itself a *praxis*, but one in which *praxis* as that which can be otherwise at any moment comes (historically, via the philosophical tradition itself) to be increasingly concealed, there lies herein an ethical directive for our era, a directive coming from the history of philosophy itself, namely for contemplation to recall and catch sight of its own activity *as praxis*, in its *singularity* and in the momentary character of its *temporal* unfolding. This "momentary" character is a kind of *stasis*, an "ek-stasis," a stretching of time, as

Heidegger would say. Contemplating must turn back—not in representational reflection, but protoethically, acknowledging the recoil of history, the historical recoil that thinking is now called upon to take: a genealogical retrieval of its own concealments—it must return to its own beginning and origin that will also have been its end: the experience of wonder, of the wonder that inhabits every human being as such, and that need only be awakened. This wonder we "see" in the eyes of another human being (in his or her living embodiment, in their *ēthos*) as a radiance, a shining whose provenance is obscure and which may itself become largely concealed. The practice and *art* of philosophizing (which is therefore something other than teaching theories of existence), as practised by Foucault and Heidegger, seems to us to be nothing other than the attempt to be attentive to this wonder, to nurture its awakening, in oneself and in others, as one's access to a world. For to experience wonder in one's existence is to pause, to hesitate before something unknown, it is to have time, to be given or granted time. A time for what? A time to dwell for a moment in the presence of other beings, a time to deliberate, to think. To deliberate as one acts, to hesitate amid the commitment of one's existence, before being committed entirely and in advance to a particular cause or end: to pause before rushing headlong, with all guns blazing, as we say, into a particular future offered to us by the present moment or the present age. To cultivate, perhaps, a sense of time.[18] Thus, what is crucial to practical wisdom (*phronēsis*), and to being able to act well (*eupraxia*), says Aristotle, is the ability to take the right or appropriate time to deliberate. This means that deliberation should neither be too quick (one should not simply be moved to act spontaneously, by the first thought that enters one's head) nor too slow (for this would be to let an opportunity pass us by). But this time—the right time and duration—must above all be responsive to the situation as it unfolds before us. It must be responsive to—but not dominated or dictated by—the time of other beings, to the time of the present and of one's age or historical era.

To dwell for a time, in the company of others; to be granted time to deliberate. . . . We ought to remind ourselves that the original meaning of *ēthos*, as Aristotle records and as Heidegger attempts to reawaken, is related to habit, to habitat and dwelling. One's *ēthos* refers to where one dwells ontologically, the place from which we emerge and to which we return in showing ourselves in a particular manner of Being in each case. But this ethical or protoethical dwelling is not simply god-given: it has to be cultivated (*erwandert*, Heidegger will say),[19] in and through experiences and practices of the self. And what is crucial is that none of these abilities essential to discerning the right *logos* of one's action can simply be taught. They must be learned or acquired by practices of the self, practices of self-formation, exercises in which one's own singularity is engaged, renewed, and where necessary transformed. Ethical existence is therefore never simply the application of laws, rules, or techniques one has learned to a particular situation; it is not the application of theory to *praxis*.[20] For the situation of *praxis* is precisely that which is not knowable beforehand, since it always engages and puts in question my own existence as something new, something other at every moment. It demands a singular response that no one else can make, for no one else is addressed here, no one else is in my place.

It is in memory of this beginning of philosophizing, perhaps, that Foucault in his interview invokes Socrates as "the man who truly cares for others" (7). For the wisdom of Socrates, the first true teacher, lies in his acknowledgment that he knows nothing. This does not mean, as we can see very clearly, that he has no knowledge. It means that knowledge is not simply an accomplishment or achievement, that knowledge is not an answer but the point of departure for an ever-renewed questioning, that what we already know is never the whole story; in short, that knowledge, like human existence itself, is a task, the task of ongoing transformation and revision of what we once thought we knew, and even now think we know concerning ourselves. Whereas the ordinary free citizen, once he or she has learned a craft or acquired a technical training, settles into a routine way of Being and of relating to him- or herself on the basis of this more or less secure knowledge and acquired place in the world, the philosopher is precisely unwilling to let the relationship to self stagnate or become complacent in this manner. He or she continually creates and transforms the relation to self anew; and this *ēthos* of the self is also what Foucault has called an "aesthetics of existence."[21] Philosophical existence is nomadic: It is the presence of the stranger in the midst of the routine business of the *polis*; as the word *theōrein* once indicated, it draws the experience of the foreign into the very heart of the relation to self.[22] This strange journey of coming to be a stranger to oneself is also the ontological condition for a genuine openness to the foreign, not just to other cultures, but to every other human being as a stranger who puts my self in question. To say that the appropriate care for self is a philosophical task is simply to reiterate that ethical existence has never been accomplished by anyone. It finds its fitting essence as a task, not as something that ever could be accomplished once and for all. An existence comes to be ethical, it accomplishes our originary *ēthos*, only insofar as I strive to hold myself, in advance, within the dimension of ontological freedom. But precisely the same goes for philosophical existence, for existence is truly philosophical only when its knowledge is appropriately attuned to that which cannot be known, to a destiny that exceeds oneself. Both Heidegger's and Foucault's discourses seem to us to instantiate and accomplish this *praxis* of thinking, of philosophizing—of the *work* of philosophizing as a finite enactment of existence. Care for the self as a kind of "mastery" over self entails above all a prior acknowledgment of the finitude of existence. As Foucault expresses it:

> [P]hilosophy is precisely the challenging of all phenomena of domination at whatever level or under whatever form they present themselves—political, economic, sexual, institutional, and so on. This critical function of philosophy, up to a certain point,[23] emerges right from the socratic imperative: "Be concerned with yourself, i.e., ground yourself in liberty, through the mastery of self." (729/20)

THREE

Apportioning the Moment
Time and Ēthos *in Heidegger's Reading of* Aristotle's Nicomachean Ethics *and* Rhetoric

Having raised, in our last chapter, the question of selfhood primarily in terms of the ontological relation to self (albeit a relation that
remains grounded in the ontic-existentiell) and in terms of the
question of freedom, the present chapter seeks to develop further
a theme already broached in chapter 2: that of the concrete practice
of self-formation contributing to the cultivation of one's *ēthos*. Specifically, we shall try to follow an earlier, 1924 account of *ēthos* in
Heidegger's work that raises the question of the relation between
the moment of action and the role of ethical virtue in concretely
bringing about one's ethical stance and conduct. In particular, how
does Heidegger's understanding of Dasein's temporality as ekstatic,
finite, and primarily futural impact the traditional, Aristotelian
understanding of virtuous *praxis* as entailing both ethical and intellectual virtues? Heidegger's early, phenomenological analysis, we
shall suggest, initiates a certain displacement of an ontology of
presence-at-hand operative in Aristotle's accounts of ethical *praxis*
(an ontological perspective that, while it may not be entirely exclu-
sive of other perspectives, nevertheless—as Heidegger would
go on to claim—obfuscates the distinctive temporality in which
the *kairos* of human action is enclosed), and does so in opening
Aristotle's account of *ēthos* onto the fundamentally unsettled and
unsettling dimension of the distinctive temporality and historicality
of human existence.

Heidegger's reappropriation of Aristotle's account of *phronēsis*,
or practical wisdom, in the *Nicomachean Ethics* is by now well known.
Focusing on the temporality of *phronēsis*, Heidegger's phenomenological analyses in the *Sophist* course of 1924–25 showed how this
dianoetic virtue of deliberative excellence with regard to ethical
praxis must be understood as responsive to what presents itself in
the particular, finite moment or *Augenblick* of action. The analytic
of Dasein in *Being and Time* (1927) and in the Marburg lecture
courses of 1927–30 deepen these phenomenological analyses in

relation to the finite temporality of Being-in-the-world, where the
world is understood, not as a constantly present backdrop to the
human being's temporal actions unfolding in an ever-changing
"now" (as in Aristotle), but as immanent to the temporality of
Being-in-the-world itself. The phenomenology of Dasein as Being-in-the-world shows that the *Augenblick* itself, as "held" and
attuned in advance by the fundamental attunement of *Angst*, is,
over and beyond the circumstances of the moment, exposed in
advance to the presencing of a historically determined world. The
Augenblick of action can "hold and keep its world in view"[1] only
because it is itself already held within the originary dimension of
the presencing of a world, attuned by the *Angst* that "holds the
Augenblick at the ready," brings us before repeatability itself
(*Wiederholbarkeit*) as the repeated suspension of presence that holds
us in the indeterminacy of possibility, free and open for the moment of a possible decision.[2] As noted in chapter 1, the primary
disclosure of the presencing of a world is thus, on this account,
accomplished not by intellectual or philosophical knowledge, but
by a fundamental *pathos* or attunement (*Befindlichkeit*); and such
pathos is fundamental in attuning, in advance of any explicit deliberation or discursive understanding, the way in which we are
held in the presencing of the moment—in short, in attuning our
entire *ēthos*. If Heidegger's analyses in the *Sophist* course focused
on the dianoetic virtues, and in particular on *phronēsis* and *sophia*,
to the relative neglect of the ethical virtues, this was not only in
order to show how and why *phronēsis* itself was not a purely
intellectual virtue—not a *hexis meta logou monon*, as Aristotle puts
it—but, more fundamentally, responsive to the *Augenblick* of a
practical *nous*, itself oriented in advance toward an end that must
already have been seized in a *proairesis*. It was also because in the
course delivered just prior to this in the summer semester of 1924,
"Fundamental Concepts of Aristotelian Philosophy," Heidegger
had already given a detailed analysis of *ēthos* and *pathos* in relation to a number of Aristotelian texts, in particular the *Rhetoric*. In
the present chapter we shall examine the account of *ēthos* and
pathos given in that course, in order to address the question of
how Heidegger's interpretation understands the specific place and
role of ethical virtue, specifically in relation to the *proairesis* that
always already guides any action. In raising this question, we are
interested in particular in how Heidegger's understanding of the

temporality of human existence implies a certain displacement of Aristotle's understanding of *ēthos* and the ethical.[3]

KOINŌNIA: *ĒTHOS* AND COMMUNITY

As with the *Sophist* course, Heidegger's 1924 course centering on Aristotle's *Rhetoric* is especially notable in that it already translates much of Aristotle into a discourse that, several years later, would appear as the rigorously formulated terminology of *Being and Time*. Although much of the language will therefore appear familiar to the reader acquainted with *Being and Time*—key terms such as "Being-in-the-world"; "Being-with-one-another" (as existing in the community or *koinōnia* of the *polis*); "attunement" (the phenomenon of *pathos* as *Befindlichkeit*); the "one" (*das 'Man'* as the realm of *doxa*); "open resolve" (*Entschlossenheit* as the accomplishment of a *proairesis*); the Augenblick (as the critical time or *kairos* of *praxis*)—this does not mean that we can simply translate *Being and Time* back into Aristotle, as it were, thus to claim that the 1927 treatise is nothing more than a rendition of Aristotle. Not only is the scope and register of some of these terms used in the 1924 course distinctly different ("Being-in-the-world," for example, is used of both animals and humans alike, and is not restricted merely to the Dasein of human beings as in *Being and Time*), but the 1927 treatise brings to bear on the analysis of Dasein much that is quite foreign to Aristotle and that is at best at work only implicitly in the 1924 course (the context of the destructuring of the history of ontology; the developed analysis of originary truth as unconcealment; the analyses of Dasein as ekstatic temporality and historicality; and the projection of authentic Being-toward-death, to name but a few). Nevertheless, both the 1924 and 1924/25 courses let us see how the ethical, political, and aletheic dimensions of Aristotle's thought are implicitly taken up into and inscribed within the discourse of *Being and Time* and the analyses of Dasein presented there. In *Being and Time* itself these dimensions are hinted at in the important footnote citing *Nicomachean Ethics*, Book VI, and *Metaphysics*, Book IX, as documenting Aristotle's understanding of primordial truth as unconcealment, accessible via *aisthēsis* and *noein*,[4] and in the identification of Aristotle's *Rhetoric* as "the first systematic hermeneutic of Being-with-one-another in everydayness," in the public disclosedness of the 'one' (SZ, 138).

The analysis of fear that follows is explicitly developed on the basis of Book II of the *Rhetoric*.[5]

For Aristotle, the human being is *zōion politikon*, a living being whose authentic Being-in-the-world as a Being-with-one-another is conducted in the *polis*. Our concrete way of Being-there in the *polis*, the distinctive way in which we manifest ourselves in each case, is our *ēthos*. *Ēthos* names our "self-conduct" and "stance" (*Sich-halten, Haltung*) in the world. Ethics, the study of human *ēthos*, is not merely a branch or part of political science, but is intrinsic to political science as a developed knowledge of "the Being of human beings in their authenticity." Rhetoric, the study of the possibilities of persuasion, is likewise intrinsic to ethics.[6] The human being is *zōion politikon* because he is *zōion logon echon*; thus, the properly or authentically human life is, as Heidegger elucidates it, a "Being-in-the-*polis*" as "Being-with-one-another," as *koinōnia*, or community (GA 18, 46). Such Being-with-one-another is itself grounded in the "having of a common world," as "a *koinōnia* of what is *sumpheron* and *agathon*," a community oriented toward a common good (49). In a living being, whether animal or human, the world is primordially "there," given in the manner of being affected by it: in animals, via *aisthēsis* and *phōnē*, sensory apprehension and sound, that disclose the world in the manner of pleasure and pain; in humans, the common world is disclosed and constituted primarily through the *logos*, on the basis of a *legein*: the having of a common world and a common good is a speaking "with" the world as a speaking with one another (50). In human existence as *praxis*, what is advantageous and conducive (*ōphelimon, sumpheron*) to the human good— the world itself as conducive to accomplishing the good—is disclosed through discursive deliberation (as operative in *phronēsis*) and thus oriented toward the *kairos*, the opportune moment of action. Deliberation, as a discursive seeking, is thus, as Heidegger explains, a "bringing-to-language":

> In this bringing-to-language of what is *sumpheron*, of the world as it is concretely there, the world is first authentically brought into the "there." The "now" and "here" of human existence [*Sein*] becomes explicit in a particular deliberation, and through this deliberation the human being is—in modern terms—in the concrete situation, in the authentic *kairos*. In this *logos*, *legein* as *logizesthai*, the Being of the human being has the world

there, in such a way that I am in the world here and now in
a particular situation. (59)

Heidegger gives the example of how the ethical virtue of friendship is actualized. I decide to bestow on my friend the pleasure of
a gift. This goal is taken up in advance in a *proairesis*, in a decision
I have already made. Now I begin to deliberate on how best to
fulfil this goal: what would my friend like, what should I give
him? I decide to give him a book. "In this deliberative process my
Dasein in this moment [*Augenblick*] orients itself within this *proairesis*.
The circumspective view within which my deliberation moves has
its world there." I go not just to any bookstore, but to this particular one, so as to procure the book quickly and thus bring my *praxis*
(here rendered as *Besorgen*) to fulfilment. The world is thus seen
from the outset *as* such and such, as conducive to the accomplishment of a certain end; human *praxis* is a *praxis meta logou*, where
the *meta*, Heidegger provocatively suggests, means "in the midst"
(*mittendrin*): *legein* is, so to speak, the very medium in and through
which *praxis* is carried out (60–61).

Two fundamental questions are implicit in Heidegger's account
of ethical existence in dialogue with Aristotle. The first concerns
the relation of this *legein* to the disclosure of beings themselves in the
happening of a world. If this deliberative bringing-to-language is
the way in which the world is first authentically brought into the
"there," the question remains of whether this disclosure of world is
indeed the most originary or primordial event of disclosure. The
term *world* is here used in the sense of the presencing of beings as
determined by their worldly context, that is, as being interpreted as
this or that in relation to a certain end; the seeing at work in *praxis*
is an interpretive, circumspective seeing (63). Interpreting or addressing the world as such and such is a *legein ti kata tinos* (60, 63);
but this deliberative bringing-to-language with oneself (*sum-
bouleuesthai*), this "taking counsel with oneself" operative in *phronēsis*
is, Heidegger insists, only one possibility of a more originary one,
namely, that of taking counsel with others, of talking something
through with others. Talking something through with oneself is a
speaking, a *legein*, a bringing-to-language, yet such speaking always
bears within itself the possibility of speaking with others, of
Mitteilung—of a communicating that is the disclosive sharing with
others of a common world, of the *koinōnia* of a world: "*Speaking is in*

itself communicating and, as communication, is nothing other than *koinōnia*" (61). Human Being in a world is intrinsically a Being-with-others; it is determined by a *legein* concerned with what is good and advantageous for human *praxis*. *Logos* is never simply individual or private, but always already has inscribed within it our being in a common world, in a world shared with others; *logos* is always the *logos* of a community. That *logos* is seen and experienced by the Greeks in this originary manner, that is, in its worldly immediacy of a communal Being-with-one-another in the *polis*, is, Heidegger notes, precisely what is testified to in Aristotle's *Rhetoric*.

Being-with-one-another, thus understood, does not mean, Heidegger remarks, that the human being is not alone, but instead is together with others, in the sense of factually getting together with others. Rather, Being-with-one-another names a "way of Being": my very Being-in-the-world is, always and intrinsically, a Being-with. In this perspective, the assertion "I am," notes Heidegger, is incorrect: one should really say: "I am one," in the sense of "I am others, I am them": " 'One' is, 'one' undertakes this or that, 'one' sees things in such and such a way." This "one," properly understood, is the "how" of everydayness, of our average, concrete Being-with-one-another; from it arise the ways in which human beings "at first and for the most part" see and are affected by and address the world. The real carrier or bearer of this way of our everyday being in the *polis* is language. Yet from this average way of Being-with-one-another there also arises the possibility of "an authentic Being-with-one-another in certain ways" (63–64).

Heidegger does not here specify the details of such authentic Being-with-one-another, but given that what is presented here is in essence a condensed foreshadowing of the analysis of *das 'Man'* that would appear in the 1925 lecture course *Prolegomena to the History of the Concept of Time* and subsequently in *Being and Time*, presumably he has in mind the "liberating solicitude" that frees the other for his or her own Being, and that would characterize precisely the ethical virtues, such as friendship: in giving my friend a gift, if this act is truly one of gift-giving, I undertake this action not because it is what "one" does, nor out of some ulterior motive, but as an end in itself and out of a genuine care for the well-being (*eudaimonia*) of my friend. Precisely as a virtuous act, as an instance of *eupraxia*, my action stands out from the norm: it is not governed by the public interpretedness of the world that specifies what "one" does.[7]

If this is the case, then our analysis suggests that in the intellectual virtue of *phronēsis*, as displaying excellence in deliberation, our deliberation cannot be governed solely or primarily by the common norms that regulate the *ēthos* of a given community and of a particular world. While deliberative excellence would certainly take such norms into account in its deliberation, it would presumably be characterized by an openness attuned to the disclosure of a world exceeding that of the "one," by a letting "oneself" be held open in advance for the appropriate measure of action at any given moment. One's *ēthos* in this situation would be attentive to the particular circumstances of action, relating to the beings disclosed therein, from out of an openness of and toward the phenomenon of world as such, that is, attuned in advance by *Angst*. And on this account, would not all of the ethical virtues be attuned by and grounded in this fundamental *pathos*? Deliberation, as a *legein*, brings the world to language, thus to the dimension or medium of public interpretedness and disclosedness; but what comes to be thus disclosed must already announce itself, speak to or address us, prior to (or as the inaugural moment of) this bringing-to-language, as the situation of action seen in the momentary light of the openness of world as such, to which deliberation is responsive.[8]

A second fundamental question that thus arises in this context is how Heidegger's interpretation understands the specific place and role of ethical virtue, first in relation to the fundamental *pathos* or attunement of *Angst*, and second, in relation to the *proairesis* that always already guides any action. For ethical virtue, according to Aristotle, is not a mere *pathos* or emotion, but rather a "disposition" or *hexis*; furthermore, it is a *hexis proairetikē*: it involves choice, or is "not without" choice (NE, 1106 a1–12; 1139 a23), choice itself being defined as the deliberative desire of actions within our power (1113 a10; 1139 a24). If, as Aristotle tells us, our *proairesis* is always the result of prior deliberation, and good deliberation determining the mean relative to us (i.e., the appropriate measure of our action) is accomplished by *phronēsis* (1106 b35f.), then this might seem to imply that ethical virtue is ultimately dependent upon the intellectual virtue of *phronēsis*. Yet our *proairesis* is not decided by thought alone, but by thought that mediates desire (1139 a32); our action will be virtuous only if our desire is already directed toward the good (the ultimate end that is wished for), and so, Aristotle explains, our *proairesis* involves both thought and a certain ethical disposition (1139 a32–35). Indeed, as it turns out in the course of the analysis of *phronēsis* in Book VI of the *Nicomachean Ethics*, ethical virtue is if anything more important than *phronēsis* for the attainment of *eupraxia*: we cannot acquire *phronēsis* without ethical virtue, Aristotle asserts, for the ultimate end or supreme good appears as such only to someone who is already good, and *phronēsis* itself is concerned not primarily with the ultimate end desired, but only with uncovering the actions conducive to accomplishing that end (1144 a29f.; cf. 1113 a15ff.). A defective disposition may let what is in fact an evil end appear (*phainetai*) as good. Thus, the primary disclosure of the end with regard to ethical and political action is attributed not to intellectual virtue, but to ethical virtue, in relation to which the disclosive power of *phronēsis* is seen to be severely restricted. While for Aristotle the ultimate end of action, true *eudaimonia* (what is truly good, as opposed to the apparent good), can be genuinely disclosed only in and through the *theōria* of *sophia*, and this *theōria* must, as it were, infuse or inform *phronēsis* if the latter is truly to be *phronēsis* (that is, a consistent and steadfast disposition whereby we hit the appropriate mark, the appropriate measure of action, not just occasionally, by chance, or arbitrarily), nevertheless the purely intellectual virtue of *sophia* does not, in and of itself, ensure that we will act virtuously: As Aristotle argues against Socrates, we can know the good and yet not do the good; doing the good—the truly virtuous accomplishment of the good—requires that the *logos* of our deliberation determine our actual conduct, that is, that virtuous action is not merely *kata ton orthon logon* but *meta tou orthou logou* (1144 b25f.).

Far from being an independent virtue, *phronēsis* is thus dependent upon ethical virtue in order to be the excellence that it is: we cannot, Aristotle affirms, be a *phronimos* without ethical virtue (1144 b30). Heidegger would indeed draw attention to this very point in his own interpretation of the intellectual virtues in the *Sophist* course:

> Someone can be *phronimos* only if he is already *agathos*. The possibility of the *alētheuein* of *phronēsis* is dependent on the one who accomplishes it *already* being *agathos* of his own accord in his Being. . . . [P]raxis is not only guided by circumspection, by the seeing that belongs to *phronēsis*. Rather, it becomes apparent that this seeing, the anticipation of the *agathon* as the way in which uncovering is accomplished, is possible only in someone

> who is themselves an *agathos*. *Phronēsis* is nothing so far as it is
> not accomplished in *praxis*, which as such is determined by
> [ethical] *aretē*, by the *prakton* as *agathon*.... To the extent that
> *phronēsis*, with regard to the possibility of its correct accomplish-
> ment, remains dependent upon its being accomplished by an
> *agathos*, it itself is not independent. (GA 19, 166–67)

Heidegger had already made the same point earlier in the same course when commenting on Aristotle's remark, *sōphrosunē sōizei tēn phronēsin*: the ethical virtue of *sōphrosunē*, "thoughtful restraint" or *Besonnenheit*, as Heidegger translates it, saves or rescues *phronēsis*, preserves the human being with respect to the uncoveredness of his or her own Being that otherwise threatens to become concealed, with respect to its ultimate *archē*, through the attunements wrought by pleasure and pain.[9]

Seen in this perspective, the situation seems clear: the ethical virtues must have priority over *phronēsis* in determining our *ēthos*. Yet while Heidegger in the *Sophist* course apparently affirms Aristotle's analysis, and proceeds to elucidate the ontological and ultimately temporal grounds for Aristotle's prioritizing of *sophia* over *phronēsis*, this should not be taken to imply that Heidegger simply agrees with Aristotle, given that the very foundation of Aristotle's ontology (the primary meaning of Being as constant or enduring presence) is precisely what Heidegger, within the broader context of a destructuring of the history of ontology, is attempting to problematize.[10] If the Being of the world, implicitly conceived by Aristotle as enduring presence-at-hand that is most properly disclosed only via the *theōrein* of *sophia*, is not being understood in a phenomenologically originary or appropriate way by Aristotle, then what are the consequences of Heidegger's more radically temporalized understanding of world-disclosure for the relation between ethical virtue and *phronēsis*? How does the 1924 course understand ethical virtue and its temporality in relation to that of *phronēsis*?

TIME AND ETHICAL VIRTUE

According to Book II of the *Nicomachean Ethics*, ethical virtue, *aretē*, is a *hexis proairetikē* located in the mean relative to us, where the mean is determined by *logos* in the manner that a *phronimos* would determine it (1106 b36). As Heidegger renders it in the 1924 course, ethical virtue as a *hexis* is the dispositional having of a particular possibility to be in such and such a way. *Hexis proairetikē* means:

> [the] "possibility of deciding for . . . [*des Entschlossenseins zu* . . .]," of being able to decide in such and such a way at a particular moment [*Augenblick*]. [It is] a *hexis* "that finds itself [*sich befindet*] in the *mesotēs*, has the middle there" *hōrismenēi logōi*, the middle as "delimited by *logos*," "determined by talking it through in deliberation." The *meson* for *praxis* is the *kairos*. (GA 18, 144)

What is notable here is not only that the language that would become that of *Being and Time* is being used to translate Aristotle's *Nicomachean Ethics,* but also that a certain displacement of Aristotle's thought appears to be underway. For what Heidegger's translation emphasizes, seizing on the temporal sense of *pro-airesis*,[11] is that *proairesis* is not so much an actual act of decision or choice, but a being directed toward something, in the manner of deliberative desire, such that what we are directed toward is there in advance (*im vorhinein*): having a goal there in the manner of anticipation (*vorweghaben*), such that this future-oriented anticipation of something already there opens up the possibility of the present moment in a particular regard, in a particular orientation: "To *proairesis* there belongs an orientation toward the entire *Augenblick—proairesis* is not a so-called act; it is the authentic possibility of being in the *Augenblick*" (145). Heidegger's interpretation here emphasizes possibility throughout: ethical virtue, as a *hexis proairetikē*, is the dispositional having of a *possibility* of the present. "*Proairesis* is always directed toward something possible, indeed toward something determinate that is possible, and that we are able to undertake and carry out now at this moment." *Proairesis* is concerned with something that is possible for us; it leads or guides us toward the *eschaton*, toward the point at which an action engages.[12]

It is important to underline that *Entschlossensein* and *sich entschließen*, which Heidegger uses here to indicate that onto which our *proairesis* opens, carry not so much the sense of willful decision, resoluteness, or resolve in the modern sense of a subjective act, as that of opening oneself to something that will in itself be decisive. This is suggested by the way in which Heidegger describes how the directionality of our *proairesis* is decisive for our very Being, for our *ēthos*, in a way that opinion is not. Merely having an opinion (*doxa*) about something does not, in and of itself, affect our *ēthos*; it "*does not affect the stance of the human being's very Being toward others.* By contrast, the manner and way in which I open myself [*mich entschließe*], that to which I open myself, which stands within a *proairesis*, is *decisive* [entscheidend] *for my Being,* for the manner and way in which I am, for my *ēthos.*"[13]

This sense of *praxis* as opening oneself onto something decisive is reinforced in Heidegger's consideration of *ēthos* and *pathos* in the context of Aristotle's *Rhetoric*. Here, the decisive *praxis* is speaking itself, *legein*—specifically, speaking that aims to persuade, to bring about a conviction—and *ēthos* and *pathos* are constitutive moments of the oratory situation. Decisive for the success of the speech are, on the one hand, the *ēthos* of the speaker himself, and on the other, the *pathos* or "attunement" (*Befindlichkeit*) of the listener. Heidegger here characterizes the *ēthos* or "stance" (*Haltung*) of the speaker as the way in which the speaker, in his very speaking, "gives himself" to his audience, such that this "giving oneself" (*Sichgeben*) and opening oneself "also speaks," contributing to the emergence of a conviction. The speaker here speaks not only through the content of his words, but "with his person," in his very *ēthos* providing testament to that of which he speaks (165). One's *ēthos*, as Heidegger puts it, "is nothing other than the manner and way in which there manifests itself what the speaker wants, wants in the sense of one's *proairesis* toward something." As Aristotle indicates in the *Poetics*, our *ēthos* reveals or manifests our *proairesis*, "the momentary resolve [*Entschlossensein*] of the one speaking."[14]

According to Book II of the *Rhetoric*, three things contribute to the formation of one's *ēthos*: (1) *phronēsis*: forming correct opinions through having the proper horizon for the issue in question, having an appropriate overview of the issue, as Heidegger elucidates it; (2) *aretē*: here, a seriousness (*spoudaiōs*) of engagement whereby one says what one really thinks, one means what one says, thus gaining the trust and respect (*epieikes*) of one's audience; (3) *eunoia*: "goodwill," whereby one actually gives one's best advice to the audience, rather than failing to convey what one knows to be best (1378 a6ff.). The first two of these, Aristotle says, may be inferred from the enumeration of the dianoetic and ethical virtues in Book I, chapter 9; the third, *eunoia*, must be considered in connection with the *pathē* or "emotions" (1378 a15).

Before pursuing the analysis of the emotions that follows in Book II of the *Rhetoric*, and in particular that of fear (*phobos*), Heidegger has recourse to several other Aristotelian texts—primarily the *Nicomachean Ethics*, but also the *Metaphysics* and *De Anima*—which, he claims, first give us the appropriate perspective for understanding the analysis of the emotions in the *Rhetoric*. The term *pathos*, he reminds us, has several meanings in Aristotle: In its most general sense, it can mean any changeable quality of something; in its specifically ontological meaning, important for the understanding of motion, it is understood as a correlate of *paschein*, as suffering or undergoing change; and in a narrower sense, that which applies to the *Rhetoric*, it means a changeable quality specifically in relation to the passions. *Pathos*, as defined in the *Nicomachean Ethics*, is a certain "attunement" (*Sichbefinden*) accompanied by pleasure or pain. A *hexis* or "disposition," on the other hand, characterizes the way in which we are disposed in respect of the emotions, "the stance that we maintain," our "composure" (*Fassung*) in regard to a particular *pathos*. A *pathos*, by contrast with a disposition, entails a certain lack of composure (*Aus-der-Fassung-Kommen*) (168). The *pathē* thus have an intrinsic relation to disposition, to the possibility of adopting a composure (171). Together with *dunameis* and *hexeis*, the *pathē* are characterized by Aristotle as *ginomena en tēi psuchē*: phenomena that come to pass in the soul, or, as Heidegger interprets this, ways of coming to be that concern the Being-in-the-world of a living being (168–69). *Pathos* is thus subject to *genesis* and *metabolē*, to arising and to suddenly changing over (*umschlagen*) into a different *pathos*. The *pathē*, Heidegger remarks, are not "states of mind" with accompanying physical symptoms; rather, they "determine our Being-in-the-world, Being-in-the-moment [*Im-Augenblick-Sein*]"; as such, they affect not just an isolated part of the human being, but "the whole human being in his *attunement* [*Befindlichkeit*] *in the world*" (192). The state of composure (*Verfassung*) in which we stand affects "our stance toward things, how we see them, to what degree and in which respects." Our shifting from one state of composure into another affects primarily the way we assume a stance toward the world, our way of Being-in-the-world. The world itself, as disclosed at first and for the most part in our *praxis*, is transparent to us in a greater or lesser degree; in this regard, attaining the right state of composure means "*attaining the middle*, coming from the extremes into the middle." "The middle is nothing other than the *kairos*," notes Heidegger, yet the *kairos*, while culminating in the moment of decision that virtuous action itself is, is not simply a moment or point, but "our entire circumstances, the how, when, for what end, and in relation to what."[15]

With regard to the relation between ethical virtue (as a *hexis proairetikē*) and the *kairos*, this entails that our *proairesis*, as our primary orientation toward the *kairos*, plays the leading role. Heidegger recalls the two senses of *hexis* (deriving from *echein*, "to have") identified in the *Metaphysics*: *hexis*, as a "having," means firstly, the *energeia* or presence of the relation between the haver and what is had, such as when we have on a garment. The garment is "there," present in what it properly is, in its fullest Being, not when it hangs in the closet, but when we wear it, when we have it present in this way. Secondly, *hexis* can mean a *diathesis* or "disposition," "in virtue of which something is disposed well or badly, either in itself or in relation to something else" (1022 b10ff.). In this sense, health is a *hexis*: we "have" health when our body is well disposed in relation to the possibility of illness. Here too, *hexis* means a way of Being: having health means being healthy, being disposed in a healthy manner. Disposition or *diathesis* means an "arrangement" (*taxis*) of that which has parts, an arrangement that has the character of order or positioning (*thesis*), and is not just an arbitrary collection (1022 b1). "Having" in this sense is an orderly arrangement of parts in various respects, and in relation to some guiding possibility. It is this second sense of *hexis* that pertains to ethical virtue: ethical virtue as a *hexis* is a *diathesis*, a *taxis*: it "springs from our *proairesis*," as Heidegger puts it; it means "finding ourselves correctly attuned in the apportionment of the moment" (*das rechte Sichbefinden im Verteiltsein des Augenblicks*) (176).

On this understanding, an appropriate ethical composure arises in the coming-into-being of our own Being as responsive to whatever shows itself in the unfolding moment of action. The Being of the moment, as the emergent presencing of the present in which I stand (and have always already assumed a stance), as this unfolding presencing of my own Being, is itself continually being distributed, arranged and ordered in its manifold respects of "our entire circumstances, the how, when, for what end, and in relation to what," and this in accordance with the deliberative accomplishment (through *phronēsis*) of our guiding *proairesis*. Heidegger thus characterizes *hexis* as a fundamental determination of our Being:

> *Hexis determines the authentic Being [Eigentlichkeit] of Dasein in*
> *its structural aspect of being composed in readiness for something:*
> the various *hexeis* as various ways of our being able to adopt
> a composure [*des Gefaßtseinkönnens*]. *Hexis* is, in an altogether
> fundamental sense, a determination of the Being of our au-
> thentic Being. . . . Our being composed is not arbitrary or inde-
> terminate; within our *hexis* lies a primary orientation toward
> the *kairos*: "I am there, come what may!" This Being-there [*Da-*
> *sein*], being vigilant in one's situation with regard to one's
> issue of concern—this characterizes our *hexis*. (176)

It follows from Heidegger's interpretation here that the ethical
dispositions or *hexeis* are fundamentally futural in their Being: as
modes of our potentiality for Being, namely, for adopting a composure, they orient in advance our coming into being, our being
able to assume a particular stance or *ēthos* in response to the momentary situation of action. More precisely, their temporality must
be that of a futural having-been: as already existing orientations, as
dispositions that have already been formed in us, they must always already be at work in our Being, in our potentiality for Being,
and in such a way as to find their appropriate attunement, their
fitting measure, in the particular situation of action. As a determination of the Being of Dasein, ethical virtue as a *hexis* is thus "not
some quality we possess, not some property imported into Dasein
from the outside, but *a way of Dasein itself. Aretē* is a 'how' of
Dasein, not as a fixed property, but rather, as a 'how' of Dasein,
determined by its Being, characterized by *temporality,* by its stretching into time" (181). The Being of a *hexis* is determined by the
temporality of Dasein itself, and this point emerges most clearly,
Heidegger notes, in Aristotle's reflections on the genesis of the
ethical virtues at the beginning of Book II of the *Nicomachean Ethics*:
we do not possess them by nature, but acquire them through habit
or habituation (*hē d'ēthikē ex ethous periginetai*), becoming courageous by doing courageous actions, and so forth (1103 a17). The
ethical virtues, as dispositions, arise from the "repeated performance" of virtuous actions (*ek tou pollakis prattein*: 1105 b4), which
requires experience and time. Yet this is not a learning by routine,
or by some technique, as in art or *technē*. For in matters of conduct,
where every situation is different, there can be no fixed technique
or standard routine for arriving at the appropriate action. Thus,
Heidegger remarks, "there can be no such thing as a general army

command, an apriori ethics in accordance with which humanity would eo ipso be improved. Each person must for himself have directed his view toward that which is in the moment [*Augenblick*] and which concerns him" (182). Furthermore, although in *technē* we also acquire the relevant disposition through repeated practice and habituation, such that our ability to make or produce something becomes an acquired habit, such practice has, as Heidegger notes, precisely the sense of largely eliminating all deliberation in the interests of efficiently producing the end product. In action, by contrast, deliberation is decisive in accomplishing our *proairesis*, and furthermore must be undertaken anew on each occasion. Thus, Heidegger emphasizes,

> The manner and way of habituation in the case of action is not practice, but *retrieval* [Wiederholung]. Retrieval does not mean the bringing into play of an established skill; it means, rather, *acting anew at every moment [Augenblick] from out of a corresponding resolve.* (189)

Our resolve or *proairesis*, while oriented toward a *kairos* (toward the enactment of a particular end), is also fundamentally open in the sense of being adaptable in response to the situation of the moment, of the present in its very unfolding. Our *hexis*, as a potentiality for Being in the sense of adopting a composure toward the *pathē*, is likewise fundamentally open: open to being retrieved and reenacted in accordance with the emergent distribution and ordering of all the constituent aspects of action, such ordering being directed in advance by our *proairesis*, by our Being's being ahead of itself in an advance or anticipatory deliberation concerning the *kairos*. The appropriate measure or "middle" (*mesotēs*) of action itself is apportioned through our deliberative "speaking" with the world (*hōrismenēi logōi*: 1106 b36f.) as the accomplishment of *phronēsis* "in the manner of an anticipatory deliberation [*Vorüberlegen*] of the moment, . . . such that in this apportionment the appropriate ordering of the moment emerges" (188). Retrieval, as a reenactment of our already being ahead of ourselves in our very Being, is thus not only the manner of habituation through which a *hexis* is appropriated, it marks the temporality of action in general, the temporality of Dasein itself. Not only must such appropriation be accomplished ever anew; the happening of this appropriation is, for this very reason, responsive not only to the situation of the

moment, but to a prior disappropriation that befalls Dasein itself—
or in other words, to the happening of Dasein's freedom, to the
freedom into which Dasein has always already been thrown. As
the accomplishment of *phronēsis*, it is explicitly or knowingly responsive to that openness which marks the possibility of the new.
Whereas in all routine operation "the *Augenblick* is destroyed," such
that "every skill as established routine falls short in relation to the
Augenblick," the "how" of *praxis* has to be accomplished anew at
every moment:

> The "how" can be appropriated only in such a way that the
> human being puts himself in a position *to gain composure for
> every moment* [Augenblick]; not routine, but adopting a free
> stance [*Sichfreihalten*], *dunamis* in the *mesotēs*. All human life is
> unable to be permanently there. The possibilities at the dis-
> posal of a human existence are not permanently there within
> the stretching of Dasein; Dasein loses itself. Possibility falls
> away, and an ever new appropriation is called for, one that is
> constantly retrieved. (190)

What is peculiar to this retrieval, Heidegger notes, can also be
characterized by indicating that all action is oriented toward the
mean, a mark or target that, as Aristotle reminds us, is difficult to
attain and easy to miss. "To become angry is easy; to be angry at
the right moment is difficult." Action that attains the mean is thus
rare (191). For our Being, as determined by *Jeweiligkeit*, by its momentary character, "*there can be no single or absolute norm*"; the task
is rather to cultivate our Being in such a way that it "gains the
propensity to maintain the mean [*die Mitte zu halten*], which is to
say, to seize the moment" (186). The "mean," or middle, is to be
taken not in an arithmetical or geometrical sense, but "in the sense
of *hexis* as *taxis*: the 'arrangement' [or 'apportionment'] of whatever comes into question in relation to a decision." Ethical virtue
aims at the mean, it is *tou mesou stochastikē*:

> Aristotle designates *aretē* as *tou mesou stochastikē*, it "aims" as
> maintaining the mean, as being oriented toward the correct
> apportionment, the correct seizing of the moment [*Augenblick*].
> *Mesotēs: hexis blepousa*, a "composure that sees" and is open for
> the situation. (187)

Ethical virtue in action is thus not something separate from the dianoetic virtue of *phronēsis*, which accomplishes the way in which human Being-in-the-world sees itself as such: "Being-in-[a state of]-Care for Dasein has its way of seeing in *phronēsis*" (193). Rather, ethical virtue in its very unfolding is a propensity toward the mean that itself *sees* the mean, contributes to bringing about the correct *Augenblick*, the appropriate glance of the eye that culminates in the *kairos*. As such seeing, it is all the while an openness, a holding oneself open and free for the ever new appropriation that the time of life itself calls for.

The temporality of retrieval thus characterizes the acquisition—the appropriation, formation, and habituation—of a *hexis*, just as it characterizes action itself. This, Heidegger concludes, is the meaning of Aristotle's claim that we acquire a *hexis* through the habituation of "repeated actions" (*ek tou pollakis prattein*). "Repeated actions" does not imply that after a certain length of time we will finally or automatically have acquired the right habit, such that our dispositions would be routine; rather, "it relates to *praxis* as *proairesis*: Repeated [ever new] retrieval of our *proairesis*. The 'repeated' is precisely what characterizes the temporality of Dasein." The Being of Dasein, of human existence is not *aei*, or ever-enduring sameness, but "determined by historicity": "The '*ever*' of a being such as Dasein is the *repetition of retrieval*" (191).

The rootedness of the ethical virtues in the temporality of Dasein itself remains faithful to Aristotle's own insistence that the virtues are nothing if they are not actualized and displayed in action itself. They are virtues of action, not mere dispositions that we "have" in some indifferent manner, such that they might from time to time be activated or put into practice. As part of the emergent unfolding and fulfilment of *praxis* itself, the ethical virtues are important structural moments of the genesis and accomplishment of *praxis*, moments that must be set to work, distributed and ordered in the enactment of our *proairesis* and in relation to the *kairos* by way of our finding the appropriate measure. Ethical virtue finds its delimitation in our anticipatory deliberation of the moment (*Augenblick*), such that in this delimitation "the right apportionment of the *Augenblick* results"; and this understanding of the mean and of virtue, Heidegger remarks, shows "that it would be mistaken to grasp *aretē* as a skill [*Fertigkeit*]—this contradicts the sense of *aretē*."[16] When Aristotle determines the *pōs echōn*, the "how," of virtuous action—the way in which the actor or agent "has" him-self—in accordance with the three criteria of acting (1) with knowl-edge (*phronēsis*); (2) from out of a *proairesis*; and (3) in such a way as to be *bebaiōs kai ametakinētōs echōn*, the latter does not mean to be of a fixed and permanent disposition of character, as something one would already have, but rather to be steadfast in regard to "not losing one's composure"—which implies letting one's compo-sure be attuned in accordance with one's *proairesis* and its anticipa-tory orientation toward the *kairos*. Heidegger emphasizes that what is important in this third aspect of the "how" of virtuous action is not the state of composure already arrived at, but rather our "not being composed, our being underway [*Aus-der-Fassung-Sein, das Unterwegssein*] from one state to another, the peculiar unrest [*Unruhe*] that is given with *pathos* itself . . . ," in relation to which we have always yet to attain composure (183; 1105 a33). Ethical virtue, as future-oriented, in this sense means the retrieval of a fundamental readiness, an orientation.

In conclusion, while both Aristotle and Heidegger emphasize that ethical and dianoetic virtue are intimately connected and ul-timately inseparable, Heidegger's interpretation of ethical virtue appears to effect a displacement of the priority that Aristotle accords it in relation to *phronēsis*. Heidegger's temporal interpreta-tion of *praxis*, oriented toward the *kairos*, emphasizes the anticipa-tory, futural, and "ekstatic" character of *proairesis* over the already having of a *hexis*.[17] What is decisive in virtuous *praxis* is not the already having of a *hexis* as some fixed property or ability, but the way in which ethical virtue as a *hexis* "springs from" (*entspringt*) our *proairesis*—the way in which our potentiality for Being itself comes into Being, is retrieved, from out of the presencing of a world as disclosed in the anticipatory openness of our *proairesis*. In *Being and Time,* as we have indicated, Heidegger will attribute our fundamental openness to the world not to the *theōrein* of *sophia* but to the attunement or *pathos* of *Angst*, which, holding the *Augenblick* "at the ready" (*auf dem Sprung*), brings us before the possibility of retrieval, holds us free and open for the moment of a possible decision. In the 1924 course, his temporal interpretation of *ēthos* and *praxis* opens up the dimension of ekstatic temporality (as "stretching," *Erstreckung*, and "historicity," *Geschichtlichkeit*) within Aristotle himself, discerning the significance of retrieval in appor-tioning the moment.

FOUR

The Time of Action

From Phenomenology of Praxis *to the Historicality of Being*

Our last chapter has shown how Heidegger's early, phenomeno-logical account of ethical virtue in its relation to *ēthos* and *pathos* initiates a certain displacement of Aristotle's thought, bringing it into the dimension of the ekstatic temporality of human Dasein and its historicality. On Heidegger's account, given the temporal-ity of human existence, the emphasis must be on its open-ended, futural, and yet finite and situated character: the emphasis, in other words, is not so much on the already "having" of a virtue con-ceived as *hexis*, but on the extent to which any already acquired potentiality remains precisely that: potentiality, and thus must come into its appropriate unfolding or actualization, find its measure, in response to the (ultimately unforeseeable) circumstances of the moment. Our having-been happens, or is temporalized, from out of the future, even as it deflects the very unfolding of such futural Being; and this deflection or decision is our existing in, or as, the moment of the present. Who I can come to be—the unfolding of my very *ēthos*—will always depend in part on who, or how, I have already been: there is no escape from this thrownness of my very Being. Yet such thrownness is not only the result of my prior de-cisions and actions; the coherence of what will have been my "own" life story is, rather, from the outset and in advance exposed to, and inserted into, a historicality that far exceeds all individual decision making. The Being of a world into which I am thrown, long before I come to myself (that is, appropriate such thrownness) in any way or to any degree, is itself already historically determined by a tem-porality, or better, a destinal power, that far exceeds my own.

In this and the following chapter, we shall try to make visible something of how Heidegger's understanding of the temporality of human *praxis* develops, in his work of the 1930s, into an under-standing of the *Augenblick* not only as the site of disclosure of a world, but as the site of the historical destining of world conceived

---

In memory of Hillary Johnson, 1975–1999

as an event (or *Ereignis*) of Being. In the present chapter we shall attempt to trace something of this path by first recalling Heidegger's characterization of the *Augenblick* in his 1924–25 reading of Aristotle's *Nicomachean Ethics*, and tracing its development in subsequent phenomenological works of the 1920s. We shall then turn our attention to the reflections entitled *Contributions to Philosophy (Of Ereignis)*, dating from 1936–38, an extremely rich and productive period of Heidegger's work that is commonly regarded as marking a fundamental "turning" in his thought. What is at stake here is, we shall suggest, once again a certain displacement or shift in emphasis, in which the *Augenblick* is seen not only in regard to human action, but as belonging in advance, and always already, to a happening of world that exceeds human action and that indeed first calls it into Being. Not only is the time of the *Augenblick*—as already in the phenomenology of the 1920s—not that of a "now" or point in time that can be set before us or represented as one "moment" in a linear sequence of events; it is also now seen as historical in the sense of belonging to the *Ereignis* or event of the "history of Being," that is, to the way in which Being happens and is destined to historical human beings. Human beings, on Heidegger's account of the 1930s, first become historical and come to belong to a history through the happening of this event that is the address— the speaking—of historicality itself. The *Augenblick* or moment of authentic presence is the temporal moment in which we thoughtfully respond to the way in which Being addresses us. Whether thoughtful or thoughtless, our response to the address of Being is the essence of all human action. The time of the *Augenblick,* as the time of thoughtful action itself, is a time of genesis, creation, and passing away, of both natality and mortality: a time in which and out of which an action or a work first emerges that can then, subsequently, be taken up into a history or ordered within a chronology.[1]

THE MOMENT AS THE SITE OF HUMAN ACTION: HEIDEGGER'S READING OF ARISTOTLE AND THE PHENOMENOLOGY OF DASEIN

Heidegger's early phenomenological analyses of Aristotle, as presented particularly in the 1922 treatise "Phenomenological Interpretations with Respect to Aristotle" (PIA), the 1924 course "Fundamental Concepts of Aristotelian Philosophy" (GA 18), and in the 1924–25 lecture course on Plato's *Sophist* (GA 19), are of pivotal importance for his subsequent understanding of the *Augenblick*. For it was in these early encounters with Aristotle, as his student Hans-Georg Gadamer reports, and in particular through his discovery of the intellectual virtue of *phronēsis* in Book VI of the *Nicomachean Ethics*, that Heidegger "took his first, decisive distance from 'phenomenology as a strict science.' "[2] In Aristotle's analysis of *phronēsis*, Heidegger found a kind of knowing and understanding that was fundamentally different from—and indeed more primordial than—any form of theoretical or "scientific" knowledge, and yet absolutely decisive for the apprehension and conduct of human life. Aristotle's analyses of the dianoetic virtues as modes of the disclosure of truth (*alētheuein*) in Book VI of the *Nicomachean Ethics* had, as Gadamer notes, "for Heidegger the following significance above all: that the primacy of judgment, of logic, and of 'scientific knowledge' hit a decisive limit with regard to understanding the facticity of human life."[3] That limit became manifest above all through the analysis of *phronēsis*, practical wisdom regarding the accomplishment of factical life. As an intellectual virtue, *phronēsis* is concerned with deliberating well (*euboulia*), with finding the best action (*eupraxia*) in a given situation, the action most conducive to accomplishing the good life or living well as a whole *(to eu zēn holon)*. As such, *phronēsis* is not theoretical or formal knowledge—even though it must be informed by a *theōria* or contemplation of the whole, that is, by *sophia*, philosophical knowing—nor is it a kind of technical know-how (*technē*) that possesses the form or *eidos* of its action in advance. What is decisive, rather, is that *phronēsis* must be attuned to the particular situation, to the here-and-now circumstances of action that cannot be seen or known in advance. The situation of action can be seen only in the moment of action itself, in the moment in which one finds oneself faced with having to act, that is, to participate in disclosing the truth of one's worldly Being as best one can, and to act accordingly. *Phronēsis* is concerned with the disclosure and accomplishment of the truth of Being—for Aristotle, of one's own finite and temporally determined Being in the situation of action—and not with the discovery or knowledge of an already existing truth. For one's own, thrown Being is that which is factically otherwise at every moment, futural in the sense that it not only already is, but has always yet to come, so long as one continues to exist.

In Book VI of the *Nicomachean Ethics,* Aristotle identifies the kind of practical seeing that belongs to *phronēsis* and is attuned to the situation of action as a kind of *nous* or *aisthēsis.* It is a sheer seeing or apprehending of the circumstances as a whole in the light of one's ends and one's general orientation toward the world. In both the 1922 treatise and the 1924–25 course, Heidegger translates this practical *nous* as the *Augenblick* of action, as that moment of presence in which one's ownmost, worldly Being is held open for a possible decision. As he puts it in the *Sophist* course:

> *Phronēsis is a catching sight of the here-and-now,* of the concrete here-and-now character of the momentary situation. *As aisthēsis it is the glance of the eye, the momentary glance* [der Blick des Auges, der Augen-blick] *at what is concrete in each specific case and as such can always be otherwise.* (GA 19, 163–64)

What is decisive in *phronēsis* is the *Augenblick* itself. It is decisive in the sense of being that starting from which and toward which the entire deliberation and practical judgment of *phronēsis* proceeds, its *archē* and *eschaton.* Practical deliberation, although crucially informed by a wider context that goes beyond the particular situation of action (most notably, it is informed by one's ethical dispositions or *hexeis;* by one's goals, both immediate and general; and by one's view, or *theōria,* and understanding of the whole of life), has the task of responding appropriately to whatever is given in the situation itself, that is, of responding to that which is disclosed in and through the *Augenblick,* and of determining the *kairos* of the *Augenblick.* The *kairos* refers to the opportune moment of action: it is the "most extreme" point or *eschaton* in which the *Augenblick* of *phronēsis* culminates or peaks, the decisive moment in which an action engages.[4]

The time of the *Augenblick* as the moment of genuine *praxis* informed by *phronēsis* is thus a moment of knowing and seeing oneself—one's own Being—as addressed and called to decision by one's worldly situation as a whole. It entails an authentic understanding of the Being of oneself as *praxis,* that is, of one's being futural in such a way that one's own having-been—who and what one has been up to that moment—is not left behind as a past that can never be retrieved except by recollection, but approaches one as that whose Being is now to be decided, held open for decision.

As the time of authentic action, the *Augenblick* as the moment of authentic presence is distinguished from the ordinary representation of the "objective" time of nature (conceived as a linear sequence of homogeneous "now"-points unfolding before an independent or outside observer) in being finite and unrepeatable, unique and singular, bound to the finite Being of the individual in these particular circumstances and at this particular place and time, and—as this protoethical moment—essentially inaccessible to others. The phenomenon of the *Augenblick* has certainly been seen in the history of philosophy, yet according to Heidegger not fully appreciated in its radical implications, in large part because of the dominance of the theoretical view of the world. Indeed, even Aristotle, "the last of the great philosophers, who had eyes to see," and who saw most clearly here, did not fully fathom the temporality that announces itself in this phenomenon (GA 24, 329). As Heidegger remarks in his lecture course *The Basic Problems of Phenomenology* (1927), "Aristotle already saw the phenomenon of the *Augenblick,* the *kairos,* and delimited it in Book VI of his *Nicomachean Ethics*, although without succeeding in connecting the temporal character specific to the *kairos* with what he otherwise knows as time (the *nun*)" (GA 24, 409). Similarly, Heidegger acknowledges the significance attributed to the *Augenblick* in Kierkegaard's thought, but emphasizes that Kierkegaard understands the moment only as the "now" of the ordinary concept of time, that is, he does not explicate the originary temporality specific to the *Augenblick* (GA 24, 408).[5]

In the hermeneutic of Dasein presented in *Being and Time*, Heidegger attempts to explicate phenomenologically the originary and authentic time of the *Augenblick* in terms of the "ekstatic" temporality proper to it, by contrast to the ordinary concept of time that issues from an "inauthentic" self-understanding of Dasein. Ordinary understanding too indeed "sees" the *Augenblick,* but sees it only as an instant, as a fleeting moment that is simply present-at-hand, and not as the decisive time of action itself (GA 29/30, 427). Just as it interprets the Being of the self inauthentically, in a manner phenomenologically inappropriate to it, by regarding it as something present-at-hand or ready-to-hand, so too it misinterprets the originary time and presence of human existence—the moment—as something objectively and independently present, thus failing to see it fully or perspicuously, in the degree of transparency possible with regard to the phenomenon itself. The authentic presence of Dasein's existence, however, as Heidegger elucidates in *Being and Time*, is neither a fleeting instant nor an objectively ascertainable "now":

> That *presence* [Gegenwart] which is held in temporality proper and which is thus itself authentic, we call the *Augenblick*. This term must be understood in the active sense as an ekstasis. It means the rapture of resolute openness [*die entschlossene Entrückung*] in which Dasein is carried away toward whatever possibilities and circumstances are encountered in the situation, but a rapture that is *held* in this resolute openness. The *Augenblick* is a phenomenon that *in principle* can *not* be clarified in terms of the "now." The "now" is a temporal phenomenon that belongs to time as within-time-ness: the "now" "within which" something arises, passes away, or is present-at-hand. Nothing can occur "in the *Augenblick*"; rather, as authentic presence or waiting-toward [*Gegen-wart*], the *Augenblick* lets us *first encounter* whatever can be "in a time" as ready-to-hand or present-at-hand. (SZ, 338)[6]

The *Augenblick* is not a formal, already-existing framework within which events then occur or phenomena appear; it is, rather, the moment of concretion, of the coming-into-presence of an event or action itself and thus *is* the presence of that event or action in its very unfolding. Such presence is not only not that of a fleeting moment or instant, inasmuch as it is "held" within future and having-been and thus has a certain duration (again, one that cannot be formally determined in advance, since it pertains to the finite situation of action), but is a presence that is held in an openness to the authentic future, that is, to the originary closure that enables it to exist as the thrown "ground" of a nothingness or nullity (SZ, 330). As such, the *Augenblick* is a "waiting toward"—as the German *Gegen-wart* (presence) suggests when hyphenated—the unforeseeable that may be encountered in a given situation, a being held ready and open for whatever may be encountered. Such being held at the ready is the accomplishment of the fundamental attunement of anxiety or *Angst*. In such an attunement, which first brings it before the world as world and before the fundamental possibilities of its Being (SZ, 187–91), Dasein has always already anticipated, and thus is opened to the authentic possibility of understanding itself from out of, the "most extreme" possibility of its ownmost Being. Such is a possibility that cannot itself be determined in advance (in the sense of "outstripped" or "bypassed": *überholt*), the possibility whose moment or *Augenblick* cannot be known, except as "indeterminate," "possible at any moment [*Augenblick*]," the possibility of the impossibility of any retrieval (*Wiederholung*) of the possibility of Being-in-the-world as such and as a whole. Yet this means that this anticipatory Being-toward-death, in which Dasein holds itself in resolute openness (*Entschlossenheit*) and in readiness for the retrieval of its ownmost, singular, and individuated Being (that is, for "action"), is always already exposed to a "decision" or closure within the happening of Being itself, namely, that closure that belongs to (and indeed "is") the action or accomplishment of the originary future, the closure of that which is and has been, of that which is now present, the closure that is the opening of the moment itself, the possibility of the new, of origination. The *Augenblick*'s proceeding toward, or unfolding into, the absolute *eschaton*, the moment of an open decision (*Entschluß*) in which an action engages, itself responds not only to the necessities of the situation of action, but to a more originary necessity and decision within Being itself. And this in itself tells us that human existence or Being as "action" is not reducible to "the decided action of a subject," as Heidegger later emphasized in his essay on "The Origin of the Work of Art" (H, 55), since Being itself gets decided whether or not we "act" as subjects or as individuals, whether or not we (*Dasein*) choose to take action or not. For Being is that which has not only always already been decided, but, at one and the same moment, has always yet to be decided. And how Being comes to be decided is indeed a matter of indifference, one might say, to Being—though not, presumably, to us. While as human beings we cannot but "care" about our Being, fundamentally and in the sense of *Sorge* outlined in *Being and Time*, so that we cannot fundamentally be indifferent to it, there is nevertheless something about Being itself, about its very event, its happening or unfolding, that strangely fails to touch us, that withdraws from us, that remains indifferent to us. We, as human beings, are those who stand and are held in the moment of Being's decision, whether authentically and knowingly or not. The *Augenblick* is not itself something that is decided by the human being's power of thought or decision alone, nor indeed in the first instance. For even in the situation of human action guided by *phronēsis*, human judgment can only respond to what already presents itself in the situation, that is, to the *Augenblick* itself.

What is especially significant here is the way in which these provisional phenomenological analyses of Dasein—provisional with respect to the interpretation of authentic time as the horizon of any understanding of Being in general (not merely of the Being of Dasein)—already point back into the originary dimension of presencing (of the presencing of a world) in which Dasein is held and to which it remains exposed in advance of any action or activity of its own. All activity on the part of Dasein—whether that of ethical or political action, or that of thinking, knowing, or judging, or indeed that of making or producing—all such activity as in each case a mode of coming-into-Being is shown to be primarily *responsive* in its very origination. This does not mean, of course, that Dasein or the Being of the human being is thereby reduced to a mere passivity that would stand over and against the activity or action of "Being itself" conceived as a subject. "Being itself" is neither a hypostatized "subject" nor something that stands opposite to and independent of human being, but refers to the worldly horizon or field of presencing, the open expanse in which beings first show themselves and appear as such. The primordial responsiveness of all human existing and action to the openness of Being does, however, mean that human action of whatever kind cannot be adequately conceived as having its originating ground in an already existing self or subject, or in human understanding or judgment alone. Rather, human action first comes into its own (*eigenes*), authentic Being in response to the more originary happening or event (*Er-eignis*) of Being itself, in response to a necessity and decision within Being. There is, in this sense, not a logical or hierarchical priority of Being over beings, but a *precedence* of Being itself, a precedence that is the happening in which Being "sends" or destines itself, a precedence that is the history or historicality of Being. Such precedence unfolds as an event of difference, of the originary differentiation of the "ontological" difference whereby beings are, in their coming into being and passing away, differentiated from this very event of their presencing.

We may briefly consider the significance of Heidegger's phenomenological recovery of the originary time or Temporality (*Temporalität*) of Being itself from two sides: with respect to Aristotle's ontology, and with respect to the so-called "turning" within Heidegger's own thinking that leads from his work of the 1920s into the more mature work of the 1930s and beyond. First, with regard to the basic distinction between *phronēsis* and *sophia* that guides Aristotle's ontology of factical human life, it is especially important to note how Heidegger's analyses integrate the phenomenon of world into the radical temporality disclosed in the phenomenological analysis of *phronēsis*. The world is no longer seen as that which is permanent (*aei*), as that which always is as it is, which can be disclosed in its Being only via the pure, untroubled, contemplative gaze of *theōrein,* and which is thus to be contrasted with the Being of that which can be otherwise than it is, the factical life of human concerns that is disclosed in *phronēsis*. The Being or Dasein of the human being and of the realm of human affairs is not to be contrasted with the Being of the *kosmos* or of nature in its presence-at-hand; rather, the world is that which, insofar as it can be disclosed at all, is only ever disclosed within and through the temporality of factical human existence: it is temporalized in that very temporality as its "horizon." Dasein's Being is intrinsically "Being-in-the-world," and not that of an individual subject or knower that stands opposite the "world," conceived as the totality of what is permanently present-at-hand and simply there as a potential object to be known or disclosed scientifically or philosophically. On the other hand, a corollary of this is that Aristotle's focus in the *Nicomachean Ethics* on human beings insofar as they can be regarded as the origin (*archē*) of their actions, the focus of the analyses of action on the importance of judgment, knowledge, and *proairesis* (prior choice or "intention"), and thus the bringing about of a individual "subject" of action, while not simply opposed by Heidegger (since Dasein's projective or "proairetic" understanding plays a crucial role in the disclosure and happening of the self), is likewise complicated by the orientation of the analysis of Dasein toward the worldly and thrown character of Dasein's temporal individuation. Dasein's actions and decisions are determined much more by its coming toward itself from out of its already having been thrown into the happening of a world and finding itself in the midst of that world than by any "subjectivity." The *Augenblick* as ekstatic presence in each case designates the authentic and originary presence of world in the midst of the factical situation of action. As Heidegger elucidates in *The Basic Problems of Phenomenology*, it names the way in which the world is authentically disclosed in the resolute openness of Dasein for action:

> In the *Augenblick* as an ekstasis, the Dasein that exists as openly resolved is transported on each occasion into the factically

determinate possibilities, circumstances, and contingencies of
the situation of its action. The *Augenblick* is that which, spring-
ing from resolute openness, first and solely has an eye [*Blick*]
for what comprises the situation of action. It is that mode of
existing in resolute openness in which Dasein as Being-in-the-
world holds and keeps its world in view [*im Blick*]. (GA 24,
407–408)

This phenomenological retrieval of world as the temporally determined, open horizon of the presence or Being of beings as a whole
as that starting from which factical Dasein first comes to be, that is,
to enact itself in each instance, not only dislodges theoretical contemplation from its privileged position as granting primary access to
the world, however. It also means that, while the temporal Being of
Dasein that finds its pivotal focus in the *Augenblick* must indeed be
understood as action (*Handeln*) or *praxis,* such *praxis* must be taken
in an originary sense that encompasses or underlies all of Dasein's
modes of Being. It should not, as in Aristotle, be restricted to ethical
or political *praxis* understood in a narrow sense as contrasted with
the *praxis* of theoretical contemplation or philosophizing.

    With regard to the second question, that of the transition of
Heidegger's own thinking from the preparatory, hermeneutic phenomenology of the Being of Dasein in the 1920s into the thinking
of Being itself that gains ascendancy from the early 1930s on, a
twofold shift occurs. The first aspect concerns the manner of thinking; the second, the issue or *Sache* that becomes the focus of thought.
On the one hand, what is left behind as inadequate to the issue or
matter itself (the question of Being) is the conception of phenomenological ontology as a science—as "the science of the Being of
beings" (SZ, 37)—that is, the entire venture of a theoretical representation and thematization of the Being of beings, the objectification of Being upon the horizon of its givenness.[7] For this very
aspiration to develop a science of Being soon showed itself, as
Heidegger would concede in the "Letter on 'Humanism,'" to be
"inappropriate" (GA 9, 357). The horizon of givenness of the Being
of beings showed itself phenomenologically to be neither a stable
entity (the "subject" as ground of the act of presentation or theoretical objectification), nor the permanent presence (*nous*) of the
world, but the temporal event of the presencing of world whose
horizon, as originary and futural, and thus essentially open, is
simultaneously one of the closure and concealment of Being itself.

This event of presencing is the way in which Being is originarily "given" or destined; as in each case singular and finite, bound to a particular worldly context and showing itself only in the *Augenblick,* it cannot by its very nature become the object of theoretical contemplation or thematization. Commensurate with this, the *Sache* or issue of this thinking has also changed accordingly. In place of the attempt in the 1920s at a thematic and scientific objectification of Being starting from the analytic of Dasein, where Being is conceived metaphysically as the horizon of givenness belonging to beings—an attempt that, at least in its scientific and methodological aspirations, is itself already historically determined by subjectivity—Heidegger's work of the 1930s and beyond constitutes the continually renewed endeavor to stand thoughtfully within and to think from out of the event or *Ereignis* of Being as presencing, that is, to assume a stance within the *Augenblick* as the originary "site" of this event. It emerges from the attempt to think this very event, and indeed, to understand thinking itself—the most proper action or activity of the thinker—as nothing other than a finite response to this event. The resolute openness of the *Augenblick* is from here on seen not so much as belonging to the Being of Dasein conceived as one particular, albeit distinctive entity among others; rather, the Being of Dasein, as of all other entities, is now understood as belonging, always already and in advance, to the *Augenblick* as the site of the disclosure of a world and of the historical destining of the event of Being. Furthermore, the *Augenblick* itself is now seen to be historically determined, not primarily by the historicity of Dasein, as it was in *Being and Time,* but by historicality understood as the happening of Being itself, to which human actions are responsive.

The so-called turning within Heidegger's thinking is thus itself a response to a turning within Being itself, that is, to a change in the way in which Being shows itself and addresses itself to the thinker. No longer showing itself as a temporal horizon whose temporal character (*Temporalität*) was to be thematically illuminated and objectified by theoretical-scientific study—as though this kind of thinking were itself fundamentally untouched by its object; as though such contemplation were not itself already a response to a historical address and destiny of Being—Being now appears in its historical precedence as the event of presencing that announces itself in the *Augenblick* in its finitude and singularity and which, precisely as this singular and finite event in each case, cannot itself become something present. It thus remains inaccessible to theoretical apprehension, which for its part can contemplate only that which already *is*, that which is already present, and whose Being, moreover, always is as it is (*aei*): that which is constantly present in its sameness. Accordingly, Heidegger indicates in the *Contributions*,

> the task was . . . above all to avoid an objectification of Beyng, on the one hand by *holding back* the "Temporal" [*temporalen*] interpretation of Beyng, and at the same time by attempting to make "visible" the truth of Beyng independently thereof. . . . Thinking became increasingly historical. . . . Beyng itself announced its historical essence. (GA 65, 451)[8]

A key transitional text in this respect, on the way from Heidegger's early phenomenology to the thinking of the *Contributions*, is the last lecture course of the 1920s, the course of winter semester 1929–30 entitled *The Fundamental Concepts of Metaphysics: World, Finitude, Solitude*. Toward the end of that course, Heidegger raises the critical question of the appropriate "dimension" for thinking the ontological difference, that is, for thinking the distinction between Being and beings. It is inappropriate, he now insists, to think this distinction in the manner of objectifying thinking, as though we could simply place "Being" and "beings," and the difference between them, all before us on the same level, as though they simply lay independently there to be contemplated by our theoretical gaze. For metaphysical thinking has in essence always represented Being and beings in this manner, in their difference, although without thinking this difference radically enough (and thereby tending to reduce Being to what Heidegger calls "beingness," an existent quality or ground of beings) or paying heed to the difference as such. Not only does the ontological difference not lie before us as an object that lies present-at-hand within the field of presence; it is also, Heidegger emphasizes, not something first created by a particular way of thinking (philosophy). Rather, "we are always already moving *within* the *distinction as it occurs*. It is not *we* who make it, rather, *it* happens *to us* as the fundamental occurrence of our Dasein." Furthermore, not only is this differentiation of Being (presence) from beings (that which is present) something that happens constantly, whether with or without any explicit intervention or conscious action on our part, but it must, Heidegger stresses, "*already* have occurred" simply for us to be able to apprehend beings in their being such and such. "In a metaphysical sense, therefore, the distinction stands at the origin [*Anfang*] of Dasein" (GA 29/30, 519). In these statements we see at once an explicit recognition of the precedence of the event of presencing as an event of differentiation, and an insight into this event as lying at the origin of the Being of Dasein, as that starting from which Dasein can first be open for the approach of beings themselves. Finally, and most importantly, Heidegger here makes the decisive call to set aside the thematic coining of the distinction, and to "venture the *essential step* of transposing ourselves into the *occurrence of this distinguishing* in which the distinction occurs" (GA 29/30, 524), that is, into the dimension of the happening of world, the occurrence in which world is "formed." This is, in effect, the first formulation of what Heidegger would later refer to as the call for the "step back" out of metaphysics (founded on this distinction) into the "essence" of metaphysics as the dimension from which the distinction first arises.[9]

THE MOMENT AS THE TIME OF *EREIGNIS*: FROM PHENOMENOLOGY TO THE HISTORY OF BEING

When, therefore, Heidegger alludes to the *Contributions* in a marginal note to the "Letter on 'Humanism,'" as "a path begun in 1936, in the '*Augenblick*' of an attempt to say the truth of Being in a simple manner,"[10] his highlighting of the *Augenblick* here indicates that it is central to the very stance of this thinking, and not to be understood in the ordinary sense of a chronological moment. On the other hand, as we have tried to indicate, while chronologically speaking, the said path may have its immediate beginning in 1936, its true origins and commencement lie much earlier in the chronology of the thinker's work. Indeed, on Heidegger's self-understanding, the true origins of this new endeavor of thinking lie in the history of Being itself that unfolds in a destinal and epochal manner from out of the first beginning or commencement (*Anfang*) of Western philosophical thought, the beginning of metaphysics itself. The transition in Heidegger's thinking outlined above corresponds, in effect, to the historical transition that thinking now finds itself called upon to accomplish, the transition from this first beginning to what Heidegger calls an "other beginning." The *Augenblick* of thinking must therefore understand itself as "histori-cal" in precisely this sense, namely, that of belonging to the way in which Being itself unfolds or "happens." Thus, in the opening sections of the *Contributions* Heidegger writes that "the historical *Augenblick* of transition must be accomplished from out of the knowledge that all metaphysics . . . remains incapable of placing the human being into any foundational relations toward beings" (GA 65, 12). For insight into the essence of metaphysics, founded on the ontological difference, has shown that metaphysical thought itself fails to think back into or from out of that very dimension that first founds it: it remains closed off in advance from the originary happening of Being and thus remains condemned to think and to relate toward beings themselves in a reductive manner.[11] Similarly, writing the archaic "Beyng" (*Seyn*) to indicate that Being (*Sein*) is here thought otherwise than in metaphysical representa-tion, Heidegger here emphasizes that:

> The thoughtful question concerning the truth of Beyng is the *Augenblick* that carries the transition. This *Augenblick* can never be ascertained as something actual; still less can it be calcu-lated. It first establishes the time of *Ereignis*. (GA 65, 20)

The question concerning the truth of the happening of Being, as *Ereignis*, itself occurs as the *Augenblick* of a historical transition to another thinking of Being, a thinking whose time is that of its own enactment, of its coming into its own Being, of its being "enowned." The "singular simplicity" of this transition, Heidegger goes on to say, can never be grasped historiographically or by our ordinary concept of history—since these merely represent objectively what has already occurred and lies present. They belong to metaphysical thinking. The transitional thinking of the *Contributions*, by contrast, belongs to a time that can never become present as such, to what Heidegger calls "the concealed moments [*Augenblicken*] of the his-tory of Being" (GA 65, 92). On the other hand, is it not only by virtue of its becoming misrepresentable as a possible object of metaphysical or historiographical representation that this *Augenblick*, as Heidegger puts it, "has a long future in store for it"—granted, he adds, that Being's abandonment of beings can once more be ruptured? The *Augenblick* of this thinking, which first "sets" or establishes (*setzt*) the time of *Ereignis*, is also the *Augenblick* of this thinking's being established within Being, that is, becoming a *work* that itself henceforth *is* and remains to be read—a work whose time has always yet to come. Such thinking becomes a being (*Seiendes*) that "is," not in the sense of being a fixed entity, but of being a work, that is, of being something at work, something that manifests the event of its own coming into Being as an event that precedes and carries it, that remains always yet to occur. The thinking "of," that is, from out of *Ereignis* that is the work of the *Contributions* has thus, in this sense, always yet to happen, always yet to be accomplished—which accomplishment (*Vollbringen*) of Being is the authentic action of thinking.[12] The event or *Ereignis* of this thinking is thus, astonishingly enough, an event that demands its own faithfulness, that calls for its own historical *Augenblick* as something that, in all its simplicity, remains singular, unique, repeatable only in the singularity of its unrepeatablity (or untranslatability— and this is at once this thinking's resistance to translation *and* its necessity of being translated). What is at issue here is, therefore— and this is something Heidegger stresses throughout the *Contributions*—not at all a thinking of Being or Beyng in its difference from beings (thus not at all a thinking from out of the ontological differ- ence), but a "saving" or rescuing (*retten*) of *beings themselves*, a bringing of (our experience of) beings themselves back into the "truth of Beyng." The task is that of preparing "the time of build- ing the essential shape of beings from out of the truth of Beyng" (GA 65, 5), of "*the restoration of beings from out of the truth of Beyng*" (11). This entails "letting Da-sein become possible for human be- ings and thus rescuing a steadfastness in the midst of beings, so that beings themselves may undergo restoration in the open of the strife between Earth and world" (7). The site of this possible stead- fastness in the midst of beings, in contrast to the marked lack of steadfast abode that characterizes the fleeting existence of "living for the moment" in the contemporary epoch, is the *Augenblick* as the site (*Stätte*) of the strife between Earth and world—here, the site in which the work of the thinker can first come into its own and thus authentically be the work that it is. Thus, throughout the *Contributions* the site of the *Augenblick* is identified as the "time- space" of the strife between Earth and world, and, as such, as the site of *Ereignis* itself.[13] The *Augenblick*, as the originary time of the event of Being itself in which the Being of beings attains possible steadfastness in being set to work, is in this sense *"the time of Being"* (GA 65, 508).

The originary, authentic Being of Dasein as a being held in the *Augenblick* of resolute openness is now to be thought from out of *Ereignis*. The fundamental, thoughtful attunement of such being held (*gehalten*)—an attunement that is presumably already intimated within the *Angst* that in *Being and Time* opens Dasein onto its world as world, and is said to "hold the *Augenblick* at the ready"[14]—is now understood as that of restraint or reservedness (*Verhaltenheit*).[15] Restraint is, as Heidegger articulates it, "the distinctive, momentary [*augenblickliche*] relation to *Ereignis* in having been called by the address of *Ereignis*" (GA 65, 31). It attunes the *Augenblick* in the manner of a "deep stillness" (34). Dasein's Being-a-self or selfhood— the originary dimension of Being-a-self that is to be "retrieved" for the human being (31)—indeed consists in its being "the site of the *Augenblick* of this address and belonging [to *Ereignis*]" (52). Dasein, as "the fundamental occurrence of future history," "springs from *Ereignis* and becomes the site of a possible *Augenblick* for the decision concerning man—his history or non-history [*Ungeschichte*] as its transition unto downgoing" (32). In emphasizing that "decision" here, in the context of the *Contributions*, is not to be understood as the action or activity of the human being, but in the first instance as the decision that belongs to the happening of Being itself and that addresses itself to humans in calling for their possible response, Heidegger concedes that *Being and Time* was, in this respect, open to the danger of misinterpreting Dasein's resolute openness in the "existentiell"–"anthropological" sense of "moral resolve," rather than "the other way around," as "the temporalizing-spatializing of the free play of the time-space of Beyng" (87–88). The "turning" in which Being shows itself as the historical or destinal happening of *Ereignis* responds to this danger.

In seeking to understand the historical *Augenblick* of this transition we should call attention once again to the lecture course of winter semester 1929–30 as an important intimation of the thinking attempted in the *Contributions*. In Part II of the *Contributions*, concerned with the intimation (*Anklang*) of Beyng from out of the refusal that announces itself in Being's abandonment of beings,[16] which the consummation of metaphysics in the epoch of planetary technology itself institutes as an oblivion of Being, Heidegger writes of the kind of knowing (*Wissen*) appropriate to such intimation. It is a knowing that is itself *augenblicklich*: a knowing of the *Augenblick* that is enacted from out of and as the *Augenblick* of this historical transition:

> [B]ecause in the other beginning Beyng becomes *Ereignis*, the intimation of Beyng also must be history, must pass through history by an essential disruption, and must at the same time know and be able to say the *Augenblick* of this history. (What is meant is not a characterization or description according to a philosophy of history, but a knowing of history from out of the *Augenblick* and as the *Augenblick* of the first intimation of the truth of Beyng itself.) (GA 65, 108)

If the history of Being as metaphysics can justifiably be seen as the history or happening of the oblivion of Being, then the first intimation of Beyng—as the intimation of this oblivion as such—itself emerges from, and in this sense belongs to, that history as what is withheld in it in and throughout its epochal destinings. The intimation itself, however, thus also passes through that history in disrupting it, in rupturing the concealment of the oblivion of Being and thereby first letting it be seen as such, indeed first letting that history be seen as what it has been in this regard. The intimation of Beyng, in and as this historical *Augenblick*, is that very disruption.[17]

The intimation of Beyng unfolds from out of a "compelling need" (*nötigende Not*) that issues from the oblivion of Beyng, and demands to be recognized and acknowledged as such in its highest instance: the "need of needlessness" (*Not der Notlosigkeit*: GA 65, 107). Being's abandonment of beings is an "emptiness" (*Leere*), a "telling refusal" (*Sichversagen*) that, as originarily both recollective and awaiting, opens up a presence that is directed toward the decision of Beyng itself, the presence that is the *Augenblick* (383–84).[18] In the 1929–30 course, such need and refusal were already recognized by Heidegger as the absence of any essential oppressiveness or distress (*Bedrängnis*) of contemporary Dasein as a whole. Dasein's ordinary, everyday understanding, itself historically conditioned, suppresses the profound boredom that underlies it in its continual haste to attend to every social, political, and cultural need of the day through its organizations and programs (GA 29/30, 238; 243–45). As such, it fails to let any essential need as a whole emerge, that is, to direct its view toward what is happening fundamentally in the midst of the Being of beings as a whole, namely, Being's abandonment of beings that, in profound boredom, lets all

beings recede into an indifference (215). In profound boredom—
which contemporary existence precisely does not let arise as such—
Dasein is left empty in being delivered over to beings' refusal of
themselves as a whole, in being refused any essential possibilities
of engaging with or attending to beings themselves (210–11). Yet
such refusal, Heidegger emphasizes, is intrinsically a "telling refusal" (*Versagen*) that impels and holds Dasein toward that which
originarily makes it possible, enabling its existence in the midst of
beings as a whole as a potentiality for Being, carrying and sustaining all its essential possibilities. And that is: the *Augenblick,* as "that
which is most extreme" (*Äußerste*), enabling all the possibilities of
Dasein as possibilities (215–16), and which, as "the *Augenblick* of
essential action," ruptures the temporal entrancement attuning us
in the manner of the "long while" (*Lange-weile*) or "long time" that
profound boredom originarily is (226–30). Yet which *Augenblick,*
Heidegger asks, announces itself and can thereby be intimated in
this telling refusal of beings as a whole?[19] To what must Dasein,
entranced by the need of the absence of any distress as a whole,
openly resolve itself so as to rupture such entrancement and to be
open for such need?

> To this: namely, first *bringing about* for itself once again a *genu-*
> *ine knowing concerning that wherein whatever properly makes Dasein*
> *possible consists.* And what is that? The fact that the *Augenblick*
> [Heidegger's emphasis] in which Dasein brings itself before
> itself as that which is properly binding must time and again
> stand before Dasein as such. . . .
>   What, therefore, is demanded by the *Augenblick* simulta-
> neously announced in this absence of any distress as a whole?
> That the *Augenblick* itself be understood, and that means seized
> upon, as the *innermost necessity* [Notwendigkeit] *of the freedom*
> *of Dasein.* (GA 29/30, 247)

What is needed above all is a genuine knowing (*Wissen*) and understanding of the *Augenblick* itself as the ground of Dasein's freedom, that is, as that wherein the possibility of all its possibilities is
gathered in each case. Yet this knowledge of the *Augenblick* is here
already seen as a knowledge that is called for by the "need" of the
contemporary situation itself, of the historical moment in which
Dasein finds itself. And this entails, as Heidegger had expressed it
in 1928, a "historical recollection." The activity of philosophizing,
he insisted in *The Metaphysical Foundations of Logic,* must itself re-

spond to the "necessity of the *Augenblick*" (GA 26, 11). And this means that it must understand itself in terms of the historicality of its own Being. Historical recollection of the history of philosophy occurs not in a theoretical or speculative-dialectical seeing, but "thrives only in understanding oneself in terms of the *Augenblick*" (*im augenblicklichen Sichselbstverstehen*). It is "at once recollective and *augenblicklich*," grounded in the "originary unity . . . of the temporality of the factical Dasein that is philosophizing" (GA 26, 9–10). What Heidegger in the *Contributions* names "the concealed moments [*Augenblicken*] of the history of Being" (GA 65, 92) is, toward the end of the 1928 course, foreshadowed in his remarks on the significance of Kant's discovery of the productivity of the transcendental imagination—a productivity that, from Heidegger's perspective, belongs originarily not to the "subject," but to the temporalizing of ekstatic temporality itself, in which what is "produced" or brought forth is not a being or entity, but nothing less than the *nihil originarium* of the phenomenon of world, the unity of the ekstatic horizon, that is, of the Temporality of Being. In the 1929–30 course this productivity will be thought as the event of world-formation (*Weltbildung*). Kant's discovery of the productivity of the transcendental imagination, the temporal significance of which is not fully fathomed by Kant himself, is, Heidegger comments, "the first *Augenblick* in the history of philosophy in which metaphysics attempts to free itself from logic." And yet, he adds, "this *Augenblick* passed." "Perhaps the true happening in the history of philosophy is always only a temporalizing of such *Augenblicke*, moments that, irrupting and cast at distant intervals, never actually become manifest in what they properly are" (GA 26, 272–73).[20]

In view of Heidegger's growing recognition of the inappropriateness of understanding the phenomenological thinking of Being as the science of the Being of beings, section 76 of the *Contributions*, in which Heidegger presents a number of theses concerning "science," is especially significant. Heidegger here not only acknowledges that "science" (*Wissenschaft*) does not constitute genuine knowing (*Wissen*), but, alluding to the 1929–30 course, identifies the implicit oblivion and abandonment of Being that announces itself in profound boredom as being the "concealed end" or goal of modern science—even though science itself has not the slightest intimation of this state of "complete boredom" toward which it rushes in bringing about Being's "yawning abandonment of beings" (GA 65, 145; 157). The science referred to here is presumably that of the ontic sciences that determine the historical era of modernity (since philosophy in the form of Heidegger's attempted grounding of a phenomenological science of Being precisely leads to an intimation of this concealed end): those sciences that objectify beings upon the horizon of their Being (subjectivity). But Heidegger's critique of science also extends to his own conception of ontology as an objectifying science of Being. In section 73, he concedes that, with regard to any attempt to theoretically lay the ground or foundations of science, or in other words to thematically and theoretically account for the activity of science as such, "[e]very kind of theoretico-scientific (transcendental) attempt to lay the ground has become impossible. . . ." Commensurate with this comes the insistence that the very notion of "science" must be "freed from its historical indeterminacy," and ascertained with respect to its specifically modern essence (142).[21] In short, the activity of science itself must be seen in terms of its own historicality, as determined by the history of Being; the very horizon of the thinking of Being is itself historical and as such cannot be theoretically ascertained, but apprehended only in a recollection that is *augenblicklich*.

Being's abandonment of beings, according to Heidegger, constitutes a "unique era" in the history of the truth of Beyng, the era of "the long time" in which the truth of Beyng hesitates to bestow its essence clearly (GA 65, 120). But this long time, which is that of the concealed, profound boredom that draws back and forth in the abysses of contemporary Dasein, is not that of a genuine steadfastness in the midst of things. It goes hand in hand with the modern phenomena of speed, acceleration, and rapidity that entail "fleetingness," "rapid forgetting," and "losing oneself" in the next newest thing—in short, with the entire *ēthos* of "living for the moment" which, Heidegger reminds us, is in truth only "a blindness toward what is truly *augenblicklich*, toward that which is not fleeting, but opens up eternity" (121). The "eternity" in question here is not that of the *nunc stans*, the vision of a divine *praesens intuitus*, but that of the *Augenblick* itself: the "eternal," as Heidegger later indicates, does not refer to that which is ceaselessly prolonged, but to "that which can withdraw in the *Augenblick*, so as to return once again . . . not as the *identical* [*das Gleiche*], but as that which is transformed ever anew, this one and singular thing: Being [*Seyn*]" (371).[22]

That which can thus return remains, to be sure, a child of its time—but a child, nevertheless. Of Mnemosyne, perhaps.

FIVE

Historical Beginnings

Moment and Rupture in Heidegger's Work of the 1930s

*Das Geschichtliche aller Geschichte geschieht in jener großen Stille,
für die der Mensch nur selten das rechte Ohr hat.*

The historical in all history occurs in that great stillness for
which the human being only seldom has the right ear.
—Heidegger, *Basic Questions of Philosophy*

*Die stillsten Worte sind es, welche den Sturm bringen. Gedanken,
die mit Taubenfüßen kommen, lenken die Welt.*

It is the quietest words that bring the storm. Thoughts that
come on doves' feet change the world.
—Nietzsche, *Thus Spake Zarathustra*

In the preceding chapter we have seen that in his Marburg and Freiburg lectures of 1927–30, Heidegger's thinking of the Being of Dasein as temporality (*Zeitlichkeit*) shifted increasingly toward understanding that temporality, not in terms of the historicity of Dasein (as though Dasein were the "subject" of its own historicity), but in terms of the Temporality of Being itself (*Temporalität des Seins*) and of the transcendence of world. In the 1930s, he began to conceive Dasein's Being—that is to say, its time—in terms of the way in which the Being of a world is itself historically determined in the coming to pass, or *Ereignis*, of world-horizons. In the following remarks we shall try to examine more closely Heidegger's developing understanding, in the early to mid-1930s, of how worlds are historically determined by focusing on the issue of historical beginnings. The task is to shed further light on what we have seen Heidegger describe as "the concealed moments [*Augenblicken*] of the history of Being" (GA 65, 92), or, more specifically, "the historical moment of

115

transition" from the first beginning of Western philosophy to an "other beginning."[1] The term *historical beginnings* is ambiguous: on the one hand, it implies that all beginnings, in the realm of human activity, are already and inevitably historically determined; on the other hand, it refers to the beginnings of historical worlds, epochs, or human actions, the moments of disruption and irruption in which those worlds, epochs, or actions emerge and are sent or destined into their own historicality.

Ēthos and Concealment: The Power of Beginnings

We might begin, perhaps, with a question of translation. Such a beginning is necessary, indeed, not only on account of an apparently terminological difficulty in the present instance, where we are faced with the task of rendering some of Heidegger's German usage into English, but because wherever there is a question of beginning or of beginnings, translation will inevitably be the issue facing us, an issue that we may confront or evade in various ways. This is simply another way of saying that, for mortals, there can be no possibility of any pure or absolute beginning; that translation, in the broadest sense (which is not restricted to the largely paradigmatic case of translating between different languages), is itself the very enactment of beginnings.

Such issues should become somewhat clearer in the course of this chapter. Let us start, however, with the particular and quasi-technical difficulty that should at least be remarked upon here. The difficulty concerns the fact that what, in the title of this chapter, is referred to as "beginning" is intended as a rendition of the German *Anfang*, the meaning of which Heidegger himself explicitly distinguishes from that of *Beginn*, the Germanic counterpart of our English word "beginning." For this reason, "beginning" might appear not to be the best choice for translating the German *Anfang* into English. Moreover, *Anfang* is etymologically derived from the verb *fangen*, to catch or seize hold of something (and thus secure it or set it in place), as in to catch a ball, and thus carries connotations that are not immediately conveyed in the word *beginning*.[2] It is presumably for such reasons that Heidegger translators have sometimes sought to convey the meaning of *Anfang* in other ways, rendering it as "commencement" or "inception," to name but two.[3] And yet, one should also be cautious before leaping to the conclusion that the word *beginning* should be avoided as a translation of *Anfang*. For despite their etymological proximity, or even identity, the English "beginning" does not carry the same sense exactly as the German *Beginn*, nor are the two words *Anfang* and *Beginn* necessarily so clearly differentiated in German usage. Thus, what is decisive is ultimately not so much the word that we choose as a translation of *Anfang*, but the semantic resonance that we are able to lend to it (what Heidegger elsewhere calls its *Schwingungsgefüge*):[4] in other words, how we then respond in turn to the task of translating *that* word—say, the word *beginning*—into English. It is beginning to seem as though, despite the fact that we have always already begun, or that a beginning has always already happened with us, we were always faced anew with the task of beginning again.

Let us turn for a moment to a passage where Heidegger very clearly delineates the sense in which he wishes to understand the word *Anfang* and distinguishes it from the ordinary use of *Beginn*. The passage occurs in the 1934–35 Freiburg lecture course on Hölderlin's hymns "Germania" and "The Rhine." In his initial, introductory remarks Heidegger insists that Hölderlin himself must initiate (*beginnen*) and determine the endeavor to be undertaken, and he proposes therefore to start by simply reading Hölderlin's hymn "Germania," to which the first part of the lecture course will be devoted. And yet, before reading the poem and thus letting Hölderlin's poetry simply speak for itself, Heidegger immediately interrupts Hölderlin, distancing himself from this proposed start, as it were, by offering a series of prefatory remarks, the first of which concerns the question of beginning itself. Heidegger writes (we first cite the German):

> Was bedeutet dieser Beginn mit dem Gedicht "Germanien," und was bedeutet er nicht? 'Beginn'—das ist etwas anderes als 'Anfang.' Eine neue Wetterlage z.B. beginnt mit einem Sturm, ihr Anfang aber is die vorauswirkende, völlige Umwandlung der Luftverhältnisse. Beginn ist jenes, womit etwas anhebt, Anfang das, woraus etwas entspringt. Der Weltkrieg fing an vor Jahrhunderten in der geistig-politischen Geschichte des Abendlandes. Der Weltkrieg begann mit Vorpostengefechten. Der Beginn wird alsbald züruckgelassen, er verschwindet im Fortgang des Geschehens. Der Anfang, der Ursprung, kommt dagegen im Geschehen allererst zum Vorschein und ist voll da

erst an seinem Ende. Wer vieles beginnt, kommt oft nie zum
Anfang. Nun können wir Menschen freilich nie mit dem Anfang
anfangen—das kann nur ein Gott—, sondern müssen beginnen,
d.h. mit etwas anheben, das erst in den Ursprung führt oder
ihn anzeigt. Dieser Art ist der Beginn dieser Vorlesung.

Wir stellen das Gedicht "Germanien" an den Beginn, um
auf den Anfang vorzudeuten. Damit ist gesagt: Dieses Gedicht
weist hin auf den Ursprung, das Fernste und Schwerste, was
uns da zuletzt unter dem Namen Hölderlin begegnet.

In the following translation we shall translate *Anfang* as "beginning" and *Beginn* as "start":

> What does our starting with the poem "Germania" mean, and
> what does it not mean? The "start" is something other than the
> "beginning." A new weather situation, for example, starts with
> a storm. Its beginning, however, is the complete change of air
> that brings it about in advance. A start is the onset of some-
> thing; a beginning is that from which something arises or
> springs forth. The world war began centuries ago in the politi-
> cal and spiritual history of the Western world. The world war
> started with battles in the outposts. The start is immediately
> left behind, it vanishes as an event proceeds. The beginning,
> the origin, by contrast, first appears and comes to the fore in
> the course of an event and is fully there only at its end. Who-
> ever starts many things often never reaches a beginning. Of
> course, we human beings can never begin with the beginning—
> only a god can do that. Rather, we must start with, that is, set
> out from, something that will first lead into or point to the
> origin. Such is the nature of the start of our lecture course.
>
> We place the poem "Germania" at the start in order to
> point ahead to the beginning. That means: This poem points
> toward the origin, to what is most remote and most difficult,
> to that which we ultimately encounter under the name
> Hölderlin. (GA 39, 3–4)

In these remarks, then, *Anfang* or "beginning" is equated with
Ursprung or "origin," and is distinguished from *Beginn* as the start
of something or the onset of an event. As we have noted elsewhere, these remarks also suggest that for Heidegger the term
Anfang or "beginning" does not imply a determinate point of onset
in either a spatial or temporal sense, but has the sense of a more

remote, more indeterminate gathering that leads to the emergence of an action or of a historical epoch.[5] Or rather, although every historical beginning is also instituted or grounded in a certain place and time (and thus also has a start)—something indicated by Heidegger in "The Origin of the Work of Art" (1936)—what this grounding opens up is the as yet unfathomed, and perhaps ultimately unfathomable (*unergründlich*), approach of the historical vocation or destiny withheld for a historical people or community—their very *ēthos* (H, 62–64). Moreover, Heidegger's remarks here indicate that a beginning or origin is something whose full significance and import necessarily conceals and withholds itself— precisely *as* the power of the origin that holds sway. Yet this means that an altogether enigmatic temporality also pertains to the nature of a beginning: whereas a start is fully transparent, as it were, and has nothing more to reveal—it is nothing more than the sheer fact or "that it is" of an action or event—a genuine beginning, even though it has already come to pass and thus has already happened, has also always yet to manifest itself.

Two further texts of Heidegger's from around the same period help shed further light on the time of a beginning. The first excerpt, from the 1933 "Rectoral Address," makes the claim that all science remains tied to the beginning (*Anfang*) of philosophy, to "the emergence [*Aufbruch*] of Greek philosophy" (SDU, 11)—thus to what, a few years later, in the *Contributions to Philosophy*, Heidegger will identify as the "first beginning" of Western philosophy. Here Heidegger writes:

> But does not this beginning already lie two and a half thousand years behind us? Has not the progress of human activity also changed science? Certainly! The subsequent Christian-theological interpretation of the world, as well as the later mathematical-technical thinking of modernity, have temporally and substantively distanced science from its beginning. Yet the beginning itself is by no means thereby overcome, or even abolished. For granted that original Greek science is something great, then the *beginning* of this great event remains what is *greatest* about it. The essence of science could not even become empty and eroded, as it is today, despite all its results and "international organisations," unless the greatness of the beginning *still* persisted. The beginning still *is*. It does not lie *behind us* as something that has long since been; rather, it stands

before us. The beginning, as what is greatest, is what continues
to come over everything in advance and thus is what has also
already passed over beyond us. The beginning has fallen into
our future; it stands there in its distant prevailing [*ferne
Verfügung*] upon us to retrieve its greatness. (SDU, 12–13)

The Greek philosophical beginning is thus in this sense an event
that marks the emergence of what Heidegger, by the mid-1930s,
will think in terms of a history of Being and subsequently in terms
of a destining of Being. The Greek beginning is an event that, far
beyond the moment and circumstances of its own emergence, destines far in advance (at least two and a half thousand years) the
way in which Being itself will appear and be historically enacted.
This first beginning, instituted by Greek philosophy, thus has—
like every genuine beginning—the sense of an overarching, historical claim that attunes and configures in advance the fundamental
possibilities, stance, and comportment—the entire *ēthos*—of a particular humankind. This configuring is indeed the sense of what
Heidegger here calls the distant "prevailing" or *Verfügung* of the
first beginning, the way in which it fits or plies us into a particular
way of Being. In this respect, the "Rectoral Address" reformulates
in terms of the history of Being itself what was already stated in
Being and Time (1927) in relation to Dasein's historicality. Broach-
ing the task of a "destruction" of the history of ontology, Heidegger
had there explained that Dasein *is* its past, the latter understood
not as something independent that pushes along behind Dasein, as
it were, from time to time having a kind of residual, causal "effect"
on it. Rather, Heidegger writes, "Dasein 'is' its past in the manner
of *its* [Dasein's] Being which, to put it roughly, in each case 'happens' from out of its future." Yet Dasein's past is never simply its
own, individual past, but is also and before this the historically
determined past of a particular historical community and historical
world, a past destined to it in advance and into which it is thrown:
a past that approaches Dasein in its very facticity. Thus, Heidegger
continues, "Its own past—and this always means that of its 'gen-
eration'—does not *follow after* Dasein, but in each case *already* precedes it." This precedence of a historically determined vocation
always already guides and orients Dasein in advance. For Dasein
is inevitably born into, emerges and grows up within, an interpretation of existence that has been handed down, an interpretation
that affords it its basic understanding of the world. This under-

standing, Heidegger notes, "discloses the possibilities of its Being and regulates or governs them" (SZ, 20).

What would be "at work" in and throughout every *ēthos*, with its historically determined or destined understanding of Being, and in every action and comportment undertaken in the light of such an understanding, then, would be nothing other than the concealed power of a beginning (or perhaps, as we shall suggest in a moment, of multiple beginnings), of a beginning that orients in advance our fundamental perspectives and possibilities, and thus the concealed grounds of our concrete actions and attunements. If, for example, the biology scientist in today's American university sets to work on a Tuesday morning on deciphering the genetic code that determines the entire development of a turtle embryo, then her actions occur not just because she decided to go to work that morning, or because some years ago already she decided to "do biology," but because she has fundamentally been persuaded—most likely without knowing it, or understanding or ever stopping to contemplate the full range of its implications—of a conception of the truth of beings that first emerged and instituted itself in the Greek philosophy of Plato and Aristotle (namely, truth as the underlying eidetic structure and form concealed behind beings as they initially appear, an eidetic structure first to be discovered by "science").[6] Her modern institution or research institute, and the actions of her fellow beings undertaken therein, find their original grounds in this more primordial institution of Being itself in the works of Greek philosophy. It is these original grounds, then, that constitute the "greatness" and magnitude of the beginning that Heidegger in the "Rectoral Address" calls upon the scientific community of the German university to "retrieve." We must, as he puts it, "place ourselves once again under the power [*Macht*] of the *beginning*," of the emergence of Greek philosophy, we must "ply ourselves [*uns fügen*] resolutely and openly to this distant prevailing [*Verfügung*]"—if, that is, we are to "remain equal to this beginning" (and thus ultimately to ourselves). For otherwise science "remains a contingency that we happen into, or the smug comfort of a secure occupation that promotes a mere progress of knowledge" (SDU, 11–13). Here again the continuity with *Being and Time* is evident: Attaining an authentic historical understanding of one's own Being, and thus coming to be authentically historical, entails *"delivering oneself over to inherited possibility, taking over one's own thrownness, and being* in the manner of the Augenblick *for 'one's time'* " (SZ, 385). We must first find and learn a fitting relation to our own destiny.[7] We are neither born free, nor do we demonstrate our freedom through mere self-assertion or decision. Rather, we must first come to be free in coming to understand the force of our own destiny, the futural claim of the historical grounds (or grounding) into which we have been thrown.

At this point, we may turn to a third text from the period, one to which we have already alluded, and that sheds further light on Heidegger's conception of beginnings. This third text, the mature version of "The Origin of the Work of Art" (1935), brings together themes both from the first Hölderlin course and from the "Rectoral Address." On the one hand, it develops further the theme of the poietic instituting or founding of the truth of Being in a work, in a being, in terms of the relation between world and Earth: a theme already prominent in the Hölderlin course. On the other hand, it takes up in more detail the distancing from the Greek beginning mentioned in the "Rectoral Address" and the subsequent transformations of that beginning via Christian theology and mathematical-technical thinking of the modern era. Thereby, it helps us approach more carefully the difficult question of the "Being-at-work" of the concealed power that prevails as the first beginning.

HISTORY AND ORIGIN: THE IRRUPTION OF WORLDS

In the closing pages of his essay "The Origin of the Work of Art," Heidegger elaborates the essence of *Dichtung*, of the poietic, as the founding or instituting of the truth of beings, the term "instituting" (*Stiftung*) to be understood in a threefold sense: instituting as bestowing, as grounding, and as beginning (*Anfangen*). In setting the truth of beings into a work, so that this truth may henceforth be at work, art (in the sense of great or originary art) opens up what Heidegger calls the "extraordinary," a new configuration of truth that overturns the dominance of what has become ordinary and usual, and that can never be deduced or derived from what went before. It does not come about through some kind of causal relation, nor through the logic of dialectical mediation. The instituting of a new truth of Being is in this sense a free bestowal, an "excess," as Heidegger puts it. Yet this instituting is also a "grounding," insofar as what it opens up is cast toward a particular historical humankind. What such instituting opens up is a *world* (the truth of beings as a whole as such), a world that configures the relation of a historical community to the Earth, to the self-concealing ground (thereby opening up the Earth itself in a particular way). Our thrownness into the Earth, upon this self-concealing ground, Heidegger indicates, must itself be grounded and comes to be grounded only in and through a poietic projection (*Entwurf*) that itself grounds the fundamental possibilities of our relation to this first, more originary, more primordial ground. Yet this projection itself, even though it cannot be derived causally from what went before, does not come from nothing, Heidegger insists. It is, he states, only the "withheld vocation" (*die vorenthaltene Bestimmung*) of historical Dasein itself: a vocation withheld, presumably, in and through the prevailing of an earlier destining of Being.

Both bestowal and grounding, Heidegger continues, contain within them "the unmediated character of what we call a beginning." Yet, he states,

> this unmediated character of a beginning, the peculiarity of a leap from out of what cannot be mediated, does not exclude but rather precisely entails the fact that the beginning prepares itself for the longest time and wholly inconspicuously. A genuine beginning, as a leap, is always a leap ahead in which all that is to come is already leapt over, albeit as something veiled. The beginning already contains the end in a concealed manner. (H, 63)

These remarks not only reiterate the futural temporality of beginnings that we have already seen emphasized in the Hölderlin course and in the "Rectoral Address," but amplify, as it were, the potential resonance of beginnings. Beginnings, the text here makes clear, have themselves beginnings, so to speak: they have their own "beginnings," their own origins, their own slow, quiet, lengthy maturation (one thinks of Nietzsche's "doves' feet" . . .); moreover, each beginning, according to these words, has its end—an end at which, as the introductory remarks to the Hölderlin course put it, the beginning would first be fully "there," fully manifest in what it really was. But then, if there is no such thing as a beginning ex nihilo, if even a "first" or "great" beginning begins from something previously withheld, if there is, therefore, no such thing as a pure or uncontaminated beginning—what exactly marks a beginning as such, for Heidegger? What makes a beginning "great" or "genuine"? Where does one beginning end and another begin? How self-contained is the destinal power withheld in and as the prevailing of a particular beginning? We may approach these questions, perhaps, in considering what Heidegger in the same essay goes on to say regarding the transformations that occur in the course of that history—our history—destined by the Greek beginning:

> Whenever beings as a whole, as beings themselves, demand to be grounded in openness, art comes into its historical essence as instituting. This happened in the West for the first time in Greece. What was in the future to be called Being [Sein] was set into work in a manner that gave the measure. Thus opened up, beings as a whole then came to be transformed into beings in the sense of that which was created by God. This occurred in the Middle Ages. Such beings were again transformed at the start [Beginn] and during the course of the modern age. Beings became objects that could be controlled and become perspicuous through calculation. On each occasion a new and essential world irrupted. On each occasion the openness of beings had to be established in beings themselves by setting truth into place in the figure [of a work]. On each occasion unconcealment of beings occurred. Unconcealment sets itself to work, which setting is brought to accomplishment by art. (H, 63–64)

It is interesting here that Heidegger, writing of the transformation from the Middle Ages into modernity, uses the word *Beginn* and not *Anfang*. Initially one might be tempted to read this as implying that the only true beginning is the first one, the Greek beginning, and that the epochal changes that transpire within the overarching sway of that beginning are at best "starts," transformations of what was destined in and through the Greek beginning, perhaps, but not themselves attaining the status of genuine beginnings. Yet closer consideration reveals that Heidegger is indeed attributing the status of a beginning to each of the transformations mentioned: *on each occasion*, he writes, a new world irrupted; on each occasion, art accomplished the setting into work of truth, instituting the openness of beings in beings themselves. Indeed, Heidegger continues, "Whenever art happens, i.e., when there is a beginning [*Anfang*], a thrust [*Stoß*] enters history; history first begins *or begins again*" (H, 64; emphasis added). This suggests, therefore, that the epochal transformations mentioned are not merely transformations of the first beginning (although they are that also), but are themselves beginnings, bringing a thrust or interruption into history, participating in the irruption of a new historical world. All of which suggests, not so much that we might have difficulty distinguishing between one beginning and another beginning, but only that we have to ask: How other can any "other" beginning be?

This, of course, was an issue not lost on Heidegger himself, as we shall recall in a moment. But with respect to the questions just posed we may perhaps surmise the following: while there is indeed no such thing as a pure or absolute beginning for historical human beings, what we recognize as beginnings are, for Heidegger, always marked by what he here calls a "thrust" (*Stoß*), by a sudden or momentary interruption of what might otherwise—from a theoretical perspective, or in a retrospective writing of history—appear to be a continuous or dialectical unfolding. Beginnings are marked by the unmediated irruption (*Aufbrechen*) of a new world, a new fundamental configuration of the truth of beings as a whole and as such. What makes a beginning "great" is presumably the fact that it sets up and opens up a *world*, that is, the enduring power of the claim that issues from the beginning. And a "genuine" beginning would be one that is precisely open to the claim of the new that speaks, albeit as unspoken, in and through the already prevailing destining of Being. It would make little sense, then, if these theses are tenable, to understand the "end" of a beginning in terms of a *telos* or of completion, or to speak of the destinal power withheld in and as the prevailing of a particular beginning as being self-contained—even though every such destining would be that of a determinate configuration of the power of Being. Rather, what Heidegger remarks elsewhere concerning the essence of a unitary temporal horizon is true here also: that the horizon of an age or of a historical world is not only determinate, but also open: it itself prevails as a peculiar openness out of which new possibilities of Being may come to pass. Thus, with respect to the epochal transformations of the first beginning mentioned in the "Rectoral Address" and again in "The Origin of the Work of Art," we may say that the subsequent epochal irruptions of the Middle Ages and of modernity—as irruptions of a new world in each case, of a world that had no intrinsic necessity to its emergence—are indeed genuine beginnings, but, as mere transformations thereof, they do not

attain the greatness of the first, Greek beginning, since they remain
within the overarching sway of its claim that posits the truth of
beings in terms of the correctness of human thought and representation. Far from departing from this claim, they merely deflect it,
setting it upon another path, to be sure, but remaining entirely
within its orbit. They are in this sense far from being great beginnings, but are rather, as Heidegger suggests, renewed beginnings,
recommencements of the *same* history of Being, beginnings in which
that history begins again.

In a text composed in 1938–39 and now published under the
title *Besinnung* (meaning "reflection," not in the metaphysical sense
of representation, but as a thoughtful reflecting or meditation in
which philosophy ponders its own provenance and thereby prepares an other beginning), Heidegger more explicitly discusses the
suddenness or abruptness (*Jähe*) that marks historical beginnings
in terms of the *Augenblick* conceived as the clearing of Being that
first opens history and enables a world:

> Why is this abrupt *Augenblick* of "world history" essentially
> and abyssally different from all the "millions of years" of
> worldless events? Because this abruptness clears the singular-
> ity of Beyng, and that which, beyond Being and non-Being,
> neither was nor was not, receives the abyss of a grounding for
> beings. More void than the most fleeting character of that
> *Augenblick* is the presumed duration of those "beings" that are
> without Being, that one would seek to ascertain as that which
> already lies present-at-hand and to call "nature" retrospectively
> from out of the clearing of that *Augenblick*, so as to be able to
> reckon with the fleetingness and apparentness of that *Augenblick*
> by measuring it against them. Yet even apparentness and the
> shining of semblance [*die Scheinbarkeit und das Scheinen*] is a
> clearing, is Beyng that alone bestows the human being into his
> essence and removes him from all comparison with the animal
> and with the merely living. (GA 66, 113)

Once again, the *Augenblick* is conceived, not as a event within
time or history, but as that ekstatic displacement or removal which
first opens the time of Being and of a world, an opening that
becomes the "abyssal" grounding of beings that are first granted
appearance in and through that very opening or clearing.
The human being, as displaced in advance (in his or her very

"essence" or manner of presencing) into that opening, is removed from all comparison with the animal or with the merely living in the sense that, as we indicated in our first chapter, there is no merely existent ground for comparison—all grounds being displaced in advance into this abyssal dimension. Positing an undifferentiated phenomenon called "life," as a kind of "primal soup" in terms of which living beings could then be determined in their specific differences or qualities, remains eminently problematic in that it fails to recognize what Heidegger goes on to call "abyssal events concerning essential origins." Yet Heidegger's own characterization of the abyssal difference "between" the human essence and other living beings, as we noted, cannot then be conceived as the positing of an existent difference either. The abyss is an abyss of Being itself—the opening up of an abyss in the midst of *all* beings, human, animal, or other—as an abyss that first calls the human being into the distinctiveness of his or her own Being. This call and its concomitant displacement or removal, Heidegger implies, has always already happened wherever appearing and semblance have come to pass. Yet whether this call comes to be heard as such, as a call of Being itself, is a matter of what Heidegger here calls "decision":

> *Yet decision is*: whether we are able to bring about a hearing and telling of Beyng [*das Seyn erhören und sagen*], or whether, in a remarkable oblivion of Being, we first of all set about calculatively removing the human being from beings. . . .
>   *Yet decision is*: whether we preserve an inherent stance within Beyng as the abyssal ground of all groundings of beings and refuse our essence to common-sense reckoning. (113)

Decision does not here mean that such issues are at our free disposal to decide or choose, but rather that we have already been transported into one or other way of Being in our very *ēthos*, in our very attunement, and yet in and through this very transport remain open to possibility, to the possibility of other ways of Being, to participating in how Being comes to be decided. Notably, Heidegger here uses the language of assuming and "preserving" an "inherent stance" within the clearing event of Being that we find in "The Origin of the Work of Art," and his elucidation of "decision" proceeds to appeal to the strife of world and Earth:

> *Decision is* this; which is to say: already come into its own
> through Beyng. No mere choice, rather, determinacy attuned
> through fundamental attunements by virtue of which the es-
> sence of the human being is removed [*entrückt*] from animality
> so as to first assume a stance in the midst of the strife of Earth
> and world. This removal is an event that comes into its own
> from Beyng [*Er-eignung aus dem Seyn*]. The *Augenblick* of world-
> history, i.e., of the *Ereignis* of the truth of Beyng, does not
> permit itself to be evaluated by means of the historiographical-
> technical reckoning of time. What is essential is not duration
> or fleetingness, nor indeed mere fullness or emptiness, but the
> abyssal character of ground as ground for the encounters of
> the varied assignment of gods and the human being in the
> decisiveness of their essence that can in each case be grounded.
> (113–14)

The work of art is what grounds the way in which human beings
and gods are assigned or directed toward one another—the word
assignment (*Zuweisung*) here suggesting, as did the word *Weisung*
in "The Origin of the Work of Art," the instituting of an ethical
directive in the originary sense of *ēthos*, a directive that comes to be
set into and opened up within the work itself, and that calls us into
a particular way of dwelling.[8] We shall discuss this reciprocal assignment of humans and gods in our next chapter in connection
with Heidegger's reading of Hölderlin.

In Heidegger's thinking of the abruptness of the clearing of
Being that opens us to the abyss of dwelling, he goes so far as to
characterize the moment or *Augenblick* as the origin of time, conceived as ekstatic temporality:

> The "*Augenblick*" is the abruptness of the sudden descent of all
> that can be grounded yet has never yet been grounded into the
> clearing of Beyng.
>
> The "*Augenblick*" is the abruptness of the human being's upris-
> ing into an inherent stance within the midst of this clearing.
>
> The "*Augenblick*" has nothing to do with the "eternity" of that
> which is, in the metaphysical sense of the *nunc stans* that bears
> with it all the signs and distorted signs of calculative time.
>
> The "*Augenblick*" is the origin of "time" itself—the latter as the
> unity of removal [*Entrückungseinheit*] that itself merely plies
> itself to the clearing and *for this reason* can be adopted as the

projective realm for a first interpretation of Being, albeit not recognized as such a realm. (114)

Once again, the *Augenblick* is here thought "historically" in the sense of the sudden opening up of possibility belonging to the happening or clearing of Being. In this sense, Heidegger explains, the *Augenblick* that in *Being and Time* was conceived as the ekstasis of originary presence is thought more appropriately as the abruptness of the clearing of Being:

> Just as time conceived as originary ("ekstatic") is merely the closest proximity of the clearing of Beyng, the "nearest" thing that comes over us in our reflecting on the metaphysical interpretation of Being, so the *"Augenblick"* remains only the temporal name given to *the abruptness* of the clearing of Beyng in this sense of time. (114)

To draw these reflections to a close, and to approach more directly the question of the possibility of an "other beginning," let us now turn to one or two other texts from the same period, specifically the *Contributions to Philosophy* of 1936–38, which we shall mention only briefly, and more importantly to the 1937–38 Freiburg lecture course pubished as *Basic Questions of Philosophy* (GA 45). It should go without saying that, as itself a beginning, the time of the "other beginning" will in one sense be the same as the time of the first beginning. Yet the word *time* here, as we have seen, is ambiguous. It can mean, on the one hand, the futurality—or more precisely, the futural having-been (*Gewesensein*)—of all genuine beginnings, that is, the time of a futural destining of Being. On the other hand, it can refer to the time of emergence or origination of beginnings as such: the interruptive time of a historical *Augenblick* in which something essentially new comes to pass, thus henceforth to prevail for a time. Yet if such a moment or *Augenblick* is to give rise to a truly other destining of Being, itself instituting an other beginning in setting it to work, this can come to pass only by way of a long and patient preparation, by way of what Heidegger calls historical "recollection" or historical "reflection" (*Besinnung*). And this, as the *Contributions* already insist, can happen only in and as an *Auseinandersetzung* or critical encounter with the first beginning, one that, precisely because the beginning, as futural, is "unsurpassable" (*unüberholbar*) must repeat or retrieve (*wiederholen*) not just the first beginning (GA 65, 55), but the *unthought* of this first beginning via historical recollection. With respect to the destining of Being, we must ponder, as the 1937–38 course puts it, what did not happen, *what failed to occur*. Heidegger states:

> For what failed to occur at essential moments [*Augenblicken*] in history—and what could be more essential than a beginning—what failed to occur must at some point surely yet happen, not as a mere belated recovery, but in the sense of those thrusts, leaps, and jumps [*Stöße, Sprünge, und Stürze*], of that which is momentary yet simple, which we must ponder and continue to ponder if we are indeed to expect anything essential from future history. (GA 45, 123)

What failed to occur, Heidegger goes on to say, refers not just to some arbitrary contingency or other that might or might not have happened, but means "what is necessarily *held back and retained within* and *through* the beginning, that through which the beginning remains unfathomable [*das Unergründliche*], spurring us to ever renewed reflection upon it." Yet whence the imperative on us to engage in such historical reflection? The imperative, if there is one, can come only from history itself, from our own history—that is, from our own future—and only if we experience ourselves as called upon to reflect, by way of preparation, for what has yet to come. Heidegger expresses it as follows:

> *We* must here ponder the beginning of Western thinking and what did and did not occur in it, because *we* stand at the end—at the end of this beginning. And this means: We stand before a *decision between the end* and its drawn out course that may still last for centuries—*and the other beginning*, which may only be a moment [*Augenblick*], yet whose preparation requires a patience to which "optimists" and "pessimists" alike are unequal. (GA 45, 124)

The "end" of the first beginning, Heidegger explains, is to be taken in a double sense. It does not mean that the first beginning simply stops, ceases, or gets left behind. Rather it means, first, that which "gathers within itself all essential possibilities of the history of a beginning," that is, it means the coming to a close of all the possibilities that arose from the subsequent unfolding of the begin-

ning. End here has the sense of gathering and closure (*Vollendung*)—
a closure that Heidegger here identifies with Nietzsche. Second,
however, the "end" of a beginning means the continuing effect of
everything that came from that beginning, as a whole mishmash of
concepts, systems, values, and fundamental metaphysical positions
run their course. The end in this sense, Heidegger notes, will presumably have a very long duration and may still dominate things
even after another beginning has long since begun. The period of
the end in this sense will, he suspects, be characterized by a series
of "renaissances" of earlier ways of thinking (GA 45, 133–34).

To approach and prepare for a decision between the end of
the first beginning—the end that already lies within the first beginning—and an other beginning, then, we must first be able to think
this double sense of end, and to distinguish between these two
senses of end. And this means, as Heidegger puts it, that we must
be revolutionaries. "Revolution," he writes, in this sense means not
mere destruction and overthrowing, but a "creative overturning"
of the habitual that, although itself first arising from the beginning,
gives the impression of having surpassed the beginning, thus concealing its sheer uniqueness. Only through a revolutionary thinking, and not through the conservativism that seeks to preserve
what has merely followed from the beginning, can the beginning
reappear again, show its face or figure (*Gestalt*) again, and thus be
"reconfigured" as something "entirely other and yet the Same."
Only thus, Heidegger insists, can we attain the beginning and "creatively experience its law." Revolution, in this sense, constitutes
"the genuine relation to the beginning." The time of the other
beginning, then, would be the time of revolution, and whoever
would seek to prepare—thoughtfully, through historical reflection
and recollection—for another beginning would themselves have to
be: a beginner. For "to begin means: to think and act out of what
is to come [*dem Zukünftigen*], the inhabitual, renouncing the crutches
and escapes of the habitual and customary" (GA 45, 40–41).[9]

It is this sense of beginning, no doubt, that Heidegger has in
mind when, later in the same course, he suggests that our *going
back* into the beginning could, *in itself*, be the same as the temporality that marks every genuine *beginning* as such: the temporality
of the *Augenblick*, in which what has come to pass and thus already
been leaps ahead, in its very Being, into the future, thereby, in
the collision and encounter of past and future, first giving rise to

the present. Just as in "The Origin of the Work of Art" Heidegger had noted that every genuine beginning, as something unmediated, is a "leap ahead" (*Vorsprung*), so here he writes of how we must ponder the fact

> that the beginning is that which, *yet to be unfolded, in its greatness reaches ahead into the future*; that the *return into the beginning* could thus be a leaping ahead, indeed, an authentic *leaping ahead into the future*, though to be sure only under this one condition: that we *really do begin with the beginning.* (GA 45, 110)

From what has been said it should be clear that few of us, most likely, are as yet even close to the beginning (to the first beginning of Greek philosophy, that is), let alone in a position to begin with it—to say nothing of an "other" possible beginning. To close with a salutory reminder from Heidegger:

> In the realm of the history of what is *essential* it is only very seldom that anything occurs. What does occur here occurs very slowly and very quietly; its direct effects leap over the space and time of thousands of years. (GA 45, 113)

This appears to be another way of saying that a historical beginning has no direct effects—that its "direct" effects at best happen through a long and concealed destining, and while they are in one sense direct, since they have come to be destined and come to pass as a direct consequence of a particular historical beginning, they are in another sense indirect, since they do not stand in any causal or dialectical mediation to that beginning. As other beginnings, such events are at once destined and unmediated; they are marked by the "peculiarity of a leap from out of what cannot be mediated," by the time of historical freedom.

SIX

Ēthos and Poetic Dwelling
Inaugural Time in Heidegger's Dialogue with Hölderlin

Heidegger's early, phenomenological interpretations of *ēthos* in Aristotle remain knowingly and intentionally within the "scientific" or theoretical orientation toward the disclosure of the ethical dimensions of human existence, an orientation that Aristotle himself establishes in characterizing the concern of the *Nicomachean Ethics* as a kind of "science" or *epistēmē* concerned with the human good (NE, 1094 a27). Of course, within this very orientation, Heidegger's phenomenological interpretations—like those of Aristotle—themselves display the inherent limits of any theoretical or scientific approach to ethical life in pointing into the dimensions of temporal finitude, singularity, and circumstance that no theoretical *logos* can disclose. Moreover, in focusing on human action insofar as it stands within our power (our *proairesis*), insofar as the human being is understood as the originator (*archē*) of his or her *proairesis* and thus of his or her own actions, they also share with Aristotle a foreclosure of the entire realm of chance, of fortune and misfortune, of fate and of destiny, and thus of a realm that, as Aristotle himself freely admits, is rather crucial in deciding the *eudaimonia* of our life as a whole (1100 a8ff.). Yet Heidegger's readings, as we have tried to show, also shift Aristotle's decisive insights into human *praxis* into the dimension of ekstatic temporality and historicality—and ultimately into that of the destinal historicality of Being—thereby opening up those dimensions of Being that are inevitably occluded by the theoretical perspective. The question thus arises of whether there is a *logos*—presumably akin to that of *phronēsis*—that is more attuned to the happening of human *ēthos* as impacted by these other, ultimately decisive dimensions of our temporally and historically determined Being-in-the-world. In the present chapter, and in our final chapter, we shall suggest that Heidegger's work finds a response to this question in his understanding of poetic dwelling, particularly in dialogue with the German poet Hölderlin and with Greek tragedy.

This exposition, in the present chapter at least, entails a somewhat abrupt transition, an unsettling shift of terrain, from the
phenomenological Heidegger of the 1920s and from the thinking of
the history of Being in the 1930s (itself transitional) to the more
"poetic" Heidegger of the 1930s and beyond. The shift appears as
abrupt and unsettling not least because Heidegger's work, while
affording many clues and itself always on the move, nowhere makes
explicit exactly what is entailed in this transition. This suggests,
indeed, that what is at stake in this transition is nothing other than
a transition to another beginning, and that such a transition, by its
very nature, must be characterized by the suddenness and abruptness that mark all genuine beginnings as such. In part, this implies
also that any attempt to straightforwardly account for or make
explicit what this transition entails would risk merely repeating
the theoretical perspective that emerged from and remains characteristic throughout the "first beginning" of Western philosophy. It
does not, however, preclude that the "poetic" understanding of
human *ēthos* remains in perpetual dialogue with the theoretical
discourse of philosophy. In the following chapters, we hope to
display something of this dialogue and continuity.

In so doing, we knowingly risk underplaying the discontinuities,
the entire strangeness and foreignness of much of Heidegger's later
work, and the singularities of its engagement. We shall first try to
draw attention to certain continuities in Heidegger's thinking of *ēthos*
that extend from his early, phenomenological hermeneutics through
his later engagements with Hölderlin's poetizing. In view of what
has just been said, however, it must be acknowledged that we cannot remotely pretend, in the present context, to do justice to the
singularity of Heidegger's later work as a dialogue *with Hölderlin*. In
other words, our highlighting of certain continuities should not be
taken to imply that an adequate deciphering of much of Heidegger's
remarks on Hölderlin would reveal their underlying philosophical
truth and import, thereby letting us arrive at a general account or
theory of human *ēthos* extending from early Heidegger to late. What
we do wish to suggest is that while Heidegger's dialogue with
Hölderlin cannot be adequately understood without a painstaking
engagement with Hölderlin's work itself, it can and perhaps must
also be understood as a dialogue with the philosophical understanding of *ēthos*, and in particular with that understanding which emerges
through Heidegger's own phenomenological interpretations of Aristotle.

For the purposes of situating this transition, we shall first recall a number of points already made in earlier chapters, in an attempt to weave them into a further story.

TEMPORALITY, ATTUNEMENT, AND THE PHENOMENOLOGY OF WORLD

We emphasized from the outset the central importance of the phenomenon of world in Heidegger's thinking. Yet Heidegger's concept of world was continually in flux. As we noted earlier, while *Being and Time* emphasized world as a referential totality of signification, enabling the disclosure of meanings that first "found the possible Being of word and language" (SZ, 87)[1] and as a phenomenon to which Dasein was always already exposed in advance, that to which Dasein could only inevitably return in whatever degree of explicitness (76), it also highlighted the fundamental attunement of *Angst* as that which, disclosing Dasein in its primordial *Unheimlichkeit*, the fundamental "not being at home" in which all of Dasein's Being as dwelling is grounded, also "first discloses *world as world*" (187). The "peculiar temporality" of *Angst* "holds" Dasein in the presence of its ownmost thrownness, yet in such a way as to hold the moment or *Augenblick* of possible decision "at the ready" (344). The phenomenology of Dasein as Being-in-the-world shows that the *Augenblick* itself, as "held" and attuned in advance by the fundamental attunement of *Angst*, is, over and beyond the circumstances of the moment, exposed in advance to the presencing of a historically determined world. The *Augenblick* of action can "hold and keep its world in view [*im Blick*]" (GA 24, 407–408) only because it is itself already held within the originary dimension of the presencing of a world, attuned by the *Angst* that, holding the *Augenblick* at the ready, brings us before repeatability itself (*Wiederholbarkeit*)—before the possibility of the repetition or retrieval of our Being (thus also of all ritual and all reenactment, all *mimēsis*)—as the repeated suspension of presence that holds us in the indeterminacy of possibility, free and open for the moment of a possible decision (343–44).[2]

We also noted earlier that, by contrast with Greek ontology, for which the world is disclosed by *theōria* and *sophia*, the primary disclosure of the presencing of a world is, on Heidegger's account, accomplished not by intellectual virtue or philosophical knowledge, but by a fundamental *pathos* or attunement (*Befindlichkeit*); and that such *pathos* is fundamental in attuning, in advance of any explicit deliberation or discursive understanding, the way in which we are held in the presencing of the moment, our entire *ēthos*. In Heidegger's early accounts of Aristotle, as we saw in chapter 3, world is indeed disclosed within human existence as *praxis*, a disclosure occurring through discursive deliberation as operative in *phronēsis*, and thus oriented toward the *kairos*, the opportune moment or "now" of action. Deliberation, as a discursive seeking, is thus, Heidegger explained, a "bringing-to-language":

> In this bringing-to-language of what is *sumpheron*, of the world as it is concretely there, the world is first authentically brought into the "there." The "now" and "here" of human existence [*Sein*] becomes explicit in a particular deliberation, and through this deliberation the human being is—in modern terms—in the concrete situation, in the authentic *kairos*. In this *logos*, *legein* as *logizesthai*, the Being of the human being has the world there, in such a way that I am in the world here and now in a particular situation. (GA 18, 59)

Yet this practical disclosure of world is not the most original or primordial, neither for Aristotle nor for Heidegger. For Aristotle, the world is already there, authentically disclosed in what it ultimately is only via the *theōria* of *sophia*. For the Heidegger of the 1920s, world is disclosed in the ekstatic temporalizing of Dasein via the fundamental attunement of *Angst*. Deliberation, as a *legein*, *brings* the world to language, thus to the dimension or medium of public interpretedness and disclosedness; but what comes to be thus disclosed must already announce itself, speak to or address us, prior to (or, more precisely, as the inaugural moment of) this bringing-to-language, as the situation of action seen in the momentary light of the openness of world as such (an openness attuned by *Angst*), to which deliberation is responsive.

Nevertheless, a certain theoretical remnant remained in the analyses of world presented in *Being and Time*. If Heidegger there could write: "World is neither present-at-hand nor ready-to-hand, but temporalizes itself within temporality. It 'is there' along with the [Being]-outside-themselves of the ekstases" (SZ, 365), nevertheless a certain tension remained throughout between such *already* "being there" of world and what we identified earlier, in chapter 2, as the poietic or productive moment implicit within the German *sich zeitigen* (meaning "to temporalize," but also "to come about," "come into Being," "bring [oneself] into [full] Being," thus: to flourish, to flower, to mature, as in the Greek *phusis*). In *The Basic Problems of Phenomenology* too (1927), the emphasis was still on the prior givenness of world, though Dasein—problematically enough—was now said to "cast its world before it" (GA 24, 239). Yet by the 1928 course *The Metaphysical Foundations of Logic*, the problem of the temporality of world had led Heidegger to highlight increasingly (though still in horizonal and transcendental terms) precisely the productive dimension of ekstatic temporality:

> And yet the [ekstatic] displacement [*Entrückung*] as such gives itself something in advance: precisely the futural as such, futurality in general, i.e., possibility pure and simple. The ekstase produces from itself, not a determinate possibility, but the horizon of possibility in general. . . . (GA 26, 269)

And by the end of the following semester Heidegger had indeed abandoned all transcendental language and embraced the concept of "world-formation" (*Weltbildung*) as constituting the antecedent event on whose grounds the human being could first come to exist. In *The Fundamental Concepts of Metaphysics* (1929/30), as we saw in chapter 1, he writes: "For it is not the case that the human being first exists and then also one day decides amongst other things to form a world. Rather world-formation is something that occurs, and only on this ground can a human being exist in the first place" (GA 29/30, 414). "World," as we noted, is here understood not simply as a phenomenon that already exists, but as an *event* that occurs and continues to occur: it forms itself, it is intrinsically poietic, transformative. And yet, we suggested, this event does not happen without or somewhere beyond human beings either: it occurs in and through human beings, who partake in the happening of this event, although they do not originate it as "subjects." As the 1929 essay "On the Essence of Ground" clarifies, the projection of world casts world over beings in advance, and this is the occurrence in which the Being of Dasein "is temporalized" (*sich zeitigt*). To say that Dasein "transcends" thus means, more precisely, that "in the essence of its Being it is *world-forming*, 'forming' in the multiple sense that it lets world occur, and through the world gives itself an original view [*Anblick*] (form) that is not explicitly grasped, yet functions precisely as a paradigmatic form for all manifest beings, among which each respective Dasein itself belongs" (W, 55). The emphasis again is on how Dasein is not itself the already existent origin of world-formation, but rather *lets* this antecedent occurrence of world happen and in so doing first brings world before itself. As noted in chapter 2, it is in "coming toward itself from out of the world" that Dasein first "gives rise to, or temporalizes [*sich zeitigt*] itself as a *self* . . ." (W, 53).

In the 1929–30 lecture course, we saw Heidegger approach the phenomenon of world and world-formation by contrast with the so-called poverty in world of the animal. His interpretation suggests, we argued, that animal life, in being borne along by the ongoing flow of presentation, is unable to assume a free stance outside the presence of whatever is present as its environment. As Heidegger put it, that which disinhibits the animal's instinctual drives "is *nothing enduring* [kein Bleibendes] *that could stand over against the animal as a possible object*" (GA 29/30, 372).[3] Excluded from experiencing anything enduring, animal life is excluded from the possibility of assuming an *ēthos* or taking up an ethical relation to the other. It manifests an inability to "attend to" that which disinhibits its drives, which is nothing other than an inability to dwell in the element of language. For it is in being brought to language that things first attain a certain endurance and permanence of presence, whereby that which presences comes to stand in the relative and unitary constancy of its manifold presentations. This endurance or permanence, far from being atemporal, occurs in the manner of the specific temporality of historical time. Both the enduring of things and human dwelling itself presuppose, moreover, the prior forming of a world as an event that precedes us, enabling our dwelling in and through the phenomenon of attunement, in which we originarily approach and find ourselves as a situated Being-in-the-world. Attunement, Heidegger noted, is indeed the way in which living nature "holds us captive" amid the very manifestation of beings as a whole (GA 29/30, 403–404).[4] The formation and happening of world, as the manifestation of beings as a whole in their Being, is itself a poietic event: that of an originary *poiēsis* of which we are not the origin, yet which, happening in and through us, first enables our dwelling. A language and thought attuned to this arrival, to this coming to pass of a world, would presumably not yet be a discourse seeking to determine something "as" something—not a *legein ti kata tinos*—whether that of the apophantic discourse of science, the apophantic-hermeneutic discourse of Heidegger's early phenomenology, or indeed that of the hermeneutic deliberation of Aristotelian *phronēsis* itself, all of which are dianoetic, and concerned with determining that which already manifests itself in a certain way (with a view to constant laws determining the presence at hand of things; with a view to the existential-historical situatedness and engagement of the philosophizing self; or with a view to determining the best course of action under given circumstances in order to attain a certain end). It would, presumably, be a "simple naming" (*schlichtes Nennen*), the calling (*Anrufen*) of something, a straightforward *phasis* attuned to the *alētheuein* of the *poiēsis* of what Aristotle thinks as *nous poiētikos*, of a letting-be disclosive of world in general, a letting-be that, as enabling presence itself, first enables vision, letting something be seen in its Being.[5]

It is in Hölderlin's poetizing above all, we shall now try to indicate, that Heidegger finds precisely such a language and attunement.

INAUGURAL TIME IN HÖLDERLIN'S POETIZING

In his 1936 essay, "Hölderlin and the Essence of Poetry," Heidegger insists that Hölderlin is not just one poet among others, but unique in that he poetizes the essence of poetry—"essence" understood not as a universally valid concept (which is "indifferent" [*gleichgültig*] in being valid [*gültig*] in the same [*gleich*] way for every particular to which it applies), but understood as that which is essential in the sense of engaging us, demanding of us a decision as to whether we are able to stand within the sway and dominion of poetizing. It is not as though we merely stood before and outside of this poetizing, in some neutral place from where we could make a decision whether or not to participate in the power of the poetizing. Rather, Heidegger's point is that it is the originarily poetic happening of language itself that first opens us to decision, that places our very Being in decision. For language is not in the first instance a means of communication, an instrument that can be used by human beings for various purposes:

> Language is not merely an instrument that humans possess
> among many others; rather, language first grants the possibility

of coming to stand in the midst of the openness of beings. Only
where there is language, is world there, which means: the constantly changing realm of decision and work, of deed and responsibility, but also of wantonness and noise, decline and
confusion. Only where world holds sway is there history. . . .
Language is not an instrument at our disposal, but that event
[*Ereignis*] which disposes over the supreme possibility of human Being. (EHD, 37–38)

Language is originarily not a being or an entity at all, but an event
that opens us to Being—to our supreme possibility—and thus to
having to be, opening us to decision concerning our Being, concerning what we bring about (our "work") and how we act (our
"deed"), yet thereby also to responsibility, to having to assume
and be the thrown (thus nonoriginary) ground of our actions.
Language opens our Being in opening up a world, within which
we come to "stand" in the midst of the manifestness of beings
themselves. Yet how, Heidegger proceeds to ask, does this event of
language happen? He finds a response in Hölderlin's words:

> Viel hat erfahren der Mensch.
> Der Himmlischen viele genannt,
> Seit ein Gespräch wir sind
> Und hören können voneinander.

> Much has man experienced.
> Named many of the heavenly,
> Since we are a dialogue
> And can hear from one another.[6]

We humans are a dialogue: our very Being is grounded in language, yet language essentially happens as a dialogue. Dialogue
implies speaking with one another about something, a speaking in
and through which we first approach and "come to one another."
Yet, as the poet says, being a dialogue also implies being able to
hear from one another. Being able to hear is not a mere consequence of being able to speak, but is equiprimordial with it: Hearing is directed toward the possibility of the word; the word cannot
be the word without being heard. Yet to say that we are "a dialogue" (*ein Gespräch*) also means, Heidegger emphasizes: we are a
single dialogue, *one* dialogue, *ein* Gespräch. The unity of a dialogue, however, "consists in the fact that on each occasion in the

essential word, One and the Same thing is manifest, upon which we can agree, on whose ground we are united and thus are properly ourselves." The dialogue and its unity "sustain our Dasein" (EHD, 39).

Yet Hölderlin's word says more, Heidegger notes. It tells of a *time*, of a time "since" when we are, or have been, a dialogue—a time since when our Being has been, has happened. What time is this? Where there is to be a single dialogue, Heidegger remarks, the essential word must relate to One and the Same thing: even a disagreement presupposes that we are agreed in advance as to what we are disagreeing about, that we understand ourselves from the outset to be disagreeing about one and the same thing, which must thus be manifest as such in advance:[7]

> One and the Same thing, however, can be manifest only in the light of something that endures and is constant [*eines Bleibenden und Ständigen*]. Yet constancy and enduring come to the fore and appear, when persisting and presence light up. This, however, happens at that moment [*Augenblick*] when time opens itself in its stretchings [*Erstreckungen*]. Since the time when the human being has placed himself into the presence of something enduring—since then he has been able to expose himself to what is changeable, to that which comes and goes; for only that which persists can change. Ever since the "time that tears" has been torn open into present, past, and future, there has been the possibility of agreeing upon something that endures. We are and have been *one* dialogue since the time that there "is time." Since time has arisen and been brought to a stand— since then we *are* and have been historical. (EHD, 39)[8]

Since the time of Being, since the time that time itself has been, has happened—since this inaugural time we humans too have been; our Being is and has been the happening of a dialogue. The "moment" or *Augenblick* here names this inaugural time of the "event" of language, this time of the dawn of time, as the event of the time of Being and thus also of the Being of time. Yet since this time, according to Hölderlin, man has not only "experienced much," but "named many of the heavenly." The opening of our Being as time is at once the "appearing of a world" and the "coming to word of the gods," Heidegger notes. The presence of the gods and the appearing of a world are not consequences of the happening of language, but happen at one and the same time—so much so, he remarks, that this naming of the gods and letting a world come to word constitutes, properly speaking, the dialogue that we are (38). The opening up of time in its ekstases occurs as an arrival: as letting the gods and a world come to language, and thus letting them be, letting them endure.

This distinctive moment, undoubtedly immemorial, is named and commemorated in Hölderlin's poetry as the time of his poetizing, itself poetized as the moment—the "now" or *Augenblick*—of the arrival of the holy, as in the opening words of the third strophe of the hymn "As when on feast day . . .":

> Jezt aber tagts! Ich harrt und sah es kommen,
> Und was ich sah, das Heilige sei mein Wort.

> But now day breaks! I waited and saw it come,
> And what I saw, may the holy be my word.

Or, in the opening words of the "Ister" hymn:

> Jezt komme, Feuer!
> Begierig sind wir
> Zu schauen den Tag . . .

> Now come, fire!
> Eager are we
> To see the day . . .

In each case the "now" names an inaugural moment, poetizing the dawning of the day (the appearing of a world) as a distinctive coming: the approach of the heavenly fire (of the power of the gods). This "now," Heidegger remarks, names the time of this poetizing itself, as a poetizing that is called upon in advance, as its destined vocation, to poetize the essence of poetizing. The "Now come . . ." of the "Ister" hymn, he comments, appears to speak from a present into the future; and yet, "in the first instance, it speaks into what has already happened," into something that has already come to pass and been decided, something that "alone sustains all relation to whatever is coming," namely, the calling of the poets that has called upon them to poetize. The "now" is not only what is named in the poetizing; it "is itself calling," and in its naming names this coming, this approach and arrival, of what is already "there," already underway, already happening. It names, as Heidegger says, an inaugural or appropriative event (*Ereignis*) (GA 53, 8–9).

IS THERE A MEASURE ON EARTH? POETIZING AND HUMAN ĒTHOS

Hölderlin's poetizing thus becomes manifest as the letting happen, and thus letting be, of an arrival—of that distinctive arrival which this poetizing itself "is." It becomes manifest as an originary *poiēsis* whereby a world first opens itself and comes to be. Here, we find the bringing-to-language of a world, not, as in Aristotelian *phronēsis*, as something *sumpheron*, not as a *kata to sumpheron pros to telos*, that is, not in the "as" of deliberation that brings the world to language as conducive to a certain end, but in the simple naming of a poetic language that brings into Being the *poiēsis* of world itself: an originary *poiēsis* that must already be "at work" within all deliberative and apophantic interpretation, and within all everyday discourse, yet is necessarily concealed by them.

Yet the essence of poetizing can then no longer be understood as poetry in the narrow sense of poesy, as the composing of poetic works or poems.[9] In first letting a world appear and come into Being, poetizing in its essence originarily configures the dwelling site of human beings, their *ēthos*. Hölderlin thus tells of human dwelling upon the Earth as intrinsically "poetic" in this more fundamental sense:

> Voll Verdienst, doch dichterisch wohnet
> Der Mensch auf dieser Erde.

> Full of merit, yet poetically
> Humans dwell upon this Earth.

Poetizing, according to this word, is not a human accomplishment, not something humans accomplish of their own accord or of their own merit, but, as Heidegger remarks, a gift first bestowed upon us, and as such not a mere cultural achievement or phenomenon, but "the ground of human Dasein" and "the sustaining ground of history" (EHD, 42). It first grounds human dwelling and action. Poetizing in the sense of this originary occurrence of which we are not ourselves the origin is thus neither a naming of beings that are already manifest, nor a linguistic accomplishment that humans would produce by using the "material" of language. Rather, the event of poetizing, as the inaugural event of time, itself first lets language happen, lets it arrive. The essence of poetizing, Heidegger remarks, is not, therefore, to be understood from out of the essence of language, but the converse: *poetizing is the origin of language.* "Poetizing thus never takes up language as a present-at-hand material with which to work, rather, poetizing itself first makes language possible." It is "that through which all those things first come into the open that we then talk about and discuss in our everyday language." Poetizing is a naming that first institutes or founds "the Being and essence of all things"—including, therefore, the Being of language itself (EHD, 43). The poet—who on this understanding cannot be the human being conceived as a being or origin of action, but is poetized by Hölderlin as "demigod"—is the one who, in Heidegger's words, "grasps something that endures amid the time that tears and brings it to stand in the word." Hölderlin, in the closing words of the hymn "Remembrance," says:

> Was bleibet aber, stiften die Dichter.

> Yet what endures, the poets found.

Founding or instituting (*Stiften*) occurs in and through the word of language. And yet, asks Heidegger:

> Can that which endures be founded? Is it not that which is always already present? No! Precisely that which endures must be brought to a stand, secured against being torn away; that which is simple and straightforward must be wrested from confusion, the measure must be set over and against that which is without measure. That which sustains and prevails throughout beings as a whole must come into the open. Being must be opened up, so that beings may appear. (EHD, 41)

Poetizing as founding that which endures is thus a founding of Being in the word, a naming that consists, not in providing something already known with a name, but in "first naming beings to what they are," first letting them be and be manifest "*as* being." Yet, as founding, poetizing also uncovers the *measure* of human dwelling, a measure that is never simply given or present among what already is, but that must first be found. In the well-known lines of his poem "In beautiful blue . . . ," Hölderlin writes:

> Gibt es auf Erden ein Maas?
> Es giebt keines.
>
> Is there a measure on Earth?
> There is none.

This sounds, as Heidegger comments, "like a token of hopelessness and despair." And yet, he insists, it points to something else. For Hölderlin's word implies not only that there is no one measure, no single measure, but also that the measure of human dwelling is never simply a given or there for the taking, but something that must first, and time again, be found by way of thoughtfulness and what Heidegger calls "the wakefulness of an intimative scrutinizing" (GA 53, 205). Poetizing is thus "a telling finding of Being," of that which is fitting and as such can never be found in what is actual or discovered in beings themselves (GA 53, 149).[10]

Human dwelling itself is thus not a fixed state of being or predicament of human existence. Dwelling is itself, rather, a task to be undertaken and accomplished, a challenge that has to be undergone ever anew—accomplished and brought about in and through the temporality of human experience. And just as *experience* is critical to the cultivation of *ēthos* and *phronēsis* in Aristotelian ethics, so too it remains central to the poetic accomplishment of human dwelling. As the poet Hölderlin's word indicates, human experience has been possible only since the time that time itself has been, only since the moment when time opens itself in its stretchings. For this poietic opening, this inaugural moment, first enables the time of times—gathers in advance the many times into the unity of a singular time, of the arrival of one time, and thus into the possibility of one dialogue, one story, one history.[11]

THE ECLIPSE OF EXPERIENCE: EXPOSURE AND DWELLING IN GREEK TRAGEDY

The poietic accomplishment of human dwelling, our coming to be at home as brought about in and through the temporality of experience, must unfold itself in a continual exposure to a not being at home, to what the Greeks called *to deinon*, which Heidegger—in keeping with his understanding of human Being as dwelling—translates as *das Unheimliche*: the "uncanny," or literally "that which is not of the home." While in his 1924 lectures Heidegger had affirmed, with Aristotle, that we learn the virtues pertaining to human *ēthos* "not by way of some fantastical reflection upon Dasein, but by *venturing forth into Dasein* in accordance with the possibilities of the existence in question. . . . a venturing forth into the *deina* of life . . ." (GA 18, 181–82), his 1942 lectures on Hölderlin have at their center an interpretation of Greek tragedy that emphasizes the poetic accomplishment of human dwelling as a "coming to be at home in not being at home" (*Heimischwerden im Unheimischsein*). In the words of Sophocles, Antigone's counsel (*dusboulian*) to herself, what Heidegger calls "the decisive word," is: *pathein to deinon touto*, in Heidegger's translation: "to take up into my own essence the uncanny that here and now appears." The fitting self-exposure to what is *deinon*, to the *unheimlich*, in the "here and now" is a *pathein*, the *pathos* of an undergoing that, Heidegger emphasizes, is not to be understood as a passivity that one might oppose to activity, but that itself constitutes the "action" proper that is poetized in Greek tragedy. It constitutes the true essence of experience:

> Here, however, *pathein* does not mean the mere passivity of accepting and tolerating but rather taking upon oneself—*archēn de thēran*, making it through to the end, that is, properly experiencing. This *pathein*—experiencing the *deinon*—this enduring and suffering, is the fundamental trait of that doing and action called *to drama*, which constitutes the "dramatic," the "action" in Greek tragedy. Yet this very *pathein* is also the proper relation to the *deinon*. . . . (GA 53, 127–28)

What Antigone takes upon herself is a "not being at home"; this constitutes her "supreme action," not as a single act, but as an undergoing that itself is "the movement and 'drama' of coming to be at home"—of human dwelling itself. In this very movement, "not being at home" is "accomplished": again, not in the sense of being brought to a conclusion, but in the sense of first being "brought to light" in its essence (144). This bringing to light, Heidegger suggests, is itself in turn accomplished poetically, through the *phronein* of a poetic knowing that, far from enunciating a "philosophical truth," speaks in the chorus of Greek tragedy as the voice of the poet himself (138, 148). While we cannot here examine how the work of art of Greek tragedy brings to light the truth of human dwelling as poetic in a way that is neither theoretical nor philosophical, we may note for now that this bringing to light of the essence of our dwelling as a not being at home must itself be accomplished poetically precisely because we cannot experience the inaugural moment as such, in its own time, as the moment that first brings about our dwelling, that first calls us to action and to the word. In this sense, tragic drama as a *mimēsis* of action intensifies and first brings to the fore—presents—the unpresentable through the poietic unfolding of a *muthos* and a destiny. It is a *mimēsis* of *mimēsis*—of the (originary or originating) *mimēsis* that action itself is.[12] The unpresentability of the inaugural moment of time, its inevitable eclipse, is poetized by Hölderlin in three slightly different versions of the 1801–02 hymn *Friedensfeier*.[13] The first reads:

> Des Maases allzeit kundig rührt mit schonender Hand
> Die Wohnungen der Menschen
> Ein Gott an, einen Augenblick nur
> Und sie wissen es nicht, doch lange
> Gedenken sie deß, und fragen, wer es gewesen.
> Wenn aber eine Zeit vorbei ist, kennen sie es.

> Ever knowing the measure, with protective hand, a god
> Touches the dwellings of humans,
> Just for a moment,
> And they know it not, yet long
> They ponder it, and ask who it was.
> But when a time is past, they know it.

The god alone is herald of the measure, "touching" the dwellings of humans for just a moment. And yet the time of this moment is not a time that human beings can properly know as such. They know it only afterward, in retrospect, in a time after time, as it were, even though this moment gives them to ponder "who" the divinity was—calls them into thought and into language. The time of the *Augenblick*, these lines imply, as the time of a distinctive *kairos*, is outside of time as we ordinarily know it. The supreme moment of time itself, the highest presence, temporalizes as not within time at all, even though it is the most proper (divine) happening of time.[14] Notably, two different words for human "knowing" are used by Hölderlin here, namely, *wissen* and *kennen*: not "knowing" something in the sense of *wissen* implies, not being altogether oblivious to it, but knowing of it only as something concealed, something that shows itself in its self-concealing; knowing in the sense of *kennen*, by contrast, suggests implicit recognition or acknowledgment, having become familiar with something over time, in and through experience.[15] Both are contrasted with the intimate knowing or *kundig sein* that is proper to the god alone. The second version of the hymn *Friedensfeier,* however, emphasizes more the unexpected or unforeseen—and ultimately unforeseeable—character of the arrival:

> Denn schonend rührt, des Maases allzeit kundig
> Nur einen Augenblick die Wohnungen der Menschen
> Ein Gott an, unversehn, und keiner weiß es, wer?

> For protectively, ever heralding the measure, a god touches,
> Just for a moment, the dwellings of humans
> Unforeseen, and no one knows who.

Yet the third and final version of the hymn, by contrast with the first two, speaks not of the unknowable character of the gods, of the "who," but emphasizes more the unknowability of the happening of the moment itself that is indicated in the first version. Here, however, it is the unknowability of the "when," of the time of the moment, that is highlighted:

> Denn schonend rührt des Maases allzeit kundig
> Nur einen Augenblick die Wohnungen der Menschen
> Ein Gott an, unversehn, und keiner weiß es, wenn?

> . . . and no one knows when.

Again, the "when" here refers not to the time of prediction or expectation (as in: "I don't know when it's going to happen"), but to the time of the event itself as and when we stand in it, at the moment it is happening to us: at such a moment, we do not know it. What this means, however, is that the inaugural moment of the arrival of a world can only transpire historically, in and as the happening of a historical destiny. The second version of the later hymn *"Der Einzige"* ("The Only One") poetizes precisely this relation between the moment and destiny:

> Fein sehen die Menschen, daß sie
> Nicht gehn den Weg des Todes und hüten das Maas, daß einer
> Etwas für sich ist, den Augenblik
> Das Geschik der großen Zeit auch
> Ihr Feuer fürchtend, treffen sie, und wo
> Des Wegs ein anderes geht, da sehen sie
> Auch, wo ein Geschik sei, machen aber
> Das sicher, Menschen gleichend oder Gesezen.

> For humans see discerningly, that they
> Do not take the path of death, and protect the measure, that each
> May be something for themselves, the moment,
> The destiny of a time that was great too,
> Fearing its fire, they meet it, and where
> Something else goes their path, there too they see
> Where a destiny may be, but make it
> Secure, resembling humans or laws.[16]

These lines once again insist on the disjunction between divine and human destiny: humans are destined not to take the path of death, the path of the god who, in Greek tragic presentation, "is present in the form of death."[17] Yet it was in part this proximity of the *encounter* between divine and human destiny that, according to Hölderlin, marked as distinctive "the destiny of a time that was great." These words allude, of course, to the golden era of the Greeks and in particular of Greek tragedy. Compare "Bread and Wine," first version:

> Delphi schlummert, und wo tönet das große Geschik?
> Wo ist das schnelle? wo brichts, allgegenwärtigen Glüks voll
> Donnernd aus heiterer Luft über die Augen herein?

> Delphi slumbers, and where sounds destiny great?
> Where swift? where does it irrupt, full of omnipresent fortune
> In thunder from clear skies upon our eyes?[18]

By contrast with the golden age of the Greeks, who were exposed to the "fire of the heavens," "our" era and our vision, while it has the possibility of assuming a destiny, makes everything secure and law-like in accordance with the German virtue of clarity of presentation (as described in the 1801 letter to Böhlendorff).[19] Yet although our time is without destiny, or without greatness of destiny, it is neither without the possibility of destiny, nor without measure. In the fragment cited, the *Augenblik* is itself identified with the measure, and the measure is that of human freedom and abandonment: a measure that must be protected with discerning vision, with a seeing that remains mindful of human mortality.[20]

THE FESTIVAL

Heidegger's interpretations of human *ēthos* in dialogue with Hölderlin suggest that such dwelling not only unfolds poetically, but that the measure and fitting moment of action can never be mastered by human knowledge or virtue. Virtuous action, if and when it happens, depends not only on human abilities of discernment, readiness, and experience, but also on divine good fortune; the ultimate law of human dwelling is neither simply human or divine, but poietic, unfolding as the dialogue of divine and human destiny. Yet this also means, on Heidegger's readings of Hölderlin and Greek tragedy, that the primordial attunement or *pathos* of human dwelling is not simply that of (human) *Angst* in the face of death, whose moment or *Augenblick* is at once certain and indeterminate (SZ, 258)—or rather, it means that the attunement of *Angst* is itself pervaded by a more primordial attunement: that of festivity, of what Heidegger, with Hölderlin, calls *das Festliche*. The festival is, for Hölderlin, the "bridal festival" of the coming together of human beings and gods,[21] which Heidegger, in his 1941–42 remarks on Hölderlin's hymn "Remembrance," reads as the "event" (*Ereignis*) of that "primordial greeting" which at the beginning of "As when on feast day . . ." is poetized as the arrival of the "holy." This primordial greeting, Heidegger suggests, is not only the wellspring of the coming together of humans and gods. It is, he says, "the concealed essence of history." "This primordial greeting is *the* event, *the* beginning" (GA 52, 70). As such, the festive is what sustains and pervasively attunes all coming together, all encounter:

> The festive is what primordially attunes. What thus attunes, pervasively attunes and determines everything as a silent voice. . . . If the festive, as that which primordially greets, is

the holy, then what holds sway in the holy is the attuning of an attunement that always remains more primordial and originary than every attunement that pervasively attunes and determines us human beings. . . . The festive is more primordial than all attunements and their counterparts otherwise known to us. (69–71)

In these altogether remarkable claims, Heidegger identifies the festive as more "primordial" (*anfänglicher*) and more "originary" (*ursprünglicher*) than every other human attunement—including, he goes on to say, both mourning (*Trauer*) and joy, which, moreover, are not to be regarded as opposites.[22] It is that which originarily attunes (*stimmt*) and determines (*bestimmt*) our vocation and calling, and it does so as a "silent voice" (*lautlose Stimme*), as the attuning "voice of Being" that speaks in and through every fundamental attunement. As such, the festive is "the ground of celebration," not something that first arises through celebration. Thus, Greek tragedies (*Trauerspiele*), in which the tragic predicament of human action and *ēthos* is itself celebrated, are not, Heidegger reminds us, "theater" in the modern sense of the word, but "celebrations, and are therefore oriented toward the festival" (72).[23] In his 1958 essay "The Word," Heidegger begins by asking us to ponder, "for a moment," the following lines from Hölderlin's "Bread and Wine":

> Warum schweigen auch sie, die alten heilgen Theater?
> Warum freuet sich denn nicht der geweihete Tanz?
>
> Why are they, too, silent, the ancient, holy theaters?
> Why is there no joy in consecration of the dance? (UWS, 219)

Hölderlin's word tells us that the word has been exiled from the site where once the gods appeared, as the telling word in which the god himself approached. The telling of the word, Heidegger remarks, was in itself the letting appear of what had already looked upon the speakers, bringing speakers and listeners into the "infinite intimacy [*Innigkeit*] of the strife between men and gods." Yet this strife itself, he notes, was pervaded by something beyond gods and men, by that which Antigone identifies in saying:

> Not just today, nor since yesterday, but ever-enduring
> This rises into Being (*ho nomos*, directive need) and no one has
>   seen from whence it came to appear.

"Directive need," in German: *der weisende Brauch*, is the term Heidegger uses to translate *ho nomos*, the law that determines Antigone's actions. *Weisen* here means: to convey an ethical directive. *Brauch*, related to the verb *brauchen*, has connotations of both need and usage; thus, in the present context it suggests that the human being, as the one who tells, who "has" the word, is at once needed and used by the gods as the site of their appearance. But *Brauch* also means custom, tradition, and thus might equally be translated as *ēthos*, naming that poietic unfolding of *ēthos* which, exceeding the human, between humans and gods, is here said to "live" (*zēi*), to rise into Being: *aufgehen*, as Heidegger translates it, suggesting a *poiēsis* that is also of *phusis*, a *phusis* that happens as an originary, originating *poiēsis*.[24]

SEVEN

The Telling of Ēthos

Heidegger, Aristotle, Sophocles

> *Der Mensch ist jenes Nicht-bleiben-können und doch nicht von der Stelle Können.*
>
> Man is that inability to remain and is yet unable to leave his place.
>
> —Heidegger, *The Fundamental Concepts of Metaphysics*

In his "Letter on 'Humanism' " (1946), Heidegger pointed unequivo-cally to the fundamental significance of Greek tragedy from the point of view of his own thinking of Being. "The tragedies of Sophocles," he stated, "—provided such a comparison is at all permissible—shelter the *ēthos* in their sayings more primordially than Aristotle's lectures on 'ethics' " (W, 184). The more original Greek meaning of *ēthos*—more original than that of the "ethical" and of "ethics"—is one's abode, one's place of dwelling. Heidegger goes on to indicate this by reference to Heraclitus's saying *ēthos anthrōpōi daimōn*, which he translates: "The abode (of the ordinary) is, for human beings, the site that is open for the presencing of the god (of the extra-ordinary)" (W, 187). To say that Sophocles' trag-edies shelter in their sayings and in their telling the *ēthos* of human beings, of their thinking and of their actions, is thus to say that these tragedies shelter—and thus also may bring to light—the very meaning and truth of human dwelling, that is, of our Being. For already in *Being and Time* (1927) Heidegger had identified the pri-mary meaning of our Being-in-the-world as dwelling:[1]

> Being-in does not mean a spatial "containedness" of things lying present before us, nor does the word "in" originally signify a spatial relation of this kind. "In" comes from *innan-*, to dwell, *habitare*, to have an abode; "an" signifies: I am in the habit of, familiar with, I tend to something; it has the

signification of *colo* in the sense of *habito* and *diligo*. We characterized this being, to which Being-in in this sense belongs, as the
being that I myself in each case am [*bin*]. The expression *bin* is
connected with *bei*; *Ich bin* [I am] means in turn: I dwell, I have
my abode in the presence of [*bei*] . . . the world as something
familiar to me in such and such a way. Being [*Sein*] as the infini-
tive of *Ich bin* . . . means dwelling in the presence of . . . , being
familiar with . . . (SZ, 54).[2]

Dwelling, in this sense, does not refer to a "physical" place that
could be located in mathematical terms; it is precisely that which
resists any mathematical or scientific localization. Being in the world
in the sense of dwelling means being in the presence of (*bei*) other
beings, and thus also always being situated in a particular context;
it means being an open site, not just or primarily for beings, but for
beings in their presence and presencing. To exist as such a site is
also to be an exceptional presence in the midst of other beings—
exceptional because although it is the site of disclosure of other
beings as a whole, this site itself is never fully disclosed as such.
The site of un-concealment is equally, indeed even more so, a site
of concealment, itself concealed in its innermost essence.

What the tragedies of Sophocles shelter and may reveal to us
is not so much the "essence" of this site in the sense of what it is,
but the site itself in its very prevailing and occurrence, in its worldly
happening and unfolding. In other words, the tragedies shelter,
not the "essence" of dwelling in the philosophical-Aristotelian sense
of *Wesen* (of the *to ti ēn einai*), but in the verbal sense of *Wesen* as
the "essential happening" or enduring self-showing and self-concealing of something.[3] Yet the latter is unveiled—if it comes to be
unveiled at all—not as an already existent ground, but in a historical, or, as Heidegger would also say, in a destinal and epochal
manner; and such unveiling occurs, if and when it occurs, not in
a descriptive *logos* that contemplates (*theōrein*) that which is in its
permanent form (*eidos*), but poetically, in a telling and saying that
is poetic and that in its very happening not merely discloses, but
enacts and thus accomplishes the "poetic dwelling" (to use
Hölderlin's word) of human beings upon this Earth.[4] To say that it
enacts and *accomplishes* human dwelling means that the poetic telling of Sophocles' tragedies is itself originary *praxis* or "action."
Such telling does not, on Heidegger's readings, merely "depict,"
"represent," or "portray" human action. The "Letter on 'Human-

ism' " indeed begins by inviting us to rethink the essence of action or *praxis*: To act, Heidegger indicates, does not mean to cause or bring about an effect; rather, "the essence of action is accomplishment." To accomplish, *vollbringen*, means to unfold something into the fullness of its "essence," to *bring it to its full unfolding*. But if this is so, then we can bring to its full unfolding only that which in some way already "is":

> But what "is" above all is Being. Thinking accomplishes [*vollbringt*] the relation of Being to the essence of the human being. It does not make or cause the relation. Thinking brings this relation to Being solely as something handed over to thought itself from Being. Such offering consists in the fact that in thinking Being comes to language. Language is the house of Being. In its home human beings dwell. The thinkers and poets are the guardians of this home. (W, 145)

The poetic saying of Sophocles' tragedies thus accomplishes the Being of human beings as dwelling. It does so in thoughtfully enacting, that is, bringing to full disclosure, the unfolding of such dwelling in its own time and situation. The thinkers and poets, Heidegger goes on to say, "guard" or tend the homestead of human dwelling in accomplishing the manifestness of Being, in bringing such manifestness to its full unfolding, and this occurs as their thoughtful saying and telling of Being. When such telling happens, Being itself comes to the fore and is "preserved" in language.[5] Human beings become manifest in their relation to Being, which is to say, in the manner in which they dwell in the midst of beings as a whole.

A "Scarcely Pondered Word": Aristotle's Testimony

What kind of thinking and thoughtfulness is it that here accomplishes human dwelling? Why is such thinking itself originary action or *praxis*? Does this imply that for Heidegger only the action of the professional thinker or philosopher, of the Greek tragic poet such as Sophocles, or of the German poet of the homestead, Hölderlin, is authentic action—as is often claimed—and that all other kinds of action (ethical and political) are of lesser status and importance?[6] Is this just one more instance of philosophy's traditional and well-documented denigration of the political? Not at all. The action of a great thinker or poet is indeed exceptional; its greatness lies precisely in its reaching into the realm of the extra-ordinary, bringing the latter into Being in its "work." Yet this does not mean that other kinds or instances of action are of lesser status. For Heidegger's claim is neither, strictly speaking, a philosophical one; nor is there any claim to a principle upon which such a hierarchical ordering could be made. Precisely the "destinal" happening of Being's unfolding or "history," as the destinal manner of poetic and thoughtful unveiling, precludes and refuses any such principle and any transcendent ground. And this is why, ultimately, the very comparison between the telling of Sophocles' tragedies and that of Aristotle's lectures on "ethics" is problematic. More precisely, what would be problematic would be any straightforward comparison between the two tellings of *ēthos* that would claim one to be "more original" than the other, implying the continuity of an order of founding between the two. And this implies that Heidegger's claim of a "more primordial" (*anfänglicher*) telling in Sophocles should not be taken as a purely historical claim. For between these two ways of telling of the *ēthos* of human beings a fundamental transformation in telling itself (and thus also in the nature of *ēthos*) has occurred, namely, from the poetic telling of *muthos* to a primarily apophantic *logos*, such that there *is* no common measure (if Being itself indeed finds its unfolding and completion in the saying of language). Yet far from precluding any comparison, it is this very event that not only first invites, but indeed necessitates a recollective thinking of this transformation. Thinking itself must first take the measure—that is, find the measure in first bringing it to Being—of that which it has been invited to ponder: the measure of action itself. In the words of the statement that opens the "Letter on 'Humanism,'" "We are still far from pondering the essence of action decisively enough." Heidegger's essay itself is nothing other than an attempt to take the measure of this historical event.[7]

Yet why, then, does Heidegger claim that the poetic telling of Sophocles' tragedies shelters the *ēthos*, the dwelling and abode of humans, in a more primordial manner than do Aristotle's lectures on "ethics"? And what can be meant by "more primordial" (*anfänglicher*) here? Are we invited to ponder the essence of *ēthos* and of action in relation to Aristotle and to Sophocles purely as a matter of historical interest and significance? Or is something else

at stake? Heidegger's remark occurs in the context of his addressing Jean Beaufret's question of the relation between ontology and
a possible ethics. Must not ontology—in particular the fundamental ontology of Dasein presented in *Being and Time*—be supple-
mented by an ethics? In reply, having indicated the sense of
Heraclitus's saying in Fragment 119, Heidegger on the contrary
affirms that "[i]f the name 'ethics,' in keeping with the basic meaning of the word *ēthos*, should now say that ethics ponders the abode
of the human being, then that thinking which thinks the truth of
Being as the primordial [*anfängliche*] element of the human being,
as the one who eksists, is in itself originary [*ursprüngliche*] ethics"
(W, 187). "Ek-sistence," Heidegger indicates, is here meant to indicate the human being's ek-static standing and dwelling within the
truth of Being (W, 155–58).

The context makes apparent right away what is problematic
not only about Aristotle's lectures on ethics, but also about the
account of Being-in-the-world as dwelling presented in *Being and
Time*. Heidegger begins his response by addressing the relation
between ontology and ethics in terms of the historical emergence
of these disciplines. "Ethics," along with "physics" and "logic,"
arose for the first time, he recalls, in the school of Plato, at a time
when "thinking was becoming 'philosophy,' philosophy *epistēmē*
(science), and science itself a matter for schools and academic disciplines" (W, 184).[8] Four significant factors are named here: (1) the
transformation of thinking into "philosophy"; (2) the further reduction of philosophy to *epistēmē* or "science"; (3) its becoming a
scholastic affair; and (4) concomitant with these changes, the emergence of "disciplines" of thought. Each of these factors is significant for understanding the claim that Aristotle's lectures on ethics
fail to attain the more primordial telling of *ēthos* that resonates in
Sophocles' tragedies.

1. The transformation of thinking into philosophy marks the shift
   from a way of speaking and saying that simply and directly
   brings to presence what is, a telling that is thus in a certain
   harmony with Being itself as appearing [*Erscheinen*],[9] to a *logos*
   that, inquiring into the essence of what truly "is," begins to
   assert its radical independence from Being qua appearing. This
   logos of the philosophers thus severs itself from the immediate
   appearing and self-presentation of things; appearances, it says,

may deceive. The result of this different way of saying Being, of this different claim? Speaking, saying and telling, itself loses the immediacy of its authority.[10]

2. Nevertheless, one must recognize that the power and persua-
    siveness of this claim derive from the fact that this transformed
    thinking and saying—precisely in its most powerful form, the
    philosophy of Aristotle—does not institute difference between
    Being and appearing, but remains in proximity to phenomena
    themselves in their self-showing. Yet rather than saying and
    thus itself bringing to Being this self-showing of phenomena,
    the *logos* of the philosophers simply seeks what is most perma-
    nent and enduring in and throughout the self-manifestation or
    appearing of phenomena. It seeks to designate the underlying
    form (the *eidos*) that endures and in advance determines the
    entity in its Being, as long as the entity remains what it is: its
    primary *ousia*, its "substance" or "essence."

    This second consideration marks the shift of philosophiz-
    ing into secured knowledge, or *epistēmē*. In this shift, something
    further comes to be concealed, and this is indicated indirectly
    by the very term that Aristotle uses to designate the primary
    ousia: it is *to ti ēn einai*, that which already was in Being. Despite
    the fact that it remains oriented toward the truth or true Being
    of the particular entity in its "thisness," the *logos* of *epistēmē* can
    designate only that which has already been, and in so doing
    conceals the singular appearing and coming into Being of phe-
    nomena themselves. This apophantic *logos*, aimed at solely point-
    ing out and revealing that which already is, relates to itself
    primarily qua *legomenon*, as that which has been said, that is, in
    terms of the meaningful content of discourse, thereby tending
    to conceal the *logos* qua *legein*, as incipient speaking and saying.
    The meaning or "definition" (*horismos*) of the *logos*, as Aristotle
    himself says, here *is* the *eidos* or *to ti ēn einai*; and thus, as he
    reminds us, it is possible for the *logos* to be true and for us to
    have "scientific" knowledge (*epistēmē*) *without* our accomplish-
    ing a genuine beholding (*theōrein*) and unveiling of things in
    their Being.[11] For it lies in the nature of such *theōrein*, as itself a
    praxis, that it is in each case singular and unique, and thus must
    be accomplished anew on each occasion by the individual con-
    cerned. By contrast, I can learn and thus "know" the truth in a

purely formal way, indeed having the right *logos*, but without any insight into the grounds of its truth. For these "grounds" lie in the phenomenon of appearing itself. Precisely the formal nature of epistemic knowledge thus enables and prepares the severing of truth from the ethical. As a scientist, I can be "in the truth" without this truth making any ethical claim upon me.

3. The third factor mentioned by Heidegger, philosophy as "science" becoming a scholastic affair, is no less significant, and can be understood only in the context of the first two points. For the emergence and development of epistemic knowledge is possible only on the basis of a *withdrawal* on the part of the philosopher or "scientist" from being involved in and claimed by the immediate affairs of life, and in particular from the activities of speaking and acting concerned with the ultimate freedom of human beings in their worldly community and plurality, namely, the affairs of the *polis*. Epistemic or "scientific" knowledge, like philosophical knowledge itself, arose only when humans not only had leisure (*scholē*) or time free from the necessities of life, but when they used this time not for direct involvement in truly human affairs—the affairs of the *polis*—but for contemplation (*theōrein*) of the world and of its divinity. The philosophy of the schools first emerged on the basis of this use of *scholē*.

4. Fourthly and finally, the development of the "disciplines" that accompanied the rise of epistemic knowledge can likewise be understood in its fundamental significance only in relation to the first three points. For it was only on the basis of taking this time and distance from immediate involvement in human affairs, and only through the emergence of a *logos* that itself marked this very distantiation, that the philosophers could make epistemic knowledge a matter of "disciplines." The development of disciplines of knowledge becomes possible only on the basis of a withdrawal from the immediate and pressing affairs and activities of daily life, such that one's Being is no longer a dwelling *in* the world but increasingly becomes a standing before the world as something to be contemplated and investigated.[12] The dividing up of Being into various regions, each to be investigated by a regional science or "discipline," is in the first instance the result of a *decontextualizing* of one's being in

the world, of dwelling in the midst of other beings as a whole
that press upon one and address one in their immediacy. The
phenomenon of worldly *context* and situatedness becomes increasingly formalized. In dividing the Being of the world (of
beings as a whole) into regions, what presses to the fore are the
specific *differences* between beings and their different ways of
Being; the primordial element of their original belonging together—the phenomenon of world itself—recedes. In place of
the original phenomenon of the world, we find in the history
of philosophy and science only retrospective attempts to
(re)construct a world that has already been epistemically dis-
sected, not to say decimated.[13]

These remarks on some of the issues surrounding the emergence of "ethics" as a discipline perhaps let us see better what is
at stake in Heidegger's claim concerning the distance between
Aristotle and Sophocles. In each of the four factors we have com-
mented on, what comes to the fore is a *withdrawal from the immediacy of dwelling in the world and from a* legein *or saying that itself
dwells in this proximity to appearing.* What appears problematic or
less "primordial" about Aristotle's ethics is, on the one hand, that
his inquiry remains an inquiry into a restricted region of Being,
and that this regional character of the inquiry—despite the greatness with which Aristotle integrates it into the study of political
life and indeed into the subjects of his other investigations—is
problematic, because symptomatic of a certain loss of worldly
dwelling. On the other hand, as a theoretical and epistemic inquiry, it seeks formal knowledge of *praxis*, that is, of that which, by
Aristotle's own admission, can in its very accomplishment never
be reduced to or grounded in purely formal knowledge.[14] Furthermore, however, while Heidegger's own fundamental ontology of
Dasein in *Being and Time*, on account of its preliminary and
nonregional character (which also make it prior to any anthropol-
ogy), thinks the realm of the ethical or of dwelling more originarily
than the history of philosophy hitherto—precisely because it seeks
to avoid any splitting up of Being-in-the-world by insisting on the
"equiprimordiality" of Being-in as being in the presence of other
beings (the present-at-hand; ready-to-hand equipment; nature; other
Dasein-like beings)—it too nevertheless remains problematic, not
least, as Heidegger himself points out here, because of its "inap-

propriate concern with 'science' and 'research' " (W, 187). For it still speaks not only the language of philosophy, but of philosophy with—at least in part and in its preliminary self-understanding[15] — a "scientific" orientation.

Yet Heidegger's remark concerning the more primordial sheltering of *ēthos* in the telling of Sophocles' tragedies should not be read as a dismissal of Aristotle's inquiries into "ethics." Aristotle's works on ethics have their own greatness, and this greatness lies in large part in their very proximity to the prephilosophical presentation of action and of the essence of human dwelling through tragedy. Thus, Aristotle's *Nicomachean Ethics* is remarkable not least for its constant reminders about the limitations of its own inquiry, that is, of a theoretical inquiry into the general nature and truth of *praxis*, and for the emphasis it places on the fragility of all human knowledge in the face both of the human contingencies of action and of the element of fortune and destiny that lies in the hands of the gods. The *Nicomachean Ethics* emphasizes throughout that neither ethical virtue formed by habit (*ethos*),[16] nor purely intellectual virtue, can on their own ensure that we will act virtuously. What is decisive, rather, is the way in which we dwell in the moment of decision itself (the *kairos*, which Heidegger translates as *Augenblick*: GA 19, 164), our response to the singularity of the given situation as that which precisely cannot be known or "seen" in advance by a philosophical *theōrein*. Our dwelling in the moment of decision is itself determined by, or better, occurs as *phronēsis*, which, as the deliberative accomplishment of dwelling, mediates in an altogether singular manner between ethical virtue of character (formed by habit and by contemplation) and the arrival of the unknown, of that which has yet to be decided: the Being of one's dwelling in the openness of a world. Recent publications of Heidegger's early lecture courses, as we indicated in chapters 3 and 4, have shown the importance of his interpretation of Aristotle's *phronēsis* for understanding the analytic of Dasein in *Being and Time*. For what Aristotle's account of *phronēsis*—despite its being a theoretical inquiry—itself brings to the fore is precisely the temporality and finitude of human dwelling as Being-in-the-world, a finite temporality that will become concealed through the increasingly removed "theoretical" discourse of subsequent philosophy. Aristotle's *theōria* itself thus orients *praxis* in advance toward the deliberative accomplishment (*euboulia*), in *phronēsis*, of its own excellence (*eupraxia*), and it does so by first disclosing the world as the contextual whole and general horizon within which alone deliberative action can orient itself in advance toward "living well as a whole" (*to eu zēn holōs*). Such *theōrein*, which participates in an originary manner in *bringing about* the guiding possibility of *eudaimonia* for human beings, thus remains in close proximity to a *poiēsis* that lets the finitude of our Being in the world come to the fore, even if this bringing-to-the-fore occurs here through the discourse of philosophy, and not through the sensuous presentation of the theater of Greek tragedy. Poietic accomplishment, as a bringing to the fore of that which already presents and announces itself, remains intrinsic to the very sense of *theōria*, even when the latter is no longer the immediate presentation of the sensuous, but its more withdrawn, more scholarly, more philosophical presentation.[17]

And yet—Greek tragedy itself already tends in this direction of the "more philosophical." The significance of Sophoclean tragedy cannot be fully appreciated without taking into consideration precisely this proximity of poetic presentation to a thinking that is at least proto-philosophical, centering as it does on a thoughtfulness and a giving-to-be-thought that occur in the time of the ancient *theōria* of Greek theater. Heidegger himself reminds us of this very proximity when he alludes, in the same "Letter on 'Humanism,' " to a statement made by Aristotle in the context of his discussion of tragedy in the *Poetics*: "But Aristotle's word in the *Poetics*, although it has scarcely been pondered, is still valid—that poetizing [*Dichten*] is truer than the exploration of beings" (W, 193). What Aristotle actually says is that poetizing (*poiēsis*) is "more philosophical" (*philosophōteron*), as well as "more serious" (*spoudaioteron*)—because it points to more grave matters—than historical inquiry (*historia*) (P, 1451 b5). Poetizing, particularly that of tragedy, is more philosophical—it already dwells in proximity to philosophical inquiry, which is likewise distinct from a mere recounting of beings such as that found in historical inquiry. If Heidegger here writes "more true" instead of "more philosophical," it is perhaps to indicate the ambiguity in the Greek sense of "truth" (*alētheia*) during precisely this period. But this ambiguity is inseparable from concomitant transformations in the meaning and sense of *theōria* as a mode of apprehending that which is; and to say that poetizing is "more philosophical" is hardly any less ambiguous, provided we do not straightaway associate the philosophical with the discourse or *logos* of *epistēmē*, but understand *theōrein* itself, in its always ambiguous status, as the site of the necessary transgression of such a *logos*. For *theōrein* is itself a mode of *alētheuein*, one that not only, to the extent that it became subservient to *epistēmē*, became the highest mode of disclosure for Greek philosophy, but one that, in exceeding what can be appropriated by the *logos* of *epistēmē*, also transgresses such epistemic disclosure in the direction of the finite, the extra-ordinary, and the divine. And thus also of the tragic.

A brief recollection of what is at issue here in the context of Heidegger's appeal to this "scarcely pondered" word of Aristotle's own testimony may help to clarify this point. According to Aristotle, the reason that poetic disclosure is more philosophical than histori-cal inquiry is that "poetry is oriented more toward the universal, while history recounts the particular" (1451 b6–7). Poetic disclo-sure is turned more toward universal or general "truths," whereas history recounts particular facts and events. *Poiēsis* is thus turned in a more philosophical direction, toward the realm of the *katholou* which, according to Aristotle, it is precisely the task of philosophi-cal contemplation or *theōrein* to disclose and thereby bring to lan-guage—language meaning now the *logos* of *epistēmē*. "History," *historia*, by contrast, has the task of bringing into view and letting be seen particular deeds and events. And this means, as Aristotle points out, that it is concerned with what has happened, with that which has already come to be (*ta genomena*), and not, like poetic disclosure, with what may or *could* happen. Aristotle is here thinking of Herodotus's own testimony[18] at the beginning of his *History*:

> What Herodotus the Halicarnassian has learnt by inquiry [*historiēs*] is here set forth: in order that so the memory of the past [*ta genomena*] may not be blotted out from among men by time, and that great and marvellous deeds done by Greeks and foreigners and especially the reason why they warred against each other may not lack renown.[19]

The difference between a historian and a poet, writes Aristotle, is thus not that one writes in prose and the other in verse, since we could set the writings of Herodotus to verse, and they would still be a kind of history; rather, the difference lies in the different dis-closure and telling of the word in each case. Yet it is important to note that *historia*, as a seeking to know and to have seen beings, did not mean inquiry into the past in the sense of modern historiography. For it did not imply investigation into something "past" in the sense of no longer present, but was more a preservation of the great deeds that presented themselves and were deemed worthy of preservation. In particular, it did not imply research into uncovering a past, but was simply a recounting and recording of what had happened and had been seen to have happened.[20] It is important to recall this because the context in which Heidegger reminds us of Aristotle's *Poetics*—that of addressing Jean Beaufret's question "How can we preserve the element of adventure that all research contains without simply turning philosophy into an adventuress?"—should not mislead us into simply identifying *historia*, "exploration of beings" (*Erkunden vom Seiendem*), as Heidegger translates it, with "research" (*recherche*) in the modern, scientific sense. Modern research, guided by scientific "theory" in the form of a representational picturing (*Vorstellen*) of the world, is itself a particular historical transformation of the *theōria* that once commanded the attention of the philosophers. Indeed, Beaufret's association of philosophizing with an "element of adventure" suggests a problematically active sense of philosophical activity that Heidegger at once counters by pointing to the sense of advent and arrival (*l'avenant*) that adventure (*aventure*) implies, and by translating such arrival into the arrival and approach of *Being* (not beings), to which thinking is destined and bound. Presumably, what is poetically disclosed in Greek tragedy has to do with this binding relation to the arrival "of" Being, that is, to Being as itself futural. Presumably, this is what Aristotle's scarcely pondered word, mentioned by Heidegger only "in passing," gives us to think.

While Herodotus's "historical" inquiry is neither research nor adventure in the modern sense, it nonetheless remains true that traveling and journeying into the foreign are inextricably bound up with his narration. And this is itself indicative of one of the transformations that the Greek *theōria* underwent during this period, prior to the emergence of philosophy. Herodotus himself, like Aristotle after him, recounts the travels of Solon to Egypt as the undertaking of a *theōria*, a seeing and experiencing of the foreign as a seeking of worldly knowledge.[21] Here, *theōria* does not appear to carry its more original connotation entailing an encounter with the divine, with the gods. In the theater of Greek tragedy, by contrast, *theōria* not only preserves precisely this encounter with the gods; it is also the unveiling of the foreign at home, in the site of one's own worldly dwelling. It is the unveiling of the extra-ordinary in the midst of the ordinary, of the foreign that arrives *in the midst of one's own*. Like Nietzsche and Hölderlin before him, each of whom in their own way emphasize Greek tragedy as a presentation of the excess that attends the Apollonian, of the inevitable transgression that accompanies the worldly appearing of form, Heidegger too highlights Greek tragedy as enacting in human presence "the struggle of the new gods against the old,"[22] the struggle between the force of destiny that has been revealed and that which has yet to come. Such was the role of tragedy in the Classical age of the Greeks, when "the arts ascended to the supreme heights of the revealing granted to them." "They brought to shine the presence of the gods, brought the dialogue between divine and human destiny."[23] In bringing this dialogue to light (*Leuchten*), in illuminating it, they presented in the sensuous the worldly measure of human dwelling. In the tragedy, such presentation (*poiēsis*) occurred *as* enactment (*praxis*), and such enactment (action itself in its full self-presentation and encounter with its own limits, the accomplishment of its own completion: enactment as supreme *energeia*) unfolded in and as a self-showing and coming to presence that was not merely "for" an audience (as though the presentation of the action and the beholding of the spectators could be separated in reality, or exist in isolation), but *was* the *theōrein* of the audience.[24]

Here, *theōria*, *praxis*, and *poiēsis* are *one* and inseparable: they unfold in their unity as the sensuous immediacy of human dwelling in the world, and are not yet analytically separated in the manner that becomes determinative for the remainder of Western philosophy, science, and technology. It is perhaps no exaggeration to claim that the story of this separation is what has been the history of Western culture ever since. For the separation brings with it not only the reduction of meaningful human *poiēsis* to a *technē* conceived instrumentally and in terms of utility, sidelining (as Heidegger remarks in this context of "The Question Concerning Technology") the *technē* of the fine arts, but also the concealment of *praxis* as the accomplishment of human dwelling in its immediacy, a concealment that has as one of its consequences the contemporary "homelessness," in the sense of uprootedness, of human beings across the Earth. "Uprootedness" and "homelessness," Heidegger indicates in the "Letter on 'Humanism,' " should not be understood simply as a loss of provincialism or of nearness to "blood and soil," nor patriotically or nationalistically, but as a loss of "nearness to Being," of the proximity to presence that is the originary site of human dwelling (W, 168ff.). Today, the near has become the far, the remote; technological presence is tele-presence and tele-presentation, "virtual" presence, the global mediation of the technological Absolute. In the present era, Being itself, as presence, becomes worthy of thought. "Can thinking," asks Heidegger, "refuse to think Being after the latter has lain hidden so long in oblivion but at the same time has made itself known in the present moment of world history [*Weltaugenblick*] by the uprooting of all beings?" (W, 184). Where human freedom no longer finds itself bound by the immediate presence of beings, where our response to beings is conceived in advance only along the lines of "gathering and ordering all plans and actions in a way that corresponds to technology," there the desire for an ethics "presses ever more ardently for fulfillment as the obvious no less than the hidden perplexity of human beings soars to immeasurable heights" (W, 183).

Yet precisely this desire for "an ethics" remains in the thrall of the essence of technology itself, as the contemporary destiny of Being, insofar as it seeks a measure, in the form of a set of rules or principles, that will be binding in advance for all human action and self-presentation.[25] It is the essence of technology to seek the orderability of all presencing in a manner that can be calculated in advance. It is in this context, and in the face of this predicament, that Heidegger is led to recall Sophoclean tragedy as disclosive of a more primordial human dwelling, in a recollective thinking that indeed provides a pointer and a directive (*Weisung*): "Insofar as thinking limits itself to its task it directs the human being at the present moment of the world's destiny [*im Augenblick des jetzigen Weltgeschicks*] into the primordial dimension of his historical abode." This directive calls for "a descent into the nearness of the nearest" (W, 182). The "moment" or *Augenblick* of the present world-destiny is not the objective time of an infinitely substitutable "now" that could be ascertained by representational thinking as a picturing of the world from the distance of the Archimedean point occupied by science and technology, but the moment in which thinking is itself engaged in response to presence, the moment when it is itself looked upon by the face of the world and in which it attains insight

(*Einsicht*) into that which is, into Being itself as the configuration or constellation of presencing under the sway of technological ordering.[26] In such "momentary" response to presence, at once finite and ekstatic, thinking accomplishes and brings to the fore both the technological configuration of world-presencing and that which exceeds it, that which, beyond and within technological "enframing" (*Gestell*), remains to be thought.

It is in this context, as we noted, and in the face of this world-destiny, that Heidegger's thinking recalls Sophoclean tragedy as disclosive of a more primordial human dwelling. Yet this recollection not only seeks to measure the distance between these two faces of dwelling, the Sophoclean and the technological, by a reminder of what is foreclosed in Aristotle's thinking of the ethical. Heidegger reminds us also, if only by way of a passing remark, that Aristotle's "scarcely pondered word" is itself the site of a recollective thinking of human dwelling in the face of the incipient emergence of the present world-destiny through the transformation of philosophy into *epistēmē*. While Aristotle's account of *praxis* and of the "ethical" in the *Nicomachean Ethics* proceeds from the outset precisely by distinguishing *praxis* from *poiēsis* and from the *theōria* of the *bios theōrētikos*, even while emphasizing their ultimate inseparability and interwovenness in the activity of a human life, the *Poetics* recalls and preserves for us the thoughtful recollection of a more originary accomplishment of dwelling.

THEŌRIA AND TRAGEDY: ARISTOTLE'S *POETICS*

Aristotle's *Poetics* is thus a crucial resource in understanding how tragedy brings to light a sense of human dwelling in a manner more primordial than the "scientific" discourse of his treatises on *Ethics*. According to the *Poetics*, tragedy is essentially the presentation of an action (*mimēsis praxeōs*) that is serious, forms a complete whole, and is of a certain magnitude; it employs song and verse in its presentation, and through pity and fear brings about a *katharsis* of these emotions.[27] Furthermore, notes Aristotle, every tragedy has six constituent parts: the story or "plot," character, speech, thought, spectacle, and song. Of these, the story, the character of those involved, and the thought that leads to their actions are revealed through speech and song, and the overall medium of presentation is visual, the spectacle (*opsis*). The Greek *mimēsis* does not mean a mere imitation or copy of an already existing image, but an original presentation and *poiēsis* in which a general trait or feature (*katholou*) of something we have seen before is again brought to the fore, and thereby remembered and recognized. The chief accomplishment and pleasure of *mimēsis*, as Aristotle indicates at the outset, lies in facilitating the recognition of something already familiar; thus, it facilitates learning. What we are supposed to recognize is not something behind or underlying the presentation, such as a hidden meaning or a real essence that conceals itself from sense-perception, but precisely whatever is presented itself. Aristotle here mentions the delight in imitation or *mimēsis* as one that is active from childhood. As Hans-Georg Gadamer recalls in this context, when children dress up to imitate someone, "we are not supposed to recognize the child who has dressed up as someone, but rather the one whom the child represents."[28] Mimetic behaviour is thus a making-present, a bringing to presence, but this does not imply, as Gadamer notes, that in recognizing what is presented "we should try to determine the degree of similarity between the original and its mimetic representation."[29] The meaningful measure of what is presented mimetically does not lie in such comparison with an original measure, as Plato demanded in his denigration of *mimēsis* in the *Republic*. Rather, as Aristotle puts it, "[t]he reason we enjoy seeing likenesses [*eikonas*] is that, as we look [*theōrountas*], we learn and infer what each particular is, for instance, 'that is so and so' " (P, 1148 b15–17). We are simply directed toward the particular *as* this or that, that is, toward the presence of the general *in* the particular. But this seeing, or *theōrein*, is not an explicit turning toward the general form (*katholou*) as such. The highlighting of the general in the particular that occurs in mimetic presentation is a bringing-to-the-fore in the midst of the sensuous itself. This bringing-to-the-fore, as a bringing into Being, occurs not in an explicit or philosophical (epistemic) contemplation of the pure form independent of appearances, but only in an act of recognition.

Yet where, then, is the measure of a mimetic presentation to be found? Evidently, only in that which is presented, in and through the presentation itself. But what is it that is primarily presented in and through the poetic presentation of tragedy? According to Aristotle, poetic presentation differs from historical recounting precisely in presenting more the general or universal, or the whole (*katholou*), whereas history presents particulars. But what exactly is "the general" that tragic drama is supposed to present? Following his initial comparison of poetic presentation with historical presentation, Aristotle specifies: "By something 'general' I mean the sort of thing that a certain sort of person will do or say either probably or inevitably" (1451 b8–9). This could be taken to mean that what tragedy presents primarily is nothing other than certain character-types, made visible in and through their actions; thus, in the *Antigone*, Creon might be considered to represent the kind of ruler who insists on an overly rigid application of the law; Antigone, the type of human being who stubbornly follows her own will with total disregard for the law, whether human or divine. Yet although the presentation of certain *kinds* of human being and of character-type is, at least for the most part, undeniably a part of tragic presentation, it is neither the primary, nor even an absolutely necessary part; indeed, Aristotle notes, one can have a tragedy without character-types (*aneu de ēthōn*: P, 1450 a23).[30]

Aristotle's point, therefore, concerning the level of *katholou* presented in poetic drama is that it is not primarily (and certainly not exclusively) about already existing "types," but about a universally recognizable relation to the future, a relation that, when recognized, binds and founds or renews a community. His mention of the *katholou* occurs and is understandable only within the context of his main point, namely, that poetry tells not what actually happened or what actually is the case (which is the historian's task), but what *could* or *will* happen, "either probably or inevitably." What will happen is not simply the (causally determined) result of a character-type; yet character is most often not irrelevant either: it may also play a role in how someone's future comes to be determined in the way that it does. Poetic presentation is oriented toward the openness and indeterminacy of the future; it shows precisely how what is in the beginning and now as yet indeterminate gets decided, assumes a certain direction and determinacy.

It is because poetry tells, that is, reveals, not what happened, but "what might happen" that it is more philosophical and more serious or grave, more elevated (*spoudaioteron*) than historical documentation. It is in the light of this seriousness or ethical import that we must understand Aristotle's remark here about poetry revealing, not simply a "universal," but "the sort of thing that a certain sort of person *will do or say, either probably or inevitably*" (P, 1451 b9).

This, Aristotle goes on to say, "is what poetry aims at in giving names to the characters." And here, Aristotle's comparison of comedy and tragedy is enlightening: in comedy (the so-called New Comedy), he notes, the plots are first constructed out of probable incidents, and the comedy-writers then "put in any names that occur to them," but do not use the names of already existing individuals—precisely because what is important in comedy is levity, and this is better achieved through the simple presentation of freely invented "types." In tragedy, by contrast, the poets keep to already existing and familiar names. "The reason is that what is possible should carry conviction [*pithanon*]." In tragedy, the recognition that is to be brought about not only concerns a serious matter, but requires *identification* on the part of the audience with what is being presented, and this is facilitated by the familiar. We recognize only what is already in some way familiar to us, and this is something that is at once outside of us and part of us.[31] We are persuaded and feel ourselves at home in the presence of the familiar; we feel our own belonging to the familiar that is part of ourselves. Something becomes a serious matter for us only when we are precisely drawn into it and identify with it in this way, such that it becomes a determinative ground of our Being. In pure entertainment, by contrast, we seek not to be bound by what we are witnessing; we are affected in the manner of being released from ourselves. Tragedy, on the other hand, concerns self-recognition in and through identification with the fate of others.

That the presentation of character-types is not the primary or most important role of tragedy is clear from Aristotle's emphasis that the story or plot—the *muthos*—and not human beings or their character is the most important element in tragedy. The *muthos* and the actions through which and as which it emerges are the end (*telos*) at which tragedy aims (1450 a22–23); thus, "the *muthos* is the first principle [*archē*] and as it were the soul of tragedy" (1450 a38–39). It is, so to speak, the *entelecheia* through which the tragedy presents itself in its completeness (*teleias*). Just as in a living body the soul is the first principle and primary actuality that binds together in advance each potentiality and part of the body into a single living whole or "organism," so in tragic drama the *muthos* "organizes" and brings together in advance each part of the action, weaving the actions into the unfolding of a continuous story. For tragedy is, according to Aristotle, the mimetic presentation of a

single action that is "whole and complete" (*teleias kai holēs*); furthermore, as a whole it must have a beginning, a middle, and an
end, and it must be of a certain magnitude. Something can be a
whole and yet have no magnitude, namely, the discursive whole
that is the *katholou* designated by a "type," by genus or species (a
holon legomenon). "Magnitude" (*megethos*) means that which is potentially divisible into continuous parts (M, 1020 a11); and what is
thus divisible must exist as something continuous (*sunechēs*), that
is, as a whole that is first constituted by the sum of its individual
parts—for example, a line, which is composed of the individual
points that constitute it.[32] This is important because it also indicates
indirectly that the story as a whole, which presents itself as *muthos*,
cannot be told or foreseen in advance in the *logos* of the *katholou*
that can be discerned by the *theōria* of epistemic knowledge. Because the *muthos* is the presentation of a single action-story or drama,
itself the result of numerous individual pieces of action that have
come together in a way that could not have been foreseen, calculated, or known in advance by either the audience or the protagonists, the scene is always open in principle for the unforeseeable,
the sudden change in fortune, the reversal (*peripeteia*) or sudden
recognition (*anagnōrisis*). Yet in recalling that a *muthos* does not
have unity simply because it deals with a single individual, and
that "innumerable things happen to an individual, some of which
do not go to make up any unity, and similarly an individual is
concerned in many actions that do not combine into a single piece
of action" (P, 1451 a18–19), Aristotle also indicates that the single
whole of the *muthos* is a unity that transcends the mere sum of its
component parts, although it is composed of those parts (or rather
of the most significant of them) and could not be what it is without
them. The plot, "being the presentation of an action, must present
a single piece of action and the whole of it; and the component
incidents or actions must be so arranged that if one of them is
transposed or removed, the unity of the whole is dislocated and
destroyed" (1451 a31–34).

The analogy of the *muthos* with the unity and whole of a
living being is recalled again by Aristotle when he notes that not
just in tragedy, but also in epic narrative, "the story [*muthos*] must
be constructed dramatically, around a single piece of action, whole
and complete in itself, with a beginning, middle, and end, so that
like a single and whole living being [*hōsper zōion hen holon*] it may

produce its own peculiar form of pleasure" (1459 a18–21). In this context, Aristotle further specifies why the poetic *muthos* differs from a historical recounting of events: Historical investigation reports and documents many diverse events and actions that happen within a certain time period, but these events often have a merely incidental relation to one another; they do not coalesce into any one overarching end (*telos*) and thus do not form a single story or unified whole (Aristotle again cites Herodotus, who recounts two different battles that occurred on the same day, the battle of Salamis and the Carthaginian battle in Sicily). The pleasure proper to tragedy depends not simply on the "spectacle" (*opsis*), but primarily on the *muthos* that governs it. The specific magnitude of the *muthos* must be such as to promote a beauty (*to kalon*) that is pleasant to behold, that raises the eye itself into a certain nobility. For it belongs to mimetic presentation, as Aristotle has pointed out, that we take a certain pleasure and enjoyment in seeing what is thereby presented, even if, as in the case of tragedy, what is presented is something painful or terrible: "[W]e enjoy looking [*theōrountes*] at the most accurate likenesses of things that are themselves painful to see [*ha gar auta luperōs horōmen*], such as obscene beasts and corpses" (1448 b10–12). Yet what magnitude is appropriate for the story of a tragedy? What magnitude will give the measure of the whole, conveying the appropriate balance and harmony of the middle (*meson*), of the story being woven around the central unfolding of the action, such that it will present its peculiar and uncanny beauty? Again, an analogy with living beings suggests itself: "Moreover, in everything that is beautiful, whether it be a living creature or any organism composed of parts, these parts must not only be orderly arranged but must also have a certain magnitude of their own; for beauty consists in magnitude and ordered arrangement." The appropriate magnitude, while it may vary considerably in length of time, must be such as to accommodate the key structural moment of a change in fortune. But most importantly, it must be easily taken in by the eye: it must afford an appropriate *theōria*:

> It follows that neither would a very small creature be beautiful—for our view [*theōria*] of it comes about in an almost imperceptible time and is therefore confused—nor a very large one, since being unable to view it all at once [*ou gar hama hē theōria ginetai*] we lose any view of a single whole [*oichetai tois*

theōrousi to hen kai to holon ek tēs theōrias], as in the case of a creature a thousand miles long. As then living beings and other organic structures must have a certain magnitude and yet be easily taken in by the eye [*eusunopton*], so too with plots [*tōn muthōn*]: they must have length but must be easily taken in by the memory [*eumnēmoneuton*]. (1450 b37–51 a6)

If something is very small or slight, it presents itself to us in an almost imperceptible time *(eggus tou anaisthētou chronou)*, as it were; our vision has insufficient duration within which to apprehend the object. Likewise, if the object is too large or too long, we are unable to apprehend it all at once, at one and the same time *(hama)*, and again the appropriate time for *theōria* is lacking. The time of *theōria* is the time of the *hama*, of the "simultaneity" of seeing and having seen, living and having lived, being and having been. As such, it is the authentic time of *praxis*, of the highest possibility and actuality of human life itself: the time of *bios*, of an existence that is intrinsically "historical," in the sense that at any given moment it is what it has been.[33] Clearly, "simultaneity" here does not mean pure presence or self-presence, and the "moment" that is its measure is not reducible to an isolated "instant" in which we barely see or catch sight of something. It refers, rather, to that which properly *endures* in and amid—indeed, *as*—the time of a life, of a life that is lived as *praxis*, and to the belonging together that binds future and past into the unfolding of a single and unique whole (the time of the one life that will have been one's own). But this whole of a life-time is not that of a continuity of incidents belonging to events themselves (which, taken in and of themselves, are purely successive, *ephexēs*), precisely because such a time unfolds in and as a series of *praxeis*, of actions (taken in a broad sense to include what happens to one, what one undergoes: *pathein*) that happen as "momentary" events, whose temporality is thus finite, and which can be neither foreseen nor known in their future import. Indeed, the vast majority of such events are forgotten; very few acquire the enduring significance that leads to their being seen and remembered as part of one's life as a whole; most often, such significance comes about and is seen only afterward or later. Aristotle makes it clear here that the time or simultaneity of *theōria* is not that of an instantaneity, but of a seeing that spans and stretches across the actions of the tragedy from beginning to end.

Its time is thus also that of memory, of apprehending and seeing in their togetherness (*sunopton, sunorasthai*) the events that, in the course of time, have come to belong together, to have attained a meaning and significance, in the form of a story that could not have been foreseen. The time of *theōrein*, Aristotle's account here indicates, can only ever be a time of retrospection and of memory. This does not mean, of course, that such *theōrein* and what it discloses is insignificant with respect to the future and to future actions. It does imply, however, that it entails experience of life, which in the *Nicomachean Ethics* is seen as a necessary condition of acquiring both *phronēsis* and the *theōrein* intrinsic to philosophizing.

To say that the whole of the story that is to be made visible and accessible for contemplation or *theōria* in and through the tragedy is not a continuity brought about by isolated incidents in and of themselves means, therefore, that the actual unfolding of the drama in its intrinsic implications is in large part concealed from our view until the end. If the tragedy shows what "probably or necessarily" follows as a result of certain actions and character-types, this nevertheless has nothing to do with any linear or causal necessity or likelihood that could be discerned theoretically or in advance. This is precisely the soul of the tragedy: the working or weaving of the *muthos* itself. It is only in retrospect that our *theōria* can discern what was destined to happen, and why it happened in the way that it did, why events came together in precisely this way that could not have been foreseen at the time they were done, in short, how the *muthos* itself came about. Like every story, the tragedy has a beginning and an end (for it is rooted in the finite time of human *praxis* itself), but its true middle is like the weaving of a web which, once begun, is no longer arbitrary. Aristotle indeed uses a language of weaving to describe the unfolding of the *muthos*: it occurs as the "tying" (*desis*) and "loosing" (*lusis*) of a series of incidents, a process in which they are at once bound together and yet each released into the flow of something greater that is still taking shape as it draws to an end. In the midst of this weaving are the unexpected twists and turns, the paradoxes, the sudden changes of fortune and moments of recognition. What appears to be the continuity of a story from the perspective of the whole, of the end that has now come into view (*theōria*) never was such at the time of enactment of its constitutive events. The working of the *muthos* is thus that of an unfolding enfolding, the unfolding implication of a sequence of incidents and actions. The *muthos*, as the *poiēsis* at work in the midst of all *praxis* and its "entanglement" (*plokē*: 1456 a9), first brings about and brings into Being—weaves, one might say—the *whole* in the light of which those events and actions will come to be seen, the finite Being of the world to which those actions will have belonged. And this—not certain character-types— is the whole that is presented in and through the *poiēsis* of poetic presentation, and that the dramatic poet must take into view in advance (*theōreisthai to katholou*: 1455 b2–3) as the *theōria* that will be revealed gradually to the audience.

It is because the *muthos* primarily configures both what the audience of spectators sees and how they see it, their general perspective,[34] that Aristotle deems the "spectacle" (*opsis*) as being intrinsically of lesser importance. By "spectacle" Aristotle means primarily the masks and costumes of the characters, or more precisely the visual effects these produce, their look and visible manifestation. Yet, as we all know from having seen a poor piece of theatre, a lavish spectacle replete with special effects leaves us indifferent or even annoyed in the absence of an intriguing story or plot. What we look for, that which holds our vision and attention, is the overall movement and meaningful unfolding of what is happening. Thus, Aristotle notes, spectacle is "quite foreign" to the poietic art properly speaking. Indeed, he goes so far as to say that the power of a tragedy does not depend on its performance by actors (1450 b18–19). For, he remarks,

> The plot should be so constructed that even without seeing [*aneu tou horan*] the play anyone hearing of the incidents happening thrills with fear and pity as a result of what occurs. So would anyone feel who heard the story of Oedipus. To produce this effect by means of an appeal to the eye [*dia tēs opseōs*] is inartistic. . . . (1453 b3–8)

Certainly, as one of the six main elements in tragic drama, the visual spectacle is important, but it should be dictated primarily by the story. The "ornament" that it presents (*tēs opseōs kosmos*: 1449 b32–33) must be that required to facilitate the presentation of the *muthos* itself. Precisely because the aesthetic presentation (*aisthēsis*) is an important component, the poet must attend to it with care and with an eye to the whole, for it "offers many opportunities of

going wrong" (1454 b17). Aristotle's point is not, therefore, that either the spectacle or the *theōria* are unimportant—this would of course
be absurd, since we are concerned precisely with a theatrical event—
but simply that it is what we do not see or rather *do not yet fully see*,
namely, the whole that unfolds as the story itself (and not simply
what is sensuously visible or perceivable), that primarily holds our
visual attention, *engages* our expectations and emotions. In compar-
ing tragedy to epic, Aristotle even suggests that the more we see, the
less we are able to experience the wondrous (*to thaumaston*)—that
emergence which originates a proto-philosophical experience of the
whole. For we experience wonder in the face of what is "inexpli-
cable," or without *logos* (*alogon*), and such absence, presumably, tends
to be filled (though only apparently) and thus concealed more readily
by visual presentation. In epic, by contrast, where "we do not see the
actors," the medium of the word makes more present what is *alogon*,
arousing more intensely our wonder (1460 a11–14). Again, the primacy of *logos* as *muthos* in bringing about our relation to the whole
and to that which is not yet fully perspicuous but nevertheless present
in its approach becomes manifest.

Whereas the philosophical-theological *theōria* of *sophia* and the
logos of *epistēmē* are directed toward what has been and already is,
or, in their modern scientific-technological guise, to predicting or
producing a future on the basis of what has been, the relation to an
unforeseeable future is thus what at once carries and is carried by
the *muthos*, which is also to say that this relation sustains and is
sustained by the *theōrein* of tragic theater. This, again, is why the
mimēsis of tragic presentation is not primarily concerned with bringing to the fore certain universal character-types. Aristotle makes this
point most emphatically when he indicates the overall perspective,
the whole within which the presentation of tragedy is to occur:

> The most important element is the arrangement [*sustasis*] of
> the incidents [that is, the plot or *muthos*], for tragedy is not a
> representation [*mimēsis*] of human beings, but of action [*praxis*]
> and of life [*bios*] and of *eudaimonia* and its opposite, which are
> found in action. And the end aimed at is a certain kind of
> action, not qualities of character [*poiotēs*]. For while character
> [*ēthē*] gives men the qualities that they have [*poioi tines*], it is
> their actions that make them *eudaimones* or the opposite. They
> do not therefore act to represent character; rather, character is
> included by way of the action. It follows that the incidents and
> the plot are the end at which tragedy aims. . . .[35]

Character presents people as they *are and have been* (for character is what we have come to see in and through a series of actions), but it does not wholly determine the outcome of future actions, and it is the latter that will decide our *bios*, our life as a whole, and whether it will have been blessed by well-being (*eudaimonia*). While we may strive for *eudaimonia* in and through our own actions, of which we are to some extent an origin, and in particular through the action of philosophizing, in which we strive to contemplate (*theōrein*) the divinity of the world, whether we achieve *eudaimonia* or not ultimately depends on the gods, on fate and fortune, on the forces of destiny that exceed our powers. Indeed, in the *Nicomachean Ethics* Aristotle in advance situates the possible *human* striving to bring about *eudaimonia* within the more encompassing perspective of fortune and misfortune, of possible reversals (*metabolai*) of fate and disasters—in short, *within* the realm of the tragic. Because *eudaimonia* concerns the story of a complete life (*biou teleiou*), Aristotle notes, we should heed the counsel of Solon that only in retrospect, only at the end of a life, when someone is dead, should we venture to judge that that person was happy and blessed during their lifetime. What we are judging is then that someone *will have been* happy: the living present, by its very openness, eludes the time of conclusive human judgment. Indeed, Aristotle adds, even then, at the end of a life, ancestors in a sense continue to be affected by the fortunes of their descendants (NE, 1100 a1ff.).

In presenting the story of a single and complete piece of action and of life, and in relation to *eudaimonia* and its opposite, the tragedy presents in condensed form, as it were, how the life story of each of the protagonists unfolds and materializes in relation to the forces that transcend the individual and his or her perception of the world. Whereas in the theoretical account of *praxis* and of *ēthos* in the *Nicomachean Ethics* the elements of ethical *praxis* and the *theōrein* of *sophia* are analytically separated out, even as they are seen in their necessary relation to one another (via *phronēsis* and the account of ethical virtue), in the *theōria* of tragic theater both the power of the gods and of divine destiny *and* individual *praxis* and its outcome are seen working together in their interwovenness. The *Nicomachean Ethics*—as Aristotle is well aware—is able only to contemplate what will necessarily have been the case for any action or series of actions, but is by its very nature able only to state generalities. That is, it is unable to *present* precisely the all-decisive moment of action itself. For the latter, by its very nature, cannot be presented in *logos*, but only enacted. Yet even in the theater such action, precisely as momentary, presents itself as largely concealed from the eye of the spectator; such presentation receives its duration only in and through the *muthos*: the latter gathers into presence and calls to our attention what would otherwise slip into concealment. This means, however, that mimetic presentation not only presents and makes visible words and deeds—action itself—in their significance and import; what it presents, above all, in the tragedy is the presence of such concealment in the unfolding of human life. It lets such concealment be "seen" precisely as the finitude of human knowledge, opinion, and action, as its being open to the forces of a destiny that will always exceed it.

THEŌRIA AND KATHARSIS

But we have not yet understood, perhaps, the *theōria* of tragedy in its full structure and uniqueness. In particular, we risk misunderstanding such *theōria* if we regard it simply as a neutral observing of a set of events presented on stage before us. The *theōria* of tragedy does not at all present us with knowledge that we simply glean from the events we have observed, and certainly not with knowledge that is acquired in any analytical or intellectual way. The *theōrein* of the tragic drama too opens onto the unknowable, it brings the audience precisely into *their* belonging to this unknowable, *as* participators in the great play of the world. Furthermore, the world thus unveiled in and through the time of this spectating is accessed not through a philosophical *theōrein* withdrawn from worldly plurality, but through a *theōrein* that is one and the same for everyone; the time of this *theōrein* is the time of a common world-experience, accessed in and through the work of art which first brings about a *sense* of worldly community.[36] The seeing of the tragedy is neither an isolated or solitary activity, nor that of a "subject" observing a series of events from a neutral distance. It occurs not through intellectual reflection or contemplation, but through the *pathē* or attunements of pity and fear. Pity (*eleos*) and fear (*phobos*) are thus not mere accompaniments to the tragic *theōria*, but are intrinsic to its very accomplishment.

To understand the role of fear and pity in Aristotle's theory of tragedy we must resist regarding these attunements as merely "subjective" feelings or emotions belonging to the spectator conceived as a neutral observer who simply judges what he sees before him. Rather, fear and pity are something the spectator *undergoes* (*pathein*). That is, these attunements do not primarily have their origin in an already existing self, character, or subject. On the contrary, the spectator as he already is, as he brings himself to see the tragedy, is overcome, indeed overwhelmed, by what he sees unfolding on stage, the drama itself. Of course, in coming to see such a drama we all bring with us a whole background of beliefs, expectations, views, and opinions (*doxai*); the tragic poet must precisely play along with these already held views, for it is the positive encouragement of such expectations that brings about our initial identification with the action portrayed. But the story turns to tragedy precisely at the point where such views are not only interrupted, but turned back upon themselves; when these very expectations lead to a turn of events or twist of fate that was unforeseen (but not altogether unforeseeable, for it must make sense in retrospect). Thus, Aristotle writes, "tragedy represents not only a complete action, but also incidents that give rise to fear and pity, and this happens most of all when the incidents come about unexpectedly [*para tēn doxan*] and yet one is a consequence of the other" (1452 a4). In this way, he adds, they arouse precisely our wonder, just because they are unforeseen. Of course, it is not just any unexpected event happening to just anyone that leads to this protophilosophical response; and not everyone brings with them the specific beliefs and views that are directly conducive to the experience of fear and pity and of the wonder that accompanies them at their most intense. (The power of a great tragedy will thus lie in its ability to sway into identifying with the story being presented even those who, on account of certain beliefs and opinions, would seem to be resistant to such an experience.) Aristotle makes this clear in his account of fear and pity in the *Rhetoric*. In the present context, we can recall only what is essential in this account for the purposes of our argument.

Aristotle's discussions of fear and pity in the *Rhetoric* indicate that both attunements are primarily oriented toward the future: they are aroused in us by certain intimations concerning what is likely to happen or will even necessarily happen if we do not manage to avoid it. Even when we feel pity for someone who has suffered already, it is because we recognize that that person has still to bear their misfortune, that it continues to affect them. Furthermore, both fear and pity emerge in us when a certain possibility—in each case something threatening—is perceived to be near at hand or imminent. Thus, fear is defined as a painful or troubled feeling brought about by the impression of an imminent evil or harm that causes destruction or pain; pity is defined in the same way, except that the perceived evil is regarded as likely to befall someone who does not deserve it. Moreover, Aristotle indicates, fear and pity belong together; they accompany one another, and do so because our relation to ourselves (to our own Being and well-being) always already involves our relation to the Being of others: Those things are to be feared "which, when they happen, or are on the point of happening, to others, excite pity" (1382 b24–26); "all that men fear in regard to themselves excites their pity when others are the victims" (1386 a27–29). But this is because, at a fundamental level, we recognize that our Being (the Being of ourselves and that of others) is one and the same, in the sense that it always approaches us from out of a common world. And it is the sameness of this belonging together in one world that is presented to us in and through the tragic drama. When we see others suffer or about to suffer, when we see them experience fear and foreboding (such as that of Oedipus in the presence of the oracle), we do not simply fear for them: we pity them and in so doing we fear for ourselves; we identify with their plight; we recognize that their fate could also happen to us; in short, as we say, we "feel for" their Being and for the fragility of their well-being, and in so doing feel for ourselves, for our own future. As we see it, in the time of this *theōria*, their story is also ours. This does not of course mean that the same things will actually happen to us, but that our relation to the future is the same to the extent that it necessarily opens onto the unforeseen. We have abandoned ourselves as we have been, precisely in opening ourselves for seeing the tragedy: we give ourselves over to, make time for, being absorbed into this experience, and thereby we have already left in advance any time that would be purely our own. We have left time for a time that is always also that of others, that is, of a common world. But this, of course, is what has always already happened to us in our most familiar and everyday existence in which we ordinarily dwell and feel ourselves "at home."

Of course, as Aristotle points out, we are unlikely to feel pity or compassion for someone whom we despise or regard as lesser than us, or for someone we consider to have deserved their misfortune or fall, through their own bad actions. Thus, he remarks, "whenever it is preferable that the audience should feel afraid, it is necessary to make them think that they are likely to suffer, by reminding them that others greater than they have suffered, and showing that those like them are suffering or have suffered..." (1383 a8–11). We feel confidence, the opposite of fear, "when a thing does not inspire fear in our equals [*tois homoiois*], our inferiors, or those to whom we think ourselves superior" (1383 a31–33). The same point is made in the *Poetics*: we feel no pity for someone bad who is struck by misfortune, since we pity only the undeserved misfortune, and feel fear only for someone like ourselves (*ton homoion*) (1453 a2–7). Because "emotional" identification is at stake, that is, identification of our being with and belonging to one another through feeling, tragedy should therefore depict characters who are at once like us (*homoious*) and better (*kallious*) than we are (1454 b10–11), yet not altogether perfect or preeminently virtuous and just (for that is too divine to be properly human, and we are unlikely to find such a depiction of humans convincing or persuasive), but open to *hamartia*, or "missing the mark" of the right thing to do (1453 a7–17). *Hamartia* entails being in error in one's actions, not through deliberate choice or intention (*proairesis*), but even while seeking to act well. It concerns a failure in one's practical perception of a certain fact or possibility,[37] a failure to apprehend something of crucial importance—in the Oedipus tragedy, Oedipus's failure, at the time of his action, to apprehend the true identity of his father, whom he killed. Tragedy shows precisely the horrendous, and apparently altogether disproportionate repercussions that follow from such *hamartia* (one for which Oedipus, of course, although he must be held responsible, could hardly be blamed or thought to have deserved).[38] It manifests the enormous consequences that take over the whole story and, beyond his control, eventually overwhelm the hero himself. What the tragedy presents in thus drawing attention to *hamartia* is the immeasurable weight and significance of each particular action: it shows why, in *praxis*, our perception of the practical situation is all-important, even more so than that *theōria* of the whole that orients our actions in advance. We may be wise as a consequence of our *theōria* of the world, and thus oriented toward the good of our Being-in-the-world as a whole, and yet be capable of doing harm or evil—

unknowingly and through no intention of our own. The tragic *hamartia* thus brings about a misfit, as it were, between the perception that guides one's particular actions and one's more general *theōria* of the world. This misfit is increased and intensified in the course of the plot, necessitating a moment of recognition and reversal.

The discussion of fear and pity in the *Rhetoric* also illuminates why, in Aristotle's view, tragedy tends to incorporate familiar names and known themes and stories (even if this is not absolutely necessary: *Poetics*, 1451 b15–26), and to deal with a few families, such as those of Oedipus and Thyestes, who occupy positions of "great glory [*en megalēi doxēi*] and good fortune" (1453 a7–22). It is not because tragedy befalls only these people, but because they are manifestly "doing better" than us, and yet it befalls even them. They are thus exemplary figures for the dramatic purpose of raising us to the perspective of the general "human condition." Yet this exemplarity is itself presented and brought forth poetically through the *muthos* and its *mimēsis*, the latter as a learning that involves the audience of spectators experiencing the peculiarly tragic pleasure (*hēdonē*) that comes from pity and fear (1453 b10–14). Our pity, and its accompanying fear, will arise most profoundly when suffering happens that affects those who are close to one another, "among friends and relatives [*philiais*], when for instance brother kills brother, or son father, or mother son, or son mother—either kills or is likely to kill, or does some such thing. . . ." As Aristotle reminds us in the *Rhetoric*, "[I]t is pitiable to be torn away from friends and intimates" (1386 a10–11); those who see that they themselves are likely to suffer include "those who have parents, children, or wives, for these [in their Being] are [part] of them [*autou te gar tauta*] and likely to suffer the evils of which we have spoken" (1385 b27–29). Tragic events that befall those who are presented on stage as close friends and family are most likely to arouse our pity as spectators precisely because we sense this very closeness of their belonging to one another in the depths of their Being: we ourselves as spectators are drawn into and identify with what is at stake in this very belonging to others; it overwhelms us, we pity the protagonists and fear for ourselves, for our own Being which is exposed to the very same forces and particularly to the possibility and approach of death. Of course, our identification with and recognition of this possibility to which we are now exposed does not mean that we actually *become* the tragic hero depicted in the ontic sense; we identify, rather with his or her *Being* and having to be, that is, the identification is primarily ontological.

These considerations help to illuminate the much-debated, so-called doctrine of *katharsis* in the proper context of the *Poetics*. Existing interpretations are almost invariably at a loss to explain what is meant by the term *katharsis* in a way that does justice to the phenomena of fear and pity themselves in the context of tragedy, and this is largely because they tend to take these as purely subjective emotions occurring in the spectator more or less independently of the tragedy itself, and to regard these emotions as something bad or negative. Thus, in the predominant understanding of *katharsis* in the medical sense of "purgation," the tragedy is seen as purging, that is, cleansing and ridding the spectator of these basically undesirable emotions that are aroused in him through the tragedy itself.[39] In this interpretation the human "spirit" is purged or released from its negative emotional baggage, so to speak. A second, older interpretation understands *katharsis* to mean "purification" *of* the said emotions; here, the emotions themselves are allegedly cleansed, and this cleansing is claimed to have a primarily moral sense. In this second interpretation, the emotions are not shed, but precisely retained in a morally purified form.[40] Against these first two interpretations, both of which locate the process of cleansing, however it is understood, in "the emotional reaction of the spectator,"[41] Gerald Else has more recently argued that *katharsis* is not a process that occurs "in the spectator's soul, or in the fear and pity . . . in his soul," but a process that occurs in the course of the tragic events and story being portrayed, "a process carried forward in the emotional material of the play by its structural elements, above all by the recognition."[42] According to Else, it is the hero's recognition of the tragic truth of his actions that "finally assures us of his 'purity' and releases our tears." The *katharsis*, on this reading, is "the purification of the tragic act by the demonstration that its motive was not *miaron* [polluted by blood-guilt]";[43] it is accomplished in and by the structure of the drama itself. Although it contains a wealth of material on the pollution of blood and kinship associated with the killing of one's own, and the horror such unforgiveable acts provoked for Greek society at the time, these facts need not be seen as supporting Else's interpretation, which in another respect is a very modern one. In its desire to resist locating the *katharsis* of fear and pity simply in the soul of the spectator, Else goes too far in the opposite direction in seeking to locate it in the purely objective events depicted in the tragedy. An inevitable consequence of his reading is that the spectator is reduced to a neutral observer who first sees, then judges, and only then, as a result, feels the emotion that leads to his tears. Thus, Else writes, "so far as the plot as a whole is concerned, if it is to gain his [the spectator's or hearer's or reader's] sympathy and ultimately his fear and/or pity, he must make two judgments . . . : (1) that the hero is 'like himself,' and (2) that he does not deserve his misfortune. These judgments are not after-effects of the spectator's feeling, they are the prerequisites to it, the conditions which must be satisfied *before his psyche* (that is, the rational element in his soul) *will allow the emotions to be felt.*"[44] On this view, *katharsis* becomes "a transitive or operational factor within the tragic structure itself, *precedent to* the release of pity, and ultimately of the tragic pleasure," rather than the end or goal of tragedy itself.[45] While Else's interpretation does have the merit of seeing the plot in its very unfolding as central to the experience of fear and pity and their *katharsis*, it also precisely reverses, as we shall indicate in a moment, the relation between the time of the spectator and that of the drama (that is, of the actor).[46]

In response to Else, the view that *katharsis* is indeed the end and goal of tragic drama has been defended by Leon Golden.[47] Proceeding from the observation that poetic learning through *mimēsis* according to Aristotle means the act of inferring or observing "from the particular act witnessed in the artistic presentation, the universal class to which this act belongs,"[48] Golden notes that learning through artistic presentation thus "renders clearer and more distinct the significance of the events presented in the work of art." But can this significance be understood as the clarification—that is, *katharsis*, understood as "making something *katharos* or 'clear' "—of the *katholou* conceived as a "universal class" or species? Golden's interpretation of *katharsis* as "intellectual" clarification, concerned with illuminating the *katholou* conceived as the universal, leads him to the odd conclusion that "tragedy in some way involves learning *about* pity and fear,"[49] that it clarifies our understanding of "the nature of pity and fear."[50] Although Golden sees that what, if anything, is clarified in and through the tragedy concerns "a universal condition of human existence,"[51] he reads

Aristotle's general remark that our seeing (*theōrountas*) of likenesses helps us learn and infer "what each thing is, for instance, that 'this is so and so' [*ti hekaston, hoion hoti houtos ekeinos*]" (1448 b16–17) together with the remark that tragedy "brings about the *katharsis* of fear and pity" in such a way as to reduce the *katholou* that the tragedy presents to the "universal nature" or essence that tells us what something is. But this is manifestly a much too intellectual, much too "philosophical" interpretation; or rather, it makes of tragedy itself a much too intellectual or philosophical kind of learning. For it is precisely the accomplishment of mimetic learning that it does not involve any explicit or reflective insight into what things are. What things are is indeed brought to the fore, in an originary unity with the way things are, but neither of these are raised into their own independent *logos*, nor are they analytically separated out, as occurs in philosophical knowledge.

Finally, Martha Nussbaum in her book *The Fragility of Goodness* has offered an important corrective to Golden's overly intellectual conception of *katharsis*. While affirming the root sense of the word to be that of "clarification" or "clearing up," Nussbaum argues that on Aristotle's view, clarification can certainly occur through our emotional responses, and that such clarification is not purely intellectual, but helps "to constitute the refined 'perception' which is the best sort of human judgment."[52] According to Nussbaum, the fear and pity experienced in tragedy enable their own kind of recognition of practical values and of ourselves that can inform our practical judgment in a way that is not simply intellectual. "Pity and fear," she notes, "are themselves elements in an appropriate practical perception of our situation."[53] This is, it seems, a much more convincing interpretation, although unfortunately Nussbaum does not develop it any further. In our remaining comments on Aristotle here we shall try to flesh out, as it were, how we might understand Nussbaum's suggestion in greater detail.

In contrast to the overpolarization of "actor" and "spectator," of "objective" and "subjective," and of "emotion" and "intellect" on which most of these interpretations (Nussbaum's excepted) tend to rest and which they encourage, Aristotle's phenomenological understanding of tragedy is, we would argue, much more closely attuned to the *immediacy* of the experience of tragic theater, that is, to the involvement of the spectator in the accomplishment of tragic action as a whole. It is only for modern subjectivity that the spectator becomes a neutral observer who, severed from all emotional involvement, observes the "objective" unfolding of events and then passes (purely intellectual) judgment on them. Likewise, it is only for an overly "analytical" inspection that the actor becomes an object to be judged in isolation from the common *world* in which both he and the spectator participate at one and the same time. Fear and pity are neither purely "subjective" emotions located within the spectator, nor are they facts that are "objectively" ascertained to belong to the action depicted and then judged in such a way as to elicit correlative emotions in the spectator. Rather, fear and pity are ways in which we are originarily attuned to the Being of the world that surrounds and confronts us—here, the world that presents itself to us in and through the mimetic presentation itself. While they are certainly constituted in part by the background beliefs and opinions that each of us brings with us, fear and pity arise primarily as our response to a situation that confronts us, a response that occurs more as feeling, as the emergence of *sense*, that is, of living sensibility, than as rational judgment. Fear and pity are always *of* something, of something that, as Aristotle himself puts it in the *Rhetoric*, presents itself and approaches us from out of a given situation. It is on the basis of such "emotional" response to things that move us in this way or that that we then, only subsequently, judge that something is pitiful or fearful, etc. For how will we judge that this event here is pitiful, unless we have already recognized it to be such, and unless it has already presented itself to us, in the element of sense (*aisthēsis*)? Such recognition, which puts into play what we already know and believe, is not primarily an intellectual or rational (let alone philosophical) activity. It is an attuned "seeing" (*theōrein*) and insight that is brought about in and through mimetic presentation itself, and that attests to the primacy of sense and feeling in our Being, inasmuch as such Being is a being exposed to a world, a finding ourselves situated within a specific context, finding and understanding our own Being, as Being-in-the-world, at any given moment—what Heidegger calls a *Sichbefinden*.[54]

Fear and pity are thus ways in which we participate in the Being of a world, and do so in an immediate and direct way, not mediated through rational or analytical judgment. In the case of tragic theater, the world is the world of the plot (*muthos*), of the action as a whole that is being presented to us via mimetic presentation. Greek tragedy unfolds and happens in *the same time* as the action of philosophizing (even though the *logos* of the action is very different in each case): the time of *theōria* itself, a time of "leisure" (*diagōgē*), a time when our remaining "practical" concerns and interests have been left behind, when we leave time simply for seeing, for seeing what presents itself before us. This entails in each case that we abandon or interrupt the pursuit of future ends or goals that we have set for ourselves, that we abandon our rational interests, that we simply give ourselves—our time—over to whatever presents itself to us. Of course, we do not simply step into this other world, this other time, from nowhere; we arrive there with a certain understanding of the world, of other human beings and of ourselves, and this is why, as we have indicated, we enter this other world as a world that is largely familiar: we find ourselves initially simply in seeing others who are like us, with whose Being we seek to identify. We look for and find the familiar, and thereby situate ourselves; we recognize our own Being in that of others. Yet this recognition is in no way an explicit turning toward ourselves; on the contrary, in this finding ourselves in and through the presence of others, we precisely abandon any concern with ourselves, we let ourselves be *absorbed into* the mimetic presentation itself, we lose ourselves in it, we forget ourselves. We let our own Being be carried along by the presentation itself.[55]

In so doing, we open ourselves to a future that is not only unforeseen, but that is not simply or primarily ours, the future that is brought to the fore in and through the plot itself. Through the unfolding of the *muthos*, we are *held toward* and thus held—spellbound and mesmerized, as it were—by this uncertain future. It is in this context that fear and pity arise, in and through and out of the course of events that the mimetic presentation itself unfolds, the web that is spun by the *muthos*. Fear and pity are ways in which we are held by the unfolding of the plot itself, and are thus neither simply inside us, nor something objectively depicted in the events themselves, but occur as the very element or medium of our worldly Being. In fear and pity we feel for and feel with the Being of others that approaches us from out of a world, and thereby we feel our own Being in the same world. Thereby, we find ourselves unexpectedly opened up in our own Being. Having abandoned in advance any attempt to appropriate, shape, or master our own futural having-been (what we will have been), that is, our own actions—

having given ourselves over to a world that will have been presented before us in the tragedy—we are freed for a strange return
to and opening up of our own sense of Being—strange because
venturing into the unfamiliar, the uncanny, the *unheimlich*.[56] Our
involvement in the Being of others presented in and as the world
of the *muthos* ultimately concerns our sense of worldly presence.
Opening us to a different *sense of presence* thus lies at the heart of
what Aristotle calls the *katharsis* of fear and pity. Aristotle states of
tragedy that "through fear and pity it accomplishes [*perainousa*] the
katharsis of these and associated emotions" (1449 b26). The word
perainousa here, related to *peras* (limit), means accomplishing in the
sense of bringing something to its proper end and limit, at which
it finds its completion. *Katharsis* has the fundamental sense of bringing something into the clear, bringing into the open and thus free-
ing what would otherwise be concealed. Tragic *katharsis* brings
into the open an intensified sense of fear and pity (and thereby,
albeit inexplicitly, their ultimate "essence"), and it does so in bringing to the fore their ultimate end, that with which they are ultimately concerned. And that is: our sense of the fragility of the
future, of the finitude and limits of all human attempts to appropriate, plan, and master the future by way of our rational actions.
But this bringing into the open of fear and pity in their ultimate
essence does not result in an intellectual or philosophical insight,
but simply in a clarification, and that means, transformation, of
our sense of presence and of what is at stake in it.

Let us try briefly to sketch the movement intrinsic to such
katharsis, the movement that unfolds as our involvement in the
presentation that the *muthos* itself is. For the purposes of our formal analysis of this involvement, we need not, to begin with, re-
strict ourselves to Greek tragic theater. We can also understand the
involvement of the spectator at a tragedy in the same way as that
of someone who goes to see a good movie at a movie theater.[57]
When today we go to see a film, we do so in our free time. We go
simply to see, and this entails that we open ourselves in advance
simply for the presentation of whatever shows itself to us. We
leave it time to show itself simply as it is in itself. A good movie
is one that grips us, one whose story or plot takes hold of us and
draws us in from the outset. From the beginning we identify with
what is going on, we recognize and see something of ourselves, of
our own existence, approach us from out of the screen. We find the

movie absorbing; it holds us spellbound, indeed to such an extent that for the most part we have already forgotten where we are, what we are doing, how we came into this movie theater, what we were doing before, what we had planned for later. The presentation itself takes over our Being, our very sense of presence. We identify with what we are seeing; for a time, it literally becomes us, a part of the life and world that will have been ours. And this identification through recognition occurs without any explicit analysis or second-level reflection: we *follow* the story simply because it grips our very sense of presence. Furthermore, to the extent that there is reflection at all, it is oriented not toward the present, but toward what is going to happen in the movie; the more gripping the plot is, the less reflection there will be on what has already happened. For such reflection is possible only if we are somewhat distracted, not wholly absorbed by the story. It occurs in a different time from that of the unfolding plot, in the time of an interruption. Our "reflection" oriented toward what will probably or necessarily happen is, by contrast, an *anticipation* of the future that is being unfolded by the story itself. To be gripped by anticipation is to experience both fear and pity. Although both are primarily futural, because rooted in anticipation, pity is oriented more toward the Being of what has already presented itself, the Being of other human beings that we see portrayed and for whom we feel compassion. Fear is oriented more toward that which has yet to happen, which we anticipate approaching us *on the basis of* what has already happened. Our very Being, as spectators—thus, the Being of *theōrein* itself—is tensed between these two temporal spans or "stretchings," as Heidegger would say, these "ekstases." The unity and continuity of our Being, as presence, first emerges and is sustained by this ekstatic structure of presentation. Yet the time of this temporality is itself that of a distinctive *poiēsis*: that of the *muthos* that unfolds mimetic presentation.[58]

If we now return to the theme of Greek tragedy, we can see more fully what is meant by the *katharsis* of fear and pity. Evidently, it cannot mean that the tragedy purges or relieves us of the fear and pity that we already bring with us to the tragedy, at least not in the particular form in which we bring these emotions with us. Although the process of *katharsis* does indeed begin with these modes of attunement, as fundamental forms of our sensibility to the world, they are precisely transformed in and through the poietic presentation itself. They are transformed in the sense of being re-oriented, given an orientation by the story itself. Moreover, the story that addresses and grips us not only reorients the emotions that are already there, but brings them forth and into the open in a new way. It "recreates" them, we might say. It reorients and poetically transports them in the direction of the future and of the ultimate threat that the future always holds for mortals, insofar as it escapes our control. It transports us toward the possible impossibility of our Being-in-the-world (as Heidegger in *Being and Time* characterizes Dasein's Being-toward-death), which we anticipate not as something that concerns us as individuals that stand isolated before a world, but as an involved Being-with-one-another, our very sense of Being and dwelling in the presence of others in a world. The poetic transport of the tragedy transports us into the site of our originary dwelling, our *ēthos*, in transporting us into a sense of worldly presence attuned to the approach of the unfamiliar and unforeseen. The tragic *katharsis* thus brings our sense of Being-in-the-world before us as that with which fear and pity are ultimately concerned; it *returns* us poetically to a sense of presence and of Being, spanned between having-been and future, that would otherwise remain concealed for the most part in and through our everyday involvements in the world.

Here, the sense of tragic *katharsis* reveals its proto-philosophical accomplishment. In bringing fear and pity to the fore in their ultimate depths and limits, tragedy frees them to be what they ultimately are, it releases them; but the dénouement (*lusis*) of the plot does not simply return them to what they were before, so that they can recede, as it were, into the place from which they emerged. Rather, as we have indicated, it transforms them in transforming our very sense of Being, of who we are and what we are ultimately "about." In bringing these attunements out of the depths of their everyday concealment, in which they are directed for the most part toward particulars (we fear this or that possibility; we pity this or that person), it raises them into the perspective of the whole. Does it not precisely thereby raise them into what Heidegger calls *Angst*? As Heidegger argues in *Being and Time*, whereas fear arises in the face of a determinate threat, *Angst* brings us before our Being-in-the-world as such and as a whole. In tragic presentation, as in all theatrical presentation, it is the privilege of the spectator that he or she is bound—through the element of sense unfolding through the emergence and promise of the *muthos*—into an anticipation of the whole, a whole that he or she is better able to anticipate than the actor or hero involved in his actions. The spectator experiences fear and pity *before* the actor involved—as we see clearly in the example of *Oedipus Tyrannos*—because he or she is already being led away from the protagonist's absorption in particular acts, each committed in their own present moment, toward seeing these in advance in the perspective of the as yet unfolding story as a whole, with an eye to their possible repercussions. This raising us toward a whole is nothing other than the poietic "setting up" of a sense of *world*.[59] To be transported into and to attain a kind of stance within the poietic happening of world belongs to the privilege of human "seeing" or *theōrein*, in which we dwell before that which looks upon us, sharing a time that is neither simply its time nor ours, but the time of a world. And this is also the source of what Aristotle calls the pleasure (*hēdonē*) that comes from fear and pity in this context: it is the pleasure of *theōria* itself, of seeing and having seen the whole, the overall story whose end has now been revealed and in which the piece of action as a whole finds its completion.[60] In sheer *theōria*, the pleasure we take in *mimēsis* finds its fulfilment. Despite its problematic transformation thereof, it was of course this privilege of *theōria* that Greek philosophy noticed and sought to magnify, extracting it, as it were, from the midst of the sensible. In the theater of Greek tragedy, this privilege was honored and celebrated in the midst of the sensible itself, in a recognition of the primacy of *muthos* in configuring the ultimate ends of human *praxis*.

On the understanding of *katharsis* we have proposed, the passage in the *Politics* (1341 b33ff.) is perfectly consonant with Aristotle's usage of the term in the *Poetics*. In the *Politics*, Aristotle claims that certain kinds of music can be used for the purposes of *katharsis*, specifically those that inspire sacred passion and excitation, or "enthusiasm" (*tais enthousiastikais*), and he explicitly likens *katharsis* to a medical treatment (*iatreias*). But this comparison is not meant to suggest that *katharsis* is the "purgation" of a pathological condition; rather, as the context clearly indicates, it merely makes the point that, *like* medical treatment, *katharsis* is essentially the *bringing forth* and bringing into the open of what would otherwise lie concealed and dormant, but be no less present and powerful, no less potent and "at work" for that. Such is the case precisely with such fundamental emotions as fear and pity, which Aristotle explicitly mentions in the *Politics*: any experience that occurs violently in some souls, he notes, is found in all, though with different degrees of intensity, "such as pity, fear, and enthusiasm" (1342 a5f.). It is clear that *katharsis* here has the sense of *intensifying and thus bringing to the fore an already existing "emotion," or rather, attunement.* The same kind of "katharsis" that is experienced in our enthusiasm for certain kinds of music must also occur, Aristotle remarks, in the emotions of those who experience fear and pity (namely, when the appropriate means of intensifying these passions is present): they too will experience a kind of *katharsis* and pleasurable relief (*kouphizesthai meth' hēdonēs*). Again, such pleasure and alleviation or "lightening" that transpires as *katharsis* is situated by Aristotle in the context of free time and leisure (*diagōgēn*) and of *theōria* and the theater. The continuity with Aristotle's use of the term *katharsis* in the context of tragedy described in the *Poetics* should be evident as soon as we see that *katharsis* in itself has nothing to do with the "purgation" of pathological emotional states.[61]

"THE PUREST POEM": HEIDEGGER'S ANTIGONE

What emerges from this reading of the *Poetics* is that the whole that is woven by the *muthos* itself is not foreseeable by the tragic hero. The world of the tragic hero cannot be foreseen and known by him in advance in the manner of a pure *theōrein*, for the latter can disclose only that which already is and has been, but not that which has yet to happen. The protagonist's knowledge and understanding of the whole, of the situation and world within which he acts and in which he participates is at best only partial; the finitude of his view or *theōria* of the whole, which guides his action in the moment or *Augenblick* of an anticipatory having-been (whether such temporality is appropriated in an authentic and resolute fashion or not; for, as tragedy shows, *hamartia* is possible even for one authentically, i.e., openly, resolved), is what precisely comes to the fore as such in and through the mimetic presentation of tragedy. In this respect, the *theōria* of the spectators (who are not neutral observers in any modern sense of spectating, but participate in what is seen by way of "fear" and "pity") sees more: the audience anticipates and thus foresees the unfolding of a greater whole of which the protagonists are each but a part. But this "foreseeing," once again, is intimative, and is carried by the *muthos* itself. It is not a having seen the whole in advance, for the whole story will have been seen only in retrospect. What thus becomes visible and is made manifest in and through the singular *muthos* of a tragedy is the fact that our relation to *eudaimonia*—which is, Aristotle claims, precisely what is presented in tragedy (P, 1450 a16–20)—is never secured by knowledge alone, not even by the highest philosophical knowing, that of *theōrein*. *Theōrein* itself is shown to be finite, at least for human beings: it is itself implicated in a *poiēsis* that is not merely human or within the control of the finite human perspective on the world.

The unfolding of human dwelling in and before a world that always exceeds it is thus not simply depicted poetically in the Greek tragedy, but is shown to be itself a poietic dwelling, accomplished in its Being by the *poiēsis* of a world that occurs in each case as *muthos*—as *muthos* that is at once singular, unique, and worldly, bringing about a belonging to a whole that exceeds us. In the experience of fear and pity, the audience is precisely brought before the future of the tragic hero, a future that they also recognize to be potentially theirs: they are brought before the approach of something *deinon* which the hero is about to undergo or suffer.[62] The identification (through pity and fear) of the audience with the Being and world of those involved will be all the greater, as Aristotle notes, if the tragedy presents the stories of a few families: not only or even primarily because their names will be known and thus already familiar to some, but because the tragic change in fortune threatens to rupture the belonging-together of those who are especially close to one another. It is not the *deinon* itself, but the approach and nearness of what is *deinon*, Aristotle notes in the *Rhetoric*, that arouses pity in us. And pity for others always implies fear for ourselves (R, 1386 a24–29). If the best tragedies are about a few families, and concern those "whom it befell to suffer or inflict terrible things" (*ē pathein deina ē poiēsai*: P, 1453 a22), it is because, as Aristotle indicates, the approach of the *deinon* has a special relation to *philia*, to the friendship and intimacy of those who are especially close to one another in their belonging together, in their dwelling in a world (P, 1453 b14–22).

To what extent do these reflections on the *Poetics* of Aristotle help illuminate Heidegger's understanding of Sophoclean tragedy, with which we began this essay? If, for Heidegger, Sophocles' *Antigone* rather than *Oedipus Tyrannos* (to which Aristotle pays much more attention in the *Poetics*) was the greatest of his tragedies, and certainly the one that most drew his renewed attention and interpretive commentaries,[63] the reason would seem to lie in the fact that whereas Oedipus's actions proceed from the beginning in a certain blindness or evasiveness toward the imminent approach of something *deinon*, Antigone's story begins with her taking knowingly upon herself the necessity of downgoing, her relation to the *deinon*. Heidegger's 1942 commentary emphasizes precisely the dangerous and grave counsel (*dusboulian*) that Antigone knowingly takes upon herself: *pathein to deinon touto*, "to take up into my own essence the uncanny [*das Unheimliche*] that here and now appears," as Heidegger renders it (GA 53, 127). Heidegger's translation of *to deinon*, "the decisive word,"[64] as *das Unheimliche*—a German word normally rendered as "the uncanny"—intends this word to be understood in the sense of *das Unheimische*, that which is "unhomely," something "not at home" that nevertheless belongs, in an ever-equivocal manner, to the worldly dwelling of human beings. "This *pathein*," Heidegger comments, "—experiencing the *deinon*—this enduring and suffering, is the fundamental trait of that doing and action called *to drama*, which constitutes the 'dramatic,' the 'action' in Greek tragedy" (GA 53, 128). Antigone takes upon herself, in taking it up into her own essence, that being unhomely that becomes the "all-determinative point of departure" of her actions, "that against which nothing can avail, because it is that appearing which is destined for her (*ephanē*, l. 457). . . ." What Antigone knowingly takes upon herself is her Being-toward-death, the dying that is a belonging to Being, and as such "a becoming homely within and from out of such being unhomely" (GA 53, 129). This "becoming homely," or coming to be at home (*Heimischwerden*) is the poetic journey of her dwelling as a knowing exposure to and *pathein* of that which is not at home, the *deinon* as the proper Being of the human being.

Yet what is it that thus decisively determines Antigone in her actions? What is the directive from which she takes counsel?, that of which she herself says:

> It was no Zeus that bade me this,
> Nor was it Dikē, at home among the gods below,
> who ordained this law for humans,
> And your command seemed not so powerful to me,

That it could ever override by human wit
The immutable unwritten edict of the gods.
Not just now, nor since yesterday, but ever steadfast
this prevails. And no one knows from whence it once
    appeared.[65]

What determines Antigone's actions is not only no mere human
ordinance, but lies beyond the upper and lower gods, Zeus and
Dikē, even though it is both of the gods and "pervasively attunes
human beings as human beings" (GA 53, 144). The all-determinative point of departure (*archē*) starting from which Antigone comes
to be who she is has no simple origin, and is itself nothing determinate, and yet it prevails and even "lives" (*waltet, zēi*): it is that
from which the time of human life first arises and comes to be.
And "this" is something that Antigone and the poet leave otherwise unnamed, but nevertheless point toward in these lines as the
indeterminacy of that future that steadfastly belongs to Being, and
starting from which, in taking it upon herself (*pathein*), Antigone
comes to be the one that she is. Heidegger intimates this in recalling the destined belonging of the one who is most *deinon*, the human
being, to something inevitable, a belonging that is poetized in the
famous chorus that begins "*Polla ta deina . . .*" (we cite Heidegger's
1942 translation):[66]

Vielfältig das Unheimliche, nichts doch
über den Menschen hinaus Unheimlicheres ragend sich regt . . .

Manifold is the uncanny, yet nothing
more uncanny looms or stirs beyond the human being . . .

and in its second strophe recollects this most *deinon* of beings back
toward its ownmost essence:

Dem einzigen Andrang vermag er, dem Tod,
durch keine Flucht je zu wehren . . .

The singular onslaught of death he can
by no flight ever prevent . . .

"It is this One," comments Heidegger, "to which Antigone already
belongs, and which she knows to belong to Being" (GA 53, 150). In

knowingly taking upon herself the *deinon*, Antigone first comes to be
who she will have been, and the accomplishment of her dwelling, as
the fulfilment of her potentiality for Being, becomes the "being
unhomely in coming to be at home" that unfolds poetically as the
muthos of the tragedy itself. Antigone knows neither the eventual
repercussions of her actions, nor the particular finality of her own
death: such things cannot be known in advance, for they first come
to be poetically, through the *poiēsis* of the *muthos* that accomplishes
the belonging of finite, human dwelling to a greater whole. Remarks Heidegger: "The human potential for Being (*Seinkönnen*), in
its relation to Being, is poetic" (GA 53, 150). But this poetic accomplishment of human dwelling, and thus the finitude of her actions
(*praxeis*) as the accomplishment of *her* singular Being, is precisely
what Antigone knows and acknowledges in the *phronein* that guides
her, the *phronein* of the heart (*phrēn*) that has taken upon itself the
deinon as the all-determinative origin of her actions:

> Antigone herself *is* the poem of becoming homely in being
> unhomely. Antigone *is* the poem of being unhomely in the
> proper and supreme sense. (GA 53, 151)

This poetic dwelling and knowing, of which Antigone is the embodiment, the poem itself, is not only the story of Antigone herself.
Rather, in and through the tragedy such a destiny is seen as such,
raised into the clearing of the light and of the air by the chorus,
and thus seen to be the kind of destiny (human, finite, wayward,
poietic) to which we all belong in advance. But such a destiny is
not only thereby manifested as an origin that is no determinate
origin, a directive such that "no one has seen from whence it once
appeared"; it also becomes manifest in its unique singularity, as in
each case *this* destiny, the journey and experience of this poetic
dwelling. For this reason, notes Heidegger, the chorus, which is
the "innermost middle" and "poetic gathering" of the work of tragedy itself, should not be understood as simply depicting a general
or universal content. "Poetizing," rather, in this supreme form, "is
a telling finding of Being." It brings us before "the nearest of all
that is near." What is misunderstood as the "general content" of
the chorus, he remarks, "is the singularity of the telling of the
singular *deinon*," which "appears in the singular figure of Antigone."
"She is the purest poem itself" (GA 53, 149). The chorus itself is

song, the harmony of a song that would not resonate without the singular voices that sustain it, but that raises into the light and the air a belonging to a world that will always have been more than the sum of its parts.[67]

Poetic dwelling is thus at once indeterminate and determinate, unfolding as that which comes to be decided poetically, as the finite accomplishment of the singular poem that each human being will have been. While Heidegger's early work in *Being and Time* understood the fundamental attunement of *Angst* as first bringing us before the indeterminacy of our ownmost potentiality for Being-in-the-world as such, before the *Unheimlichkeit* of our dwelling, his work from the mid-1930s onward, in constant dialogue with Hölderlin, Nietzsche, and Greek tragedy, increasingly brings to the fore the poietic accomplishment of such Being-in-the-world. In 1943, recalling the early account of *Angst* which—in bringing us before and attuning us to the "nothing" that is other than beings—brings us before "the veil of Being," Heidegger relates this to the poetic destiny of beings, that destiny whose origins lie veiled in the completion of Being, closing his Postscript with his own translation of the closing lines from *Oedipus at Colonus*, "the last poetizing of the last poet in the dawn of the Greek world":

> Doch laßt nun ab, und nie mehr fürderhin
> Die Klage wecket auf;
> Überallhin nämlich hält bei sich das Ereignete verwahrt
>   ein Entscheid der Vollendung.

> But cease now, and nevermore hereafter
> Awaken such lament;
> For what has happened keeps with it everywhere preserved
>   a decision of completion.[68]

Notes

INTRODUCTION

1. See the insightful account by Charles Scott of the original deriva-tion of *ēthos* from the *ēthea* or haunts of animals, documented in Homer and other thinkers prior to the fourth century. *The Question of Ethics: Nietzsche, Foucault, Heidegger* (Bloomington: Indiana University Press, 1990), 143–47.

2. See the interview "Practical Philosophy" in *Gadamer in Conversa-tion*, ed. and trans. Richard E. Palmer (New Haven: Yale University Press, 2001), 79.

3. See *The Glance of the Eye: Heidegger, Aristotle, and the Ends of Theory* (Albany: State University of New York Press, 1999).

4. A notable exception is the pioneering study by Joanna Hodge, *Heidegger and Ethics* (New York: Routledge, 1995). See also Krzysztof Ziarek, "The Ethos of Everydayness: Heidegger on Poetry and Language," *Man and World* 28: 4 (1995): 377–99. Dennis Schmidt's study *On Germans and Other Greeks: Tragedy and Ethical Life* (Bloomington: Indiana University Press, 2001) argues forcefully for the centrality of tragedy in Heidegger's thinking of the ethical.

CHAPTER ONE. THE PHENOMENON OF LIFE

1. In *Being and Time*, Heidegger notes the repeated and pervasive "passing over" (*Überspringen*) of the phenomenon of world throughout the history of ontology ever since its decisive beginnings in Parmenides. See especially SZ, 65–66, and 100. In the 1927 lecture course *The Basic Problems of Phenomenology*, he identifies the phenomenon of world as "that which has never yet been recognized at all in philosophy hitherto." See GA 24, 234.

2. Hannah Arendt, "Concern with Politics in Recent European Philo-sophical Thought" (1954), in *Essays in Understanding*, ed. J. Kohn (New York: Harcourt Brace, 1994), 443.

3. An earlier version of what follows has appeared under the title "Life Beyond the Organism: Animal Being in Heidegger's Freiburg Lectures, 1929–30," in *Animal Others*, ed. H. Peter Steeves (Albany: State University of New York Press, 1999), 197–248. The essay has been revised for the present study.

4. Whether this "simultaneity" of being held at the same time (*hama*) in the presence of living and having lived, of being and having been, is indeed attributable to animal life, is something we shall have to consider. See the concluding part of the present chapter, on "The Time of Life."

5. *Technē* should here be taken in the broad sense of a knowing that has seen something in advance in respect of its *eidos*, envisaged it already from a particular perspective. Thus, even the piece of wood that is to become a club, or the stone that is to become a hammer, must first come to be such by being viewed in advance with an eye to such ends.

6. For a discussion and defense of such teleology with respect to animal Being, see Martha Craven Nussbaum, "Aristotle on Teleological Explanation," in *Aristotle's De Motu Animalium* (Princeton: Princeton University Press, 1978), Essay 1, 59–106.

7. Later, this will be thought by Heidegger as the finite event or *Ereignis* of difference in Sameness, an event in which the otherness of other beings is caught sight of in the moment or *Augenblick* of world. We shall examine Heidegger's understanding of the relation between *Ereignis* and the *Augenblick* in chapter 4. On the *Ereignis* of difference, see "The Principle of Identity," in *Identity and Difference* (ID). With regard to Hegel, see "The Onto-theo-logical Constitution of Metaphysics" in the same volume.

8. See GA 29/30, 385–88.

9. We shall return to this issue in chapter 6, in relation to Heidegger's understanding of the essence of poetizing (*Dichtung*). Note that we see here a twisting-free from the conception of the Being of *logos* as independent presence-at-hand, that is, from precisely that conception which led to the Greek characterization of man or *anthrōpos* as *zōion logon echon*, the living being that "has" *logos*.

10. See especially Heidegger's comments on 287–88, and the translators' note on 182 of the English. On the question of "spirit" in relation to the 1929–30 course, see Jacques Derrida, *De l'esprit: Heidegger et la question* (Paris: Galilée, 1987). Translated as *Of Spirit: Heidegger and the Question*, by Geoffrey Bennington and Richard Bowlby (Chicago: University of Chicago Press, 1989). See also David Farrell Krell, *Daimon Life* (Bloomington: Indiana University Press, 1992). On the question of attunement in relation to Dasein and the body, see especially Michel Haar, *Le chant de la terre: Heidegger et les assises de l'histoire de l'être* (Paris: Éditions de l'Herne, 1985). Translated as *The Song of the Earth: Heidegger and the Grounds of the History of Being*, by Reginald Lilly (Bloomington: Indiana University Press, 1993).

11. It is therefore peculiarly mistaken to claim, as does Didier Franck in his commentary on the 1929–30 course, that "the ecstatic constitution of [Dasein's] existence cannot be reconciled with its incarnation." Attuned manifestation is as such always already ekstatic-existent; ekstasis is always ekstasis of a (singular and living) body. See "Being and the Living," in *Who Comes After the Subject?*, ed. Eduardo Cadava, Peter Connor, and Jean-Luc Nancy (New York: Routledge, 1991), 144.

12. Cf. GA 29/30, §54.

13. In this sense Heidegger, in the "Letter on 'Humanism,'" will later speak of our "abyssal bodily kinship with the animal," which is precisely a kinship of worldly Being in the midst of living nature. See the "Letter on 'Humanism,'" in *Wegmarken* (W), 157.

14. Cf. §§39 to 42, in particular 262–63.

CHAPTER TWO. CARE FOR THE SELF

1. An earlier version of the following remarks has appeared as an essay under the same title in *Philosophy Today*, 42: 1/4 (1998): 53–64. The published essay has been revised for the present volume.

2. References to the French are cited from Michel Foucault, *Dits et écrits*, vol. IV (Paris: Gallimard, 1994). The translation used is that by J. D. Gauthier, SJ., in *The Final Foucault*, ed. J. Bernauer and D. Rasmussen (Cambridge: MIT Press, 1988). I have modified translations where appropriate.

3. As Robert Bernasconi remarks, "The familiar accusation against Heidegger that the existential analytic of Dasein in *Being and Time* amounts to an egoism is almost as old as *Being and Time* itself." The objection of egoism, he goes on to note, "has grown in currency rather than declined." See "'The Double Concept of Philosophy' and the Place of Ethics in *Being and Time*," in *Heidegger in Question* (New Jersey: Humanities Press, 1993), 25.

4. We shall not address here the extent to which Heidegger's remarks in these and other texts of the period are not merely clarifications, but developments in the self-understanding of the grounds and limits of the fundamental ontology of Dasein. A more careful account would have to indicate, for example, that there is something of a shift in emphasis with regard to the centrality of the phenomenon of world and its role in the ontological constitution of Dasein's selfhood. Indeed, the concept of world is itself undergoing development during these years. We shall address this issue in greater detail at the beginning of chapter 6.

5. Cf. GA 26, 240f.

6. See GA 26, 243–44 and 246–47. Also, "On the Essence of Ground," Part III, in W, 59ff.

7. See GA 26, 175–76 and 244–46.

8. Likewise, the 'you' is not simply an alter ego: GA 26, 241–43.

9. This singularity belongs to the temporalizing of temporality as finite, to authentic time as the *principium individuationis*. For an early indication of this, see *The Concept of Time* (1924). BZ, 26–27; tr., 21E.

10. These words allude, of course, to the subtitle of Nietzsche's *Ecce Homo*.

11. The shortcomings include in particular the Husserlian legacy of attempting a *scientific* phenomenology which, in seeking to objectify and thematize Being (*Sein*), is inevitably drawn back to a theoretical stance at odds with the existentiell foundation of the ontological analytic of Dasein. Cf. Heidegger's admission, in the "Letter on 'Humanism,' " of the "inappropriate attempt to do science" (W, 187). This indicates that *Being and Time* itself calls for a kind of double reading, attentive on the one hand to the continued presence of the "theoretical" ideal (which should not be denied), and on the other hand to the more radical, "protoethical," existentiell foundation that is our focus here.

12. On the issue of this "neutrality" in Heidegger's text, cf. Jacques Derrida, "*Geschlecht: différence sexuelle, différence ontologique*," in *Martin Heidegger* (Paris: Cahiers de l'Herne, 1983), 419–30. English translation in *Research in Phenomenology* 13 (1983): 65–83.

13. SZ, 329, emphasis added.

14. We see hints of this in the present context, for example, in the acknowledgment of an "indirect" existentiell guidance (GA 26, 176) and in the need for an "extreme" construction in philosophical engagement.

15. This does not, of course, preclude that we may (and often must) judge an act, once "committed" or "accomplished," as good or bad; but even such accomplishment is never simply closed (unless it has fallen into sheer oblivion), but has merely entered the political, the worldly realm where it has become severed from the time of its emergence and is open to the historical interpretations of others, interpretations that demand in turn *their* ethical engagement (what Aristotle called *sunesis* or *eusunesia*, "good understanding" in judging the actions of others: see *Nicomachean Ethics*, 1142 b35f.).

16. On this point, see Hannah Arendt, "What is Freedom?," in *Between Past and Future* (New York: Penguin, 1993).

17. *Discipline and Punish*, trans. A. Sheridan (London: Penguin, 1991), 30.

18. Aristotle: *chronou aisthēsin*. Cf. *De Anima*, 433 b8; *De Memoria*, 449 b29.

19. Cf. GA 53, 36.

20. The point has been well made by Hans-Georg Gadamer in *Wahrheit und Methode, Gesammelte Werke*, Bd. 1 (Tübingen: Mohr, 1986). Translated as *Truth and Method*. Second, revised edition by J. Weinsheimer and D. G. Marshall (New York: Continuum, 1996).

21. See "On the Genealogy of Ethics: An Overview of Work in Progress." FR, 340ff.; also "An Aesthetics of Existence," in *Politics, Philosophy, Culture*, ed. Lawrence D. Kritzman (New York: Routledge, 1988), 47–53.

22. On the *theōria* of the ancients, see our study *The Glance of the Eye*, 263ff.

23. This qualification presumably cautions us to recall that philosophy also prepared the end of its originarily critical function, via its transformation of *theōria* and separation of truth from the Good and the Beautiful, a separation accomplished most conclusively in modern philosophy, in Descartes. After Descartes, Foucault points out, "I can be immoral and know the truth. . . . After Descartes, we have a nonascetic subject of knowledge. This change makes possible the institutionalization of modern science" (FR, 371–72).

CHAPTER THREE. APPORTIONING THE MOMENT

1. GA 24, 407–408.

2. SZ, 343–44: "*Vor die Wiederholbarkeit bringen ist der spezifische ekstatische Modus der die Befindlichkeit der Angst konstituierenden Gewesenheit.*" ("Bringing one before repeatability is the specific ekstatic mode of having-been constitutive of the attunement of Angst.") Cf. our analysis in *The Glance of the Eye*, 131–34.

3. GA 18. The published text, it should be noted, is based not on Heidegger's original manuscript, which has not been located, but on a number of transcripts made by his students. The high degree of homogeneity among the transcripts used, together with Heidegger's unmistakeable language and style, means we may assume that the text is largely reliable, certainly with respect to the general direction of interpretation. Full details are given in the editor's epilogue to the published volume.

4. SZ, 225; on *aisthēsis* and *noein*, see SZ, 33 and 226.

5. See SZ, 140, note.

6. GA 18, 68–69; *Rhetoric*, 1356 a25, 1359 b10; *Nicomachean Ethics*, 1094 b11.

7. Cf. Aristotle's insistence in the *Nicomachean Ethics* that virtue is an extreme (1107 a7). In Heidegger, "liberating solicitude" is not a putting oneself in the other's place (which would presuppose the other's being transparent to me in the thrownness of his or her factical Being—a transparency that, for me, remains factically unattainable), but rather a "leaping ahead" of the other (*Vorausspringen*) in his or her Being, a leaping ahead that recapitulates or reenacts the temporal leap accomplished by the temporality of *Angst*, which holds the *Augenblick* at the ready (*auf dem Sprung*). In other words, liberating solicitude entails nothing less than

acting from out of the (explicitly appropriated) freedom of, and for, a world—the same world in which the other appears and is manifest to me. It is in this sense that Heidegger, in both *Being and Time* and *The Basic Problems of Phenomenology*, insists that authentic Being-with-one-another does not arise from getting together and empathizing with the other, but springs from (*entspringt*), and is grounded in, authentically Being-a-self (SZ, 298; GA 24, 408. Cf. our analysis in *The Glance of the Eye*, 135–36).

8. Cf. the way in which, in *Being and Time*, the phenomenon of world is said to "announce itself" (*sich melden*), or to "light up" (*aufleuchten*) in the midst of our worldly concerns (75–76), where this "announcing itself" has the sense of something that does not show itself as such (namely, world) appearing or showing itself through something that shows itself (here, the referential totality of involvements). On this sense of "announcing," see SZ, §7A. This antecedent announcement or address of world will be thought more originarily by Heidegger in the context of his readings of Hölderlin, where the "now" or moment of the advent of a world will be seen as already responsive to an address or *Ereignis* of Being. See our analysis in chapter 6.

9. Aristotle appears to borrow this understanding of *sōphrosunē* from Plato's *Cratylus*, 411e4f.: *sōphrosunē de sōtēria . . . phronēseōs*. See GA 19, 51–52; NE 1140 b12ff. Cf. NE, 1151 a15ff.

10. Cf. Our remarks in *The Glance of the Eye,* chapter 2.

11. Aristotle himself notes that the term *proairesis* implies something chosen "before" something else (*pro heterōn aireton*: 1112 a17; cf. *Eudemian Ethics*, 1226 b7–8). It is not clear, however, that he understands this "before" (*pro*) as having a distinctly temporal sense; if anything, he seems, rather, to conceive it in terms of preference.

12. GA 18, 146. Cf. the similar formulation at GA 19, 157–58.

13. GA 18, 147. In the *Sophist* course, Heidegger uses the term *Entschlossenheit* to render the Greek *boulē*, a term that means resolve following upon deliberation. See GA 19, 150, and our comments in *The Glance of the Eye*, 41, for further details.

14. GA 18, 169. See *Poetics*, 1450 b8: *Estin de ēthos men to toiouton ho dēloi tēn proairesin.*

15. GA 18, 171. On the culmination or *Zuspitzung* of the *kairos*, see *The Glance of the Eye*, chapter 2, 46 and note 30.

16. GA 18, 188. The German word *Fertigkeit* suggests a skill that is "ready," *fertig*, in the sense of completed, already acquired, "polished." Cf. in another context Heidegger's use of the term in *Die Grundbegriffe der Metaphysik: Welt—Endlichkeit—Einsamkeit*, GA 29/30, 321–22.

17. On Heidegger's destabilizing of Aristotle's account of ethical virtue see the insightful discussion by Lawrence J. Hatab in chapter 5 of *Ethics and Finitude: Heideggerian Contributions to Moral Philosophy* (Lanham: Rowman and Littlefield, 2000).

CHAPTER FOUR. THE TIME OF ACTION

1. The following remarks have appeared in an essay entitled "The Time of *Contributions to Philosophy*," published in *Companion to Heidegger's Contributions to Philosophy*, ed. Charles E. Scott, Susan M. Schoenbohm, Daniela Vallega-Neu, and Alejandro Vallega (Bloomington: Indiana University Press, 2001), 129–49. The remarks have been revised for the present volume.

2. *Gesammelte Werke*. Bd. 3, 286–87. Translated by John W. Stanley under the title *Heidegger's Ways*, 141 (translation modified) (Albany: State University of New York Press, 1994).

3. Ibid., 312. Trans. 172 (translation modified).

4. See our study *The Glance of the Eye*, 39–47 for a more detailed discussion of the *Augenblick* and *phronēsis* in the context of Heidegger's *Sophist* course.

5. See also SZ, 338n. For a more charitable affirmation of Kierkegaard, see GA 29/30, 225. Karl Jaspers's analysis of the *Augenblick* in his *Psychology of Worldviews* is also acknowledged in SZ, 338n., although without further comment. Finally, the significance of the *Augenblick* in Nietzsche's thought would become central to Heidegger's reading of Nietzsche in the 1930s and beyond. See in particular the lecture course on "The Eternal Recurrence of the Same" in NI.

6. We have translated the German *Gegenwart* as "presence" rather than as "the present," since "the present" misleadingly suggests a fully constituted, determined presence, whereas Heidegger understands *Gegenwart* as entailing an essential openness in the direction of the future, an openness toward the event of presencing, and thus also an essential indeterminacy.

7. On thematization and objectification as central to the method of scientific phenomenology, see SZ, §69b) and GA 24, §20b), and our remarks in *The Glance of the Eye*, chapter 3.

8. In the present chapter, we have preferred to render the German *Seyn* by the corresponding Old English archaism "Beyng" than by the neologism "be-ing." However, in keeping with Heidegger's own practice in the *Contributions*, we have used "Being" and "Beyng" somewhat interchangeably. Here we have let the context decide the usage, sometimes preferring to emphasize the nonmetaphysical thinking by "Beyng," at other times leaving the accent on continuity by using "Being" where it should be clear from the context that "Being" is here being understood in a nonmetaphysical way.

9. On the "step back" into the happening of the ontological difference, see "The Onto-Theo-Logical Constitution of Metaphysics" (1957) in ID, 39ff. In the same lecture, Heidegger remarks that we can enter the destinal clearing or event of Being in its epochal significance only through

die Jähe des Augenblickes eines Andenkens: only through a sheer or abrupt (thus unpredictable) *Augenblick* of commemorative thinking or remembrance (59). On the association of suddenness or abruptness with the *Augenblick*, cf. our remarks in *The Glance of the Eye*, and note 17 below.

10. GA 9, 313n.

11. On this point, see especially §266 of the *Contributions* (GA 65, 465–69).

12. See the opening of the "Letter on 'Humanism.'" GA 9, 313.

13. GA 65, 29–30. See also 96–99, 260–61, 310-11, 349, 371, 391, 506–10. In later works, Heidegger underlines the intrinsic belonging together of *Ereignis* and the *Augenblick* by pointing to the original root of *Ereignis* as *Er-äugnis* (from *Auge*, the eye, as in *Augenblick*). *Ereignis* as *Er-äugnis* is Being's catching sight of human beings, catching our eye, looking upon us in the *Augenblick*. See *The Glance of the Eye*, 217 for further details. Regarding the strife between world and Earth in relation to the work, see "The Origin of the Work of Art" and our remarks in *The Glance of the Eye*, chapter 8.

14. SZ, 344. On the difficult relation between the held presence of *Angst* and that of the *Augenblick*, see *The Glance of the Eye*, 132–34.

15. Note that the term *Verhaltenheit* is used by Heidegger as early as the 1929–30 course to characterize the essence of human action and selfhood: all "comportment" (*Verhalten*), by contrast with animal "behavior," is possible only where there is *Verhaltenheit*; a stance or *Haltung* is found only where there is selfhood. See GA 29/30, 397–98.

16. We have preferred to translate *Anklang* as "intimation" rather than as "echo," since the German word has more of a sense of the arrival or advent of a discernible trace or resonance, of a ringing or sounding, while the English "echo" tends to suggest the sounding of something already past. Heidegger's usage of *Anklang*, it seems, is very much intended to convey the sense of an opening up, an initial breaking forth or arrival (in German, *Ankunft*). Cf. also note 19 below.

17. On the "abruptness" or suddenness (*Jähe*) of the *Augenblick* as a "historical" disruption and decision in the sense of an event of Beyng, see the important reflections in §39 of *Besinnung* (GA 66) from 1938–39. We shall return to this discussion in chapter 5.

18. GA 65, 383–84. For a discussion of these important pages see Daniela Neu, *Die Notwendigkeit der Gründung im Zeitalter der Dekonstruktion* (Berlin: Duncker und Humblot, 1997), 210–12.

19. Heidegger does not speak of an *Anklang* of Being in GA 29/30, but he does speak of the *Augenblick* and its extremity as something that can be *geahnt*, "intimated," by Dasein in the temporal entrancement of profound boredom (227). Whereas *Ahnung* is here understood as a responsive activity on the part of Dasein, *Anklang* refers to the intimation that is addressed to us from Beyng itself.

20. The sentence "Yet this *Augenblick* passed" (*Aber dieser Augenblick ging vorüber*) appears to be omitted from the English translation.

21. As we have indicated elsewhere, this concession concerning the limits of science should also be seen in the context of Heidegger's political involvement with the university. See *The Glance of the Eye*, 162–64.

22. This remark, which goes on to contrast Beyng as "the Same" (*das Selbe*) with *das Gleiche*, the "identical," presents itself as an apparent repudiation of Nietzsche's thinking of the eternity of the *Augenblick* in his formulation of "the eternal return of the same" (*die ewige Wiederkehr des Gleichen*). Yet Nietzsche's thought of the *Augenblick* of eternal return—as Heidegger's 1937 reading of Nietzsche well shows—itself enacts and thereby manifests the impossibility of thinking Being in terms of *das Gleiche*. See Heidegger's 1937 lecture course "The Eternal Recurrence of the Same" in NI, and our commentary in *The Glance of the Eye*, chapter 7.

CHAPTER FIVE. HISTORICAL BEGINNINGS

1. See chapter 4, 107–108.

2. *Fangen* derives from the Old High German and Gothic *fahan*, related to the Indogermanic root *pank-*, which carries the fundamental sense of securing. *Beginn,* from the Old High German *beginnan* (identical with the Old English *beginnan*), shares a common Teutonic origin with the English *begin* that is a compound of *be-* (about) and *ginnan*, with the root sense of to open or open up. A beginning thus suggests the opening up of something around a particular event.

3. See, for example, our own rendition of *Anfang* as "commencement" in the translation of GA 53.

4. See the 1934–35 course on Hölderlin's Hymns "Germania" and "The Rhine" (GA 39, 14–15). There is no precise English equivalent for *Schwingungsgefüge. Schwingung,* from the verb *schwingen*—which Heidegger in the 1928 *Metaphysical Foundations of Logic* (GA 26) uses to characterize the "movedness" or ekstatic displacement of temporality—means to oscillate, vibrate, or resonate; *Gefüge* implies a structure, here not in the sense of a rigid framework, but of a gathered articulation or configuration. In this 1934–35 course, Heidegger lends the word *Schwingungsgefüge* the sense of something like an overarching resonance that attunes in advance the poetic telling and choice of words.

5. See *The Glance of the Eye*, xviii.

6. Cf. our discussion in chapter 1, 28–29.

7. Later, as we shall see in chapters 6 and 7, Heidegger would think poetically this finding of what is fitting (*das Schickliche*), accompanying Hölderlin's words from the hymn "The Ister": ". . . long have / We

sought what is fitting." See *Hölderlin's Hymn "The Ister"* (GA 53) for further details.

8. Cf. our remarks on "The Origin of the Work of Art" in *The Glance of the Eye*, chapter 8. In this sense, one can also speak of an ethical "designing" on the part of things themselves. For a series of insightful discussions on this issue, see Issue 2, 2004 of the online journal *Design Philosophy Papers*, particularly the essay "Ethics by design, or the Ethos of Things" by Cameron Tonkinwise. http://www.desphilosophy.com.

9. In *Die Geschichte des Seyns* (1938/40), Heidegger distances himself from the discourse of revolution conceived as the opposite of conservativism, stating "No 'revolution' is 'revolutionary' enough. . . . Everything 'revolutionary' is merely the dependent counterpart to the 'conservative' " (GA 69, 23). On the *Augenblick* in relation to the time of revolution see the excellent study by Felix Ó Murchadha, *Zeit des Handelns und Möglichkeit der Verwandlung: Kairologie und Chronologie bei Heidegger im Jahrzehnt nach Sein und Zeit* (Würzburg: Königshausen und Neumann, 1999).

CHAPTER SIX. *ĒTHOS* AND POETIC DWELLING

1. This claim would later be qualified by Heidegger in a marginal note that remarks: "Untrue. Language is not layered on top, but *is* the originary essence of truth as the There."

2. *"Vor die Wiederholbarkeit bringen ist der spezifische ekstatische Modus der die Befindlichkeit der Angst konstituierenden Gewesenheit"* ("Bringing one before repeatability is the specific ekstatic mode of having-been constitutive of the attunement of Angst"). Cf. our analysis in *The Glance of the Eye*, 131–34.

3. The word *object* (*Gegenstand*) is here to be taken not in a narrow, "scientific" sense, but simply as referring to anything that could come to "stand" before, or "over against" (*gegen*), one as a being or entity—that one could thus relate to as other.

4. Cf. "On the Essence of Ground," GA 9, 155n55: "[N]ature does not let itself be encountered either within the sphere of the environing world, nor in general primarily as something *toward which* we *comport* ourselves. Nature is originarily manifest in Dasein through Dasein's existing as finding itself attuned *in the midst of* beings."

5. Cf. in particular Heidegger's analysis at GA 18, 326, which emphasizes the belonging together of *pathos* and *poiēsis* in the disclosure of world: "*Noein* is in a certain sense a *pathos*, a *being affected* by the world. This Being-thus-in-the-world . . . is possible only through world in general being disclosed, only if *nous* is determined by a *nous* that uncovers the world in general. . . . *Nous pathētikos* is possible only through *nous poiētikos*,

through a *noein* that discovers the world." Cf. also 391–92. On *nous* as a *phasis tis*, as a kind of "naming," see 279–81 and 364–65; *De Anima*, 431 a8. On the analogy of *nous poiētikos* with visibility and light, see GA 18, 391–92, and *De Anima*, 430 a16.

   6. From the second draft of *Friedensfeier*. Friedrich Hölderlin, *Sämtliche Werke und Briefe* (München: Hanser, 1992), Bd. I, 361.

   7. This insistence that all disagreement presupposes a deep common accord, as well as the understanding of language as event, would subsequently be taken up by Hans-Georg Gadamer's hermeneutics as developed in *Truth and Method*.

   8. On the "time that tears," *die reissende Zeit*, see especially Hölderlin's "Remarks on Antigone," the elegy "The Archipelagus" (*Sämtliche Werke und Briefe*, Bd. I, 304), and the fragmentary hymn "Yet when the Heavenly . . ." (ibid., 399), together with Heidegger's commentary on "The Archipelagus" in *Hölderlin's Hymn "The Ister"* (GA 53, 88).

   9. Cf. Heidegger's claims in "The Origin of the Work of Art":

> Poetry [*Dichtung*] is thought of here in so broad a sense and at the same time in such intimate essential unity with language and word, that we must leave open whether art in all of its modes, from architecture to poesy [*Poesie*], exhausts the essence of poetry.
>
> Language itself is poetry in the essential sense. But since language is that happening in which beings first disclose themselves to man each time as beings, poesy—or poetry in the narrower sense—is the most original form of poetry in the essential sense. Language is not poetry because it is the primal poesy; rather, poesy comes to pass [*ereignet sich*] in language because language preserves the original essence of poetry. (H, 61)

   10. Cf. Heidegger's essay ". . . dichterisch wohnet der Mensch . . ." (1951), where poetizing is characterized as that which first lets dwelling occur, and does so as a "taking of the measure" (*Maß-Nahme*), as a measuring that consists in "letting the measure that has been apportioned us arrive" (*in einem Kommen-lassen des Zu-Gemessenen*) (VA, 193).

   11. This moment thus itself belongs to something "more ancient than the times," as poetized in "Wie wenn am Feiertage . . .":

> Sie die kein Meister allein, die wunderbar
> Allgegenwärtig erziehet in leichtem Umfangen
> Die Mächtige, die göttlichschöne Natur.
>
> Denn sie, sie selbst, die älter denn die Zeiten
> . . . .
> Die Natur . . .

Whom no master alone, whom she, wonderfully
All-present, educates in a light embrace,
The mighty one, divinely beautiful nature.

For she, she herself, more ancient than the times

. . . .

Nature . . .

Cf. Heidegger's commentary in his essay "As when on a Holiday" (EHD, 59).

12. Cf. the analysis of *mimēsis* in the context of Aristotle's *Poetics* by Paul Ricoeur in *Time and Narrative*, Volume I. Translated by Kathleen McLaughlin and David Pellauer (Chicago: University of Chicago Press, 1984), chapter 2.

13. The three versions are given in *Sämtliche Werke und Briefe*, Bd. I, 356ff.

14. Cf. Heidegger's reading of these lines in *Hölderlin's Hymns "Germania" and "The Rhine"* (GA 39, 111–12).

15. This "not knowing" and being raised beyond time as normally familiar to us may be compared to the "evasion" of consciousness at the supreme height of consciousness that calls forth the courageous word and preserves the life of the spirit, according to Hölderlin's "Remarks on Antigone."

16. "*Der Einzige.*" Conclusion of a second version (1803-06), in *Sämtliche Werke und Briefe*, Bd. I, 458.

17. See the "Remarks on Antigone." Ibid., Bd. II, 373.

18. Ibid., Bd. I, 376.

19. Ibid., Bd. II, 912.

20. Cf. "The Rhine," 14th strophe: "Nur hat ein jeder sein Maas" ("Yet each has his measure"). Ibid., Bd. I, 347.

21. Cf. "The Rhine," 13th strophe: "Dann feiern das Brautfest Menschen und Götter . . ." ("Then humans and gods the bridal festival celebrate . . ."). *Sämtliche Werke und Briefe*, Bd. I, 347.

22. Heidegger here refers to Hölderlin's fragment "Sophocles," which identifies supreme joy within mourning. See GA 52, 72.

23. Cf. in this context Heidegger's remarks on Antigone at the beginning of his lectures on the "Ister" hymn, remarks that identify the Greek sense of *humnein* as "the preparation of the festival." Antigone's words at l. 806, which begin with *horat' em'* . . . , "Behold me, . . ." and conclude:

out' epi numpheiois pō me tis humnos
humnēsen

which Heidegger renders:

auch nicht als Bereitung des Brautfestes
feiert mich je ein Feiergesang

nor in preparation of the bridal festival
will ever a celebratory song celebrate me

imply that the celebration of the festival, *if* it occurs at all, can occur only in and through the presentation of Greek tragedy itself. See GA 53, 13–14. The earlier translation at GA 53, 1 omits the word *bridal*.

24. We cannot here enter into the detailed examination of Heidegger's understanding of *Brauch* that would be necessary for a more complete reading of this passage. Suffice to say that Heidegger's interpretations of *Brauch*—particularly as rendering *to chreōn* in "The Anaximander Fragment" and Hölderlin's usage of *Es brauchet*, discussed in *What Is Called Thinking?*—seek to understand it, not as a human accomplishment, but as an event of Being whereby something is admitted into its essence, into its presencing. *Brauch* thus names the apportioning of the while, of the moment of presence into which a being is admitted—an apportioning and dispensation that the Greeks otherwise experienced as *moira*. Thus, in "The Anaximander Fragment," Heidegger writes: "Usage [*Brauch*] dispenses to what is present the portion of its while" (H, 339). In *What Is Called Thinking?* Heidegger, noting the traditional meaning of *Brauch*, comments: "We speak of usage and custom [*Brauch und Sitte*], of what we are used to [*Brauchtum*]. Even such usage is never of its own making. It hails from elsewhere, and presumably is used in the proper sense" (WHD, 115).

Chapter Seven. The Telling of *Ēthos*

1. Parts one and three of the following essay have previously been published in an earlier form as "A 'Scarcely Pondered Word.' The Place of Tragedy: Heidegger, Aristotle, Sophocles," in *Philosophy and Tragedy*, ed. M. de Beistegui and S. Sparks (London: Routledge, 2000).

2. Cf. W, 189.

3. Cf. "*Der Ursprung des Kunstwerkes*" (H, 39). Translated as "The Origin of the Work of Art" in *Basic Writings*, ed. D. F. Krell (New York: HarperCollins, 1993), 175–76. See also "*Die Frage nach der Technik*" in *Vorträge und Aufsätze* (VA). Translated in *The Question Concerning Technology and Other Essays*, trans. W. Lovitt (QT).

4. The term *poetic* should in the following remarks be taken in the broad sense of the Greek *poiēsis* or the German *Dichtung*. It does not mean that we should be concerned primarily with "poetry" in the narrow sense, and thus might perhaps be better rendered as "poietic."

5. "Being itself" here means Being in its happening; for such preservation itself happens only when such telling happens, and the event of language is, as originary action, itself always finite, that is, singular and unique. On "preservation" (*Bewahrung*) see "The Origin of the Work of Art" (1936).

6. Such suspicions have been repeatedly voiced by Jacques Taminiaux. See, for example, his *Lectures de l'ontologie fondamentale* (Grenoble: Millon, 1989). Translated as *Heidegger and the Project of Fundamental Ontology* by M. Gendre (Albany: State University of New York Press, 1991); also *La fille de Thrace et le penseur professionel: Arendt et Heidegger* (Paris: Éditions Payot, 1992). Translated as *The Thracian Maid and the Professional Thinker* by M. Gendre (Albany: State University of New York Press, 1997).

7. On the significance of tragedy for Heidegger's thinking of history see Dennis J. Schmidt, *On Germans and Other Greeks: Tragedy and Ethical Life* (Bloomington: Indiana University Press, 2001).

8. The following discussion should be compared to Heidegger's remarks on this issue in GA 29/30, §10.

9. This "harmony" was, however, itself a *harmonious strife*, and was explicitly experienced as such precisely at the height of Greek tragedy: Thus, remarks Heidegger in 1935, "[t]he unity and strife of Being and appearance [*Schein*] held sway in an originary manner for the thinking of the early Greek thinkers. Yet all this was presented in its highest and purest form in the poetizing of Greek tragedy" (EM, 81).

10. Cf. the effect of the Socratic *elenchos*.

11. *Metaphysics*, Book VII; *Nicomachean Ethics*, Book VI, 1139 b18f. Cf. Heidegger's commentary on this in GA 19, 31ff.

12. Of course, such standing before the world as a realm for objective contemplation is still a mode of dwelling, but one that is everywhere and nowhere: Dispersed in and through a historically determined "everyday" dwelling, it remains oblivious to itself (to the "unhomeliness" of its own dispersion) as such, to the truth of its own historical Being.

13. Thus, in *Being and Time*, Heidegger notes that the worldhood of the world has been repeatedly passed over (§14); in *The Basic Problems of Phenomenology*, he remarks that the phenomenon of world has never yet been recognized in the history of philosophy (GA 24, 234f.).

14. This does not, of course, imply that Aristotle's inquiry is illegitimate; it simply emphasizes his critical awareness of the limits of all theoretical inquiry.

15. Cf. SZ, §7, and GA 24, §22. We consider this issue in greater detail in *The Glance of the Eye*, chapter 3.

16. Cf. *Nicomachean Ethics*, Book II, 1103 a15f., where Aristotle states that the term *ēthos* [ἦθος], the ethical, is derived from *ethos* [ἔθος], habit.

17. On the "poietic" accomplishment of the philosophical *theōrein*, to which Aristotle himself refers in the *Nicomachean Ethics*, see chapter 2 of our study *The Glance of the Eye*.

18. Martha C. Nussbaum, in *The Fragility of Goodness* (New York: Cambridge University Press, 1986), suggests that Aristotle must have Xenophon in mind (386, note). Yet the context surely suggests that he is thinking of Herodotus, to whom he has referred just a few lines earlier.

19. *Herodotus* Books I–II, trans. A. D. Godley (Cambridge: Harvard University Press, 1926).

20. On Heidegger's understanding of *historia*, see our remarks in *The Glance of the Eye*, Part 2, 185–86.

21. For an account of this, and of the shifts in meaning of ancient *theōria*, see *The Glance of the Eye*, Part 4.

22. "*Der Ursprung des Kunstwerkes*," H, 32; "The Origin of the Work of Art," *Basic Writings*, 168–69.

23. "*Die Frage nach der Technik*," VA, 38; "The Question Concerning Technology," QT, 34.

24. This perhaps helps one to understand why *theōria* retains such importance and primacy in Greek philosophy, why Aristotle continues to identify seeing and *theōrein* as the highest form of *praxis*, and, as noted, even to insist that it entails a certain *poiēsis*, participating in the bringing to presence of the world and of the human possibility of *eudaimonia* in the face of the divine and of the forces of suprahuman destiny. Apart from the other shifts mentioned in the sense of *theōria*, however, one can see that *theōrein* has by then also become a more active beholding, entailing the difficulty and effort of philosophizing, as contrasted with the simple apprehending of what shows itself in the theatrical presentation of tragedy.

25. As Heribert Boeder rightly remarks, Heidegger has no intention of satisfying this desire. See *Seditions: Heidegger and the Limit of Modernity* (Albany: State University of New York Press, 1997), 172.

26. See the essay "*Die Kehre*," in *Die Technik und die Kehre* (Pfullingen: Neske, 1985). Translated as "The Turning," in *The Question Concerning Technology and Other Essays* (QT).

27. *Poetics*, 1149 b24–28.

28. Hans-Georg Gadamer, *Kunst und Nachahmung* in *Gesammelte Werke*, Bd. 8 (Tübingen: Mohr, 1993), 31. Translated as "Art and Imitation," in *The Relevance of the Beautiful and Other Essays*, ed. R. Bernasconi (New York: Cambridge University Press, 1986), 98.

29. Ibid.

30. Furthermore, to claim that tragedy is *primarily* the presenting of character-types would be to identify with the Platonic understanding of tragedy propounded in the *Republic*, which, as Martha Nussbaum has pointed out, is precisely what Aristotle is resisting (*The Fragility of Goodness*, 378ff.).

Nussbaum also points out that Aristotle could be taken as saying that the characters presented and their actions must be *representative*, and not, like Alcibiades, to whom Aristotle refers in this context, overly idiosyncratic. Yet this seems again to give too much weight to character-*types* rather than to the action itself. Of course, the characters become who they are and come to be seen as such, insofar as they "have" character, only in and through their actions; but what would it mean to say that their *actions* must be representative? Isn't the point of the tragedy precisely concerned with the uniqueness of individual actions and their ultimately overwhelming implications? Nussbaum here seems to overly conflate existing character and the uniqueness of particular actions. "A particular action is what Alcibiades does or suffers," says Aristotle, but one cannot identify the *character* Alcibiades with one particular action. A particular action in itself tells us nothing about character, which is recognized only from seeing a pattern or likeness over time (which is what *mimēsis* enables). But this pattern itself is dictated by and emerges from and as the *muthos*, which is primary. It is thus primarily the *muthos* that brings forth and sustains our identification with the protagonists—an identification that is subsequently interrupted and put in question by the unforeseen and unexpected turn of events, the *metabasis* or change in fortune.

31. Cf. Gadamer, *Kunst und Nachahmung*, 32; tr., 99–100.

32. On the meaning of continuity, see *Metaphysics*, 1068b–69a.

33. See *Metaphysics* Book IX, 1048 b19ff.

34. Cf. *Poetics*, 1461 a4–9: "As to the question whether anything that has been said or done [in the tragedy] is morally good or bad, this must be answered not merely by seeing whether what has actually been done or said is noble or base, but by taking into consideration also the man who did or said it, and when and for whom and for what reason; for example, to secure a greater good or to avoid a greater evil."

35. *Poetics*, 1450 a15–23. For a discussion of this passage and its interpretation, see Nussbaum, *The Fragility of Goodness*, 378ff.

36. On this point, cf. our remarks on Heidegger's "The Origin of the Work of Art" in *The Glance of the Eye*, Part 4. P. Christopher Smith, in his reading of the *Poetics*, seeks to highlight an emergent "divorce" in Aristotle's account between tragic *theōria* and the acoustic and melodic dimensions of tragedy. On Smith's reading, the spectation of the audience becomes, in the *Poetics*, an *apathes theōria*, an "unaffected looking on" from a distance. Our own account, by contrast, seeks to emphasize the embeddedness of tragic *theōria* in the pathetic dimension. See *The Hermeneutics of Original Argument: Demonstration, Dialectic, Rhetoric* (Evanston: Northwestern University Press, 1998), 271–90.

37. Gerald F. Else has pointed out the importance of *Nicomachean Ethics* 1110 b32 and 1135 a15ff. for understanding what is meant by tragic

hamartia. See *Aristotle's Poetics: The Argument* (Cambridge: Harvard University Press, 1967), 380ff.

38. Cf. Creon's *hamartia* in the *Antigone*, identified by Teiresias at ll. 1024–25.

39. The purgation theory is that proposed by Jakob Bernays in *Grundzüge der verlorenen Abhandlung des Aristoteles über Wirkung der Tragödie* (Breslau, 1857). See Else, 225n14 for further details.

40. For an overview, see Else, 227n19.

41. Ibid., 227.

42. Ibid., 439.

43. Ibid., 439.

44. Ibid., 436.

45. Ibid., 439, emphasis added.

46. Else's interpretation also has the acknowledged disadvantage that it is not consonant with the *katharsis* passage in the *Politics*, where, he notes, the term seems to be related primarily to the emotions of the "subject" (see Else, 441ff.). This "therapeutic-subjective concept" found in the *Politics* is of course the source of Bernays's "purgation" interpretation. We shall comment below on the use of the term *katharsis* in the *Politics*.

47. Leon Golden, "Catharsis." *Transactions and Proceedings of the American Philological Association* XCIII (1962): 51–60. See also Golden's essay "Mimesis and Katharsis," *Classical Philology* LXIV: 3 (July 1969): 145–53.

48. Golden (1962), 53–54.

49. Ibid., 55, emphasis added.

50. Ibid., 58.

51. Ibid.

52. Nussbaum, 390.

53. Ibid., 391.

54. On *Sichbefinden* as finding oneself situated and attuned by a world, see SZ, §§29, 30, and 40. In §29 Heidegger emphasizes the primacy of attunement over any cognition or intuition (*Anschauen*) with regard to the disclosure of our Being-in-the-world: attunement constitutes our primary openness to the world (137); it uncovers, for instance, the presence of something threatening in a way that pure intuiting never can (138). On the ethical significance of feeling and attunement in relation to ekstatic Being-in-the-world, see Lawrence J. Hatab, *Ethics and Finitude*, chapter 6.

55. See Gadamer's remarks on *theōria* as authentic absorption, discussed in *The Glance of the Eye*, Part 4, 271–78.

56. On the operation of mimetic identification and difference in relation to *katharsis* see Dennis J. Schmidt, *On Germans and Other Greeks*, 54–55.

57. Of course, although the involvement of the spectator is similar, the different medium and means of film presentation (even disregarding the content) in reality make—quite literally—a *world* of difference.

58. Cf. Paul Ricoeur's analysis of the temporality of *muthos* in *Time and Narrative*, vol. I (Chicago: University of Chicago Press, 1984), chapter 2.

59. We mean "setting up" here in the sense of the German *Aufstellen* as used by Heidegger in his essay "The Origin of the Work of Art." See H, 32f.; BW, 169f.

60. The pleasure of the philosophical *theōrein* described in Book X of the *Nicomachean Ethics* is thereby referred beyond the particular *praxis* of this pure *theōrein* (supposedly the highest *praxis*) of human existence and integrated into the dimension of a poetic unfolding of *eudaimonia* exposed to the realm of *daimonia*, of the gods, of destiny and fate.

61. Hermann Abert, without citing Bernays by name, remarks that only more recent interpreters have conceived of *katharsis* as a kind of medical purgation; Aristotle himself, he notes, understands *katharsis* (in the context of the *Politics*) in a purely musical-religious way, in terms of intensification. *Die Lehre vom Ethos in der griechischen Musik* (Leipzig, 1899), 15–16 and 15n2.

62. *Poetics*, 1453 a22; 1453 b14ff.

63. The two main commentaries are to be found in the 1935 *Introduction to Metaphysics* (EM) and the 1942 course *Hölderlin's Hymn "The Ister"* (GA 53).

64. Decisive, that is, not only for Antigone, but, as Heidegger remarks in the same commentary, in the sense of being "the fundamental word . . . of Greek tragedy in general, and thereby the fundamental word of Greek antiquity" (GA 53, 82).

65. *Antigone*, ll. 449–97. As we have noted, a later translation by Heidegger of the same lines renders the last sentences as:

> Not just today, nor since yesterday, but ever-enduring
> This rises into Being (*ho nomos*, directive usage [*der weisende Brauch*])
> and no one has seen from whence it came to appear.

This translation, from the essay "*Das Wort*" in *Unterwegs zur Sprache* (Pfullingen: Neske, 1979), 219, identifies the Greek *tauta* as referring to *ho nomos*, the ethical "directive" that Antigone takes upon herself, and emphasizes the visual sense of *oiden*.

66. GA 53, 71–72.

67. It should be noted that hearing and the acoustical, even in Aristotle, retain a privileged relation to what the Greeks understand as *ēthos*, despite the ascendancy of the philosophical *theōria* that can be well documented in Aristotle's work. In the *Problems*, Aristotle himself asks why it is that, of all the objects of the senses, only that which is heard— sound, rhythm, and tune—displays *ēthos* (PR, 919 b25f.; 920 a5f.). The reason, he suggests, is that, like actions (*praxeis*), which are likewise indicative of *ēthos*, sound alone of all the sense-objects conveys movement—

it transports us into the very temporality of our Being, holding us in its sway. Likewise, the ethical (together with the educational and potentially cathartic) effects of music are of course documented in Book VIII of the *Politics*. Yet music in the Classical period, as Hermann Abert argues in his masterful study *Die Lehre vom Ethos in der griechischen Musik*, was never an independent art, but in chorus and drama was always attuned and subservient to the poetry, to the poetic word (56–57). For a rehabilitation of the acoustic in relation to *ēthos*, see P. Christopher Smith, *The Hermeneutics of Original Argument*.

68. W, 108.

Bibliography

Abert, Hermann. *Die Lehre vom Ethos in der griechischen Musik*. Leipzig, 1899.

Arendt, Hannah. *Essays in Understanding*. Edited by J. Kohn. New York: Harcourt Brace, 1994.

———. *Between Past and Future*. New York: Penguin, 1993.

Bernasconi, Robert. *Heidegger in Question*. New Jersey: Humanities Press, 1993.

Bernays, Jakob. *Grundzüge der verlorenen Abhandlung des Aristoteles über Wirkung der Tragödie*. Breslau, 1857.

Boeder, Heribert. *Seditions: Heidegger and the Limit of Modernity*. Translated and edited by Marcus Brainard. Albany: State University of New York Press, 1997.

De Beistegui, Miguel, and Simon Sparks, eds. *Philosophy and Tragedy*. London: Routledge, 2000.

Derrida, Jacques. *De l'esprit*. Paris: Galilée, 1987.

———. "Geschlecht: différence sexuelle, différence ontologique." In *Martin Heidegger*. Paris: Cahiers de l'Herne, 1983, 419–30. English translation in *Research in Phenomenology* 13 (1983): 65–83.

———. " 'Eating Well,' or the Calculation of the Subject: An Interview with Jacques Derrida." In *Who Comes After the Subject?*, ed. Eduardo Cadava, Peter Connor, and Jean-Luc Nancy, 112–13. New York: Routledge, 1991.

Design Philosophy Papers. Online journal. http://www.desphilosophy.com.

Else, Gerald F. *Aristotle's Poetics: The Argument*. Cambridge: Harvard University Press, 1967.

Foucault, Michel. "The Ethic of Care for the Self as a Practice of Freedom." *Dits et écrits*, vol. IV. Paris: Gallimard, 1994. Translated by J. D. Gauthier, SJ., in *The Final Foucault*, ed. James Bernauer and David Rasmussen. Cambridge: MIT Press, 1988.

———. *Discipline and Punish*. Translated by Alan Sheridan. London: Penguin, 1991.

———. *Politics, Philosophy, Culture: Interviews and Other Writings, 1977–1984*. Edited by Lawrence D. Kritzman. New York: Routledge, 1988.

Franck, Didier. "Being and the Living." In *Who Comes After the Subject?*, ed. Eduardo Cadava, Peter Connor, and Jean-Luc Nancy. New York: Routledge, 1991.

Gadamer, Hans-Georg. *Gesammelte Werke*. 10 vols. Tübingen: J. C. B. Mohr, 1985ff.

———. *Truth and Method*. Second, revised edition by Joel Weinsheimer and Donald G. Marshall. New York: Continuum, 1996.

———. *The Relevance of the Beautiful and Other Essays*. Edited by Robert Bernasconi. Translated by Nicholas Walker. New York: Cambridge University Press, 1986.

———. *Gadamer in Conversation*. Edited and translated by Richard E. Palmer. New Haven: Yale University Press, 2001.

———. *Heidegger's Ways*. Translated by John W. Stanley. Albany: State University of New York Press, 1994.

Golden, Leon. "Catharsis." *Transactions and Proceedings of the American Philological Association* XCIII (1962): 51–60.

———. "Mimesis and Katharsis." *Classical Philology* LXIV: 3 (July 1969): 145–53.

Haar, Michel. *Le chant de la terre*. Paris: Éditions de l'Herne, 1985. Translated as *The Song of the Earth* by Reginald Lily. Bloomington: Indiana University Press, 1993.

Hatab, Lawrence J. *Ethics and Finitude: Heideggerian Contributions to Moral Philosophy*. Lanham: Rowman and Littlefield, 2000.

Herodotus. *Herodotus: Books I–II*. Translated by A. D. Godley. Loeb Classical Library. Cambridge: Harvard University Press, 1926.

Hodge, Joanna. *Heidegger and Ethics*. New York: Routledge, 1995.

Hölderlin, Friedrich. *Sämtliche Werke und Briefe* (Band I–III). München: Hanser, 1992.

Krell, David Farrell. *Daimon Life: Heidegger and Life-Philosophy*. Bloomington: Indiana University Press, 1992.

McNeill, William. *The Glance of the Eye: Heidegger, Aristotle, and the Ends of Theory*. Albany: State University of New York Press, 1999.

Neu, Daniela. *Die Notwendigkeit der Gründung im Zeitalter der Dekonstruktion*. Berlin: Duncker und Humblot, 1997.

Nussbaum, Martha Craven. "Aristotle on Teleological Explanation." In *Aristotle's De Motu Animalium*, Essay 1, 59–106. Princeton: Princeton University Press, 1978.

———. *The Fragility of Goodness*. New York: Cambridge University Press, 1986.

Ó Murchadha, Felix. *Zeit des Handelns und Möglichkeit der Verwandlung: Kairologie und Chronologie bei Heidegger im Jahrzehnt nach Sein und Zeit*. Würzburg: Königshausen und Neumann, 1999.

Ricoeur, Paul. *Time and Narrative*. Vol. I. Translated by Kathleen McLaughlin and David Pellauer. Chicago: University of Chicago Press, 1984.

Schmidt, Dennis J. *On Germans and Other Greeks: Tragedy and Ethical Life.* Bloomington: Indiana University Press, 2001.

Scott, Charles E. *The Question of Ethics: Nietzsche, Foucault, Heidegger.* Bloomington: Indiana University Press, 1990.

————, Susan M. Schoenbohm, Daniela Vallega-Neu, and Alejandro Vallega, eds. *Companion to Heidegger's Contributions to Philosophy.* Bloomington: Indiana University Press, 2001.

Smith, P. Christopher. *The Hermeneutics of Original Argument: Demonstration, Dialectic, Rhetoric.* Evanston: Northwestern University Press, 1998.

Steeves, H. Peter, ed. *Animal Others: On Ethics, Ontology, and Animal Life.* Albany: State University of New York Press, 1999.

Taminiaux, Jacques. *Lectures de l'ontologie fondamentale.* Grenoble: Millon, 1989. Translated as *Heidegger and the Project of Fundamental Ontology* by Michael Gendre. Albany: State University of New York Press, 1991.

————. *La fille de Thrace et le penseur professionel: Arendt et Heidegger.* Paris: Éditions Payot, 1992. Translated as *The Thracian Maid and the Professional Thinker* by Michael Gendre. Albany: State University of New York Press, 1997.

Tonkinwise, Cameron. "Ethics by Design, or the Ethos of Things." *Design Philosophy Papers,* Issue 2, 2004. Online journal. http://www. desphilosophy.com.

Ziarek, Krzysztof. "The Ethos of Everydayness: Heidegger on Poetry and Language." *Man and World* 28: 4 (1995): 377–99.

Index

Made in United States
Troutdale, OR
12/11/2024

26280062R00139